PERFECTLY IMPERFECT

How ADHD Can Inspire Leaders and Entrepreneurs
to Burn Brighter and Not Burn Out

KIRAN VAS, ADHD

ISBN:

979-8-88759-597-9 - paperback

979-8-88759-598-6 - ebook

DEDICATION

For my mother, Blanche and late father Kevin. They, along with my wife Marianne, and our children Kristian and Kia have always encouraged me to realize I can do more than I think I can.

ACKNOWLEDGEMENTS

I owe thanks to

My late father Kevin Vas, who, with his brilliant leadership style, is, and always will be, my source of inspiration.

My mother Blanche Vas who possesses the most loveable wit; she is the unsung entrepreneur who embraced the concept of jugaad (frugal innovation) every day to make our family home, 25 Serpentine Street, a vibrant ecosystem of love, joy, and security.

My wife Marianne, without whose support I would have fallen years ago in the face of the many obstacles that come in the way of a life filled with ADHD.

My children Kia and Kristian, who expanded my capacity to love and for whom I always have to be the best version of myself as a father and a role model.

Brian Robinson, my friend and therapist who has been there for me in my darkest days and from whom I learned "Every leader must have at least one willing follower."

Jill, my late cousin, who, stricken by polio, was wheelchair bound for 53 years, is my ideal entrepreneur. A teacher par excellence, it was from her that I learned that discipline would take a hyperactive person like me a long way in life.

To a handful of rare teachers, leaders, and entrepreneurs under whom I will continue my apprenticeship to keep discovering new talents that I never dreamed I possessed.

And Stephen (Stevie) Rego and a motley crew of friends and family, who silently mentored me behind the scenes, helping me to enjoy the beauty of my fertile mind and find the guts to share my stories with the world.

FOREWORD

Jaideep Prabhu

Professor of Marketing at Cambridge Judge Business School

and

Co-author of Jugaad Innovation,
a book about innovation in adversity in emerging economies.

Over forty years ago, the author of this book and I shared a classroom in St. Joseph's Boys High School in the South Indian city of Bengaluru. From Grade 4 to 8, we had the same teachers, friends, and experiences. Then our paths diverged. I became an academic and wrote books about business, including one about the Indian phenomenon of jugaad while Kiran enjoyed a more multifaceted practical life sailing the seven seas, working in business including as an entrepreneur. Then, when we were both a shade over 50, our paths crossed again. Kiran got in touch to say he was writing a book on leadership, based on his experiences with ADHD, and I was immediately hooked for at least two reasons. First, for several years I had personal family experiences with mental health which had led me to read and think a lot about various conditions and how to deal with them. And second, my own research into jugaad instantly connected with what Kiran was telling me about how potential strategies of dealing with ADHD involved some of the same ingenuity that I had seen countless entrepreneurs from around the world adopt to deal with all kinds of adversity.

As a result, for the past two years now, we have spent many hours going over his ideas, through multiple outlines for the book and several drafts, and now this final version that you hold in your hands. What I have found so compelling throughout this process is Kiran's story and what he has to offer the world.

ADHD is often thought of as a condition that holds people back in life. However, in this book, Kiran challenges that assumption and presents a compelling argument for how ADHD can actually be an asset in the world of entrepreneurship and leadership.

ADHD, a neurodevelopmental disorder with symptoms such as difficulty with organization, impulsivity, and hyperactivity, affects approximately 5% of children and 3 to 4% of adults globally as per data compiled by NICE, UK*. The symptoms can make life challenging, especially in traditional settings like schools and offices that prioritize structure and routine. However, as Kiran points out, these same symptoms can be turned into strengths in the context of entrepreneurship and leadership. People with ADHD are often creative, spontaneous, and able to think outside the box. They are natural risk-takers and are not afraid to try new things. All these qualities are essential for success in the world of entrepreneurship, where innovation and adaptability are highly valued.

But it's not just in entrepreneurship that ADHD can be an asset. In leadership roles, people with ADHD can bring a unique perspective and energy that can inspire and motivate others. They are often excellent problem solvers, able to quickly identify issues and come up with creative solutions. They are also highly adaptable and able to pivot quickly in response to changing circumstances, a critical skill in today's rapidly changing business landscape.

Despite these potential advantages, people with ADHD still face many challenges when it comes to entrepreneurship and leadership. Kiran addresses some of these challenges head-on, offering practical advice and strategies for how he navigates them successfully. He draws on his own experiences as an entrepreneur with ADHD, as well as dialogs with other entrepreneurs and leaders, with and without ADHD, to provide insights and guidance that can help anyone with ADHD succeed in these roles.

One of the things I appreciate most about the book is the way that Kiran reframes ADHD from being a weakness to a strength. Instead of seeing ADHD as a disorder that needs to be overcome, Kiran encourages people with ADHD who have the resources and support to embrace their differences and use them to their advantage. This is a powerful message not just for people with ADHD, but for others without ADHD also.

In addition to its insights into entrepreneurship and leadership, this book is also a valuable resource for anyone who wants to better understand ADHD. Kiran provides a clear and accessible overview of the condition, debunking common myths and misconceptions and highlighting the many positive qualities that people with ADHD possess.

Perhaps what is most impressive is Kiran's courage in sharing his own story and experiences. As someone who has never experienced ADHD, I can only imagine how difficult it must be to navigate a world that is not designed with your needs in mind. By sharing his struggles and successes, Kiran is helping to break down the stigma surrounding ADHD and showing others with the condition that they are not alone.

In conclusion, this is a timely and important book that has the potential to change the way we think about ADHD and its role in entrepreneurship and leadership. I highly recommend it to anyone with ADHD, as well as to anyone who wants to better understand and support people with this condition. Congratulations to Kiran for writing such an inspiring and insightful book, and I wish him all the best with it.

NICE Clinical Knowledge Summaries, National Institute for Health and Care Excellence, United Kingdom 2023

TABLE OF CONTENTS

Part 1: Cut to the Chase

Part 2: Fertile Imagination

Strategic Time Out 1

Strategic Time Out 2

Part 3: Clumsy Creativity

Strategic Time Out 3

Part 4: Powerful Execution

THE ICE PACK

Once upon a time in a land far away, lived a man called Mr. Perfectly Imperfect who had everything he could ask for. Then one day, when he was dreaming that he was an astronaut and flying in space, he was hit on his head by a meteor. Dazed, he clung onto the meteor for dear life, and started burning out as he, along with the meteor, plummeted toward the Earth. On entering the Earth's atmosphere, he and the meteor were sucked into a fierce hurricane. Tossing and turning, magically, he made his way out of the hurricane with a huge sigh that sounded like Oh. The last thing he remembered was seeing a huge number of exotic creatures, all mumbling Oh, scattering in all directions.

When he got up, still in a daze, he was lying comfortably on a couch at the bottom of the crater, with an ice pack on his head surrounded by concerned faces that were continuously mumbling Oh this or Oh that in many strange dialects.

"Oh No! what will happen now, doctor?" asked a concerned bystander. How will he survive?"

Meet
Dr. Eye Can

The good doctor, called Dr. Eye Can, who was tending Mr. Perfectly Imperfect replied "Nothing to worry about. He will survive. I have given him an ICE pack. People in his situation, generally survive and often thrive after such an experience. Hearing this, there were more Ohs in the growing audience. "What is an ICE pack?" someone asked. Dr. Eye Can replied, "It is a pack that, if applied well, will kickstart his talents of Imagination, Creativity, and Execution. As the power of the ICE pack kicks in, he will find a network of family and friends to go on adventures within this gigantic crater and discover its beauty. "Tell us more," they urged the good doctor. "What will happen now?"

How to use an ICE pack

Perfectly Imperfect is a labor of love written over 28 months as I went through all the stages of a grief cycle after being diagnosed and labeled with ADHD on 05 January 2021. It is not a book on ADHD, leadership, entrepreneurship, meteors, or change management. It is an attempt to share with my peers my experiences of how I focus every day, using my talents and hobbies to survive and thrive with ADHD.

When the ADHD label arrives, it most often does so without a warning. I went through a horrid phase that began shortly before my ADHD label arrived and continued for many months after I received it, before I accepted it and was comfortable adorning it. What helped me most in my transition to a leader and entrepreneur with ADHD was a mix of my leadership and entrepreneurship talents primarily, a few hobbies, and a good dose of my fertile inspiration and perspiration.

Writing *Perfectly Imperfect* is one of the most challenging projects I have undertaken in my entire life. It started as a memoir, then morphed initially into a business book, and, subsequently, a fantasy book. At some point, it decided it wanted to be a self-help book and finally settled into an "inspire others like me to get off the couch and use their talents and hobbies to make an impact" book. It now incorporates a curious blend of all these genres.

To help me focus on the plethora of ideas that kept popping up in my mind, I was forced to turn to a team of reviewers whose minds are not powered by ADHD. The feedback I got was, "Kiran, there is no way a reader can keep track of all these ideas." Though the writing made perfect sense to me, and while I was determined to author a book that would inspire my peers with ADHD, I realized I had to be more structured to be relevant to our loved ones whose lives are touched by our ADHD.

As a compromise, one that will make life easier for the curious reader, the book is presented as an inter-related labeled collection of Stories, Concepts or abstract ideas, Tools that I call Toys, and Ethereal Adventures that I call ICE Packs. Each segment has a unique title, a summary and often an illustration of the character who plays the protagonist. The ICE Packs encompass interactive visual games designed to harness the power of imagination, enabling me to seamlessly integrate my stories, concepts, and toys. Each game is designed to provide me with a specific value that helps me to learn to survive and thrive with ADHD. The value compounds as I become more proficient at interconnecting the value of each individual game into a larger whole.

I have divided the book into Parts and Chapters, with Strategic Timeouts that help you reflect on the relevance of the stories, concepts, toys and visual games and their significance in dealing with the challenges of life. This fixed structure is like the repetition of a lesson; it may seem boring and often duplicates information, but it helped me to engrave the takeaways into my mind, so that they became a part of my decision-making process. At the end of the book, I have compiled an Appendix for those who might still feel the need for further reference.

Just imagine, sometime in the future, you may want to find your combination of talents and hobbies and convert the benefits embodied in your brand of ADHD into something you're passionate about. I hope you'll find my experience useful as a roadmap.

These will also be available on my website www.kiranvas.com where I dive deeper into these areas. To make your investment in this book actionable, there I also share real examples of how I use the book in everyday life, as well as templates and tools for curious readers to experiment with and develop their own. I also welcome questions from peers.

I hope that *Perfectly Imperfect* creates awareness in the minds of loved ones about the camouflaged value of our ADHD and inspires them to help us unleash this power in some concrete way.

An ADHD mind touches billions of lives every day. Together, let's convert many of the perfections and imperfections linked to our ADHD into genuine smiles. If we can do that, then, together, we have the potential to create a billion smiles every day.

PART 1

Cut to the Chase

I'm Kiran, 55, aka Mr. Perfectly Imperfect, diagnosed with Attention Deficiency Hyperactivity Disorder.

Apparently, I have a short attention span, so let's cut to the chase. Thankfully to help me remember that I have this disorder and the perfections and imperfections it encapsulates in, its pompous sounding name had already been shortened to an acronym of four letters – ADHD.

When I was diagnosed on the 5th of January 2021, which I choose to remember was a cold, wet winter day, I learned that, for more than four decades, my ADHD, or let's call it what it is, "my disorder" had lived happily, thrived and yet more importantly went unnoticed within me. All this while it used its unique strengths and positive traits such as impulsivity, creativity, and resilience to spur me on to create novel and magical moments that make me and the lives I touch smile.

Unaware that I had a disorder, and thereby the role it played in making me smile, I innocently assumed that the key reason behind my cherished smile was an invisible friend I called Oh who lived happily in my imagination. Oh, was my best friend and silently inspired me and conspired with me to do amazing things that created these novel and magical moments.

But after the 5th of January when I started to learn more about my disorder, it became apparent to me that it too was an invisible friend who played an important role along with Oh throughout my life in making me smile. But as I didn't know about my disorder prior to that date, I had given Oh all the credit for my smiles.

Fed up at not being given credit for my smiles, and to bring attention to himself, my disorder took control of my life; what had been seemingly perfect till now, was suddenly turned into its opposite, quite imperfect. I was in turmoil. I became miserable! My smile vanished; my much-loved sleep too, deserted me. Drained of energy and chronically grumpy, still unaware of my disorder, I assumed that some mysterious force had captured Oh, removed him from my life, while aiming to protect him from being infected by my contagious misery. With Oh disappearing, I stopped smiling. I was puzzled. I struggled to understand the root cause of my misery and how and why I had landed in such a situation. But if there was one thing, I was clear about, it was that I needed my smile back. Soon.

As part of my diagnosis, I learned that for many years, I had developed an unconscious skill to circumvent the worst impact of these negative traits and was able to reframe them as a strength to survive and thrive in life.

Thankfully the action of my invisible friends taking Oh captive worked and I became aware that I had an undiagnosed disorder. I quickly came to the realization that the only way to solve this puzzle and get my smile back was to work with medical professionals. In hindsight, this was a brilliant decision, if you belong to the "better late than never" school of thought, for it was this that led to a clear diagnosis. I was forced to accept that my undiagnosed ADHD was one of the probable root causes of my misery.

At this point, the professionals and I agreed on a treatment strategy, suited to my brand of ADHD, to rescue Oh and with that to bring my smile back. We defined my success criteria: I had to start sleeping well again and would have to work hard to restore my energy to its previous healthy levels. Only when this happened, would the faintest of smiles come back into my life. After that, when I was strong and felt confident enough, I could use experiences and talents, like leadership and entrepreneurship and with their continued support, formulate my own strategy on how to bring my smile, the one thing that I cherished and sorely missed, back into my life.

CHAPTER 1

OHISM

I would be lying if I said I know the exact day in 2022 when looking around the vast unexplored crater left by my meteor, I decided to go on a series of adventures to find my gifts and kickstart what I called My Odyssey to Find, Free, Bring, and Keep Oh in my life.

It was sometime in spring. One evening, walking by myself on the outer fringes of the crater, trying to find the words that fit the last few rough years of my life, the word odyssey just jumped out of my mind. I researched what an odyssey meant and finally found an audio book *The Odyssey* by Homer, to understand what it takes to go on one. For the next few weeks, the magical words of Homer, in a soothing British accent, flowed out through my headphones. Book by book, I was sold on the idea of going on my own odyssey to find, free, and bring back my invisible friend Oh and thereby my smile from his captors. Soon the phrase 'find, free, bring and keep Oh in my life' became a tongue twister, so I started calling these four steps Ohism or just bring Oh back into my life.

By now, thankfully, my treatment for ADHD had been quite effective. It had given me structures to survive and focus on building a stable life, one that would be critical to enjoying the basic benefits of my new title. That, in itself, was nice, but I knew that I wanted more: I wanted to thrive with ADHD. So, I took over the responsibility of planning and executing the next series of adventures that would shape my odyssey – how to learn to thrive with ADHD. I started by laying out my own strategy on how to bring back my smile, which I concluded had been captured by some mysterious forces.

I drafted a hypothesis. I needed to find the ideal combination of the perfect and imperfect qualities that come with my brand of ADHD, Leadership, and Entrepreneurship (together I named them Ex-Factor) that Oh uses as his input to make me smile and grimace. If I could then grasp the skills to develop Ex-Factor into a powerful force, and train Oh to use it effectively, I could do more of what I love (i.e., smile) and, by example, inspire others to smile too, thus supporting me in creating a billion new smiles every day!

In short, I wanted to become a smiling billionaire or Mr. Billion Smiles. I laid out a plan to execute this strategy in four steps - find my smile, free my smile from its captors, bring back my smile to my life, keep my smile in all situations in life, so I don't lose it again.

Like Homer, while writing my own odyssey, I used *Perfectly Imperfect* as my vehicle to document the thoughts, feelings, actions, and words that I experienced on my adventures, those that hopefully took me a step closer to bringing and keeping Oh in my life.

I also realized that if I were to be the hero of my odyssey and plan and execute it well, I would need to understand and leverage the rich and varied experiences I had already gathered over five decades, especially those that could benefit me on my odyssey. Having spent over three decades working as a leader and entrepreneur, I knew that I had them in plenty. I just had to choose the relevant experiences, sharpen them, and jump straight into my odyssey.

First, I brought out my Change Management experience and the writing on the wall was clear: "If my lifestyle is going to change as a result of my ADHD, I will learn the hard way to accept that. I will need to take responsibility for the change. I will have to face the change head-on, even though it will require me to redesign many aspects of my perfect life that for decades had dictated 'how I do what I do.'"

Fair enough, as I was trained for this. So, I made a deal with myself that as this was my odyssey, I wanted to think like an entrepreneurial leader who is going to enjoy unraveling the complexities of change and not one who gets trapped in them.

CHAPTER 2

OH, MY ALGORITHM

Bootstrapped with the fundamental principles of Change Management, I felt that my next move should be to let my fertile imagination run wild. I thought of ADHD as a series of meteors that had hit me on the head out of the blue and was about to change my life. The writing on the wall clearly said "In the future, I will be hit by many similar meteors." The key for me as an entrepreneurial leader was how to build a repeatable process (a boring corporate buzzword that I replaced with a 'fancy machine'), that could not only withstand the potential disruptive impact of future meteors, but also help me discover how to mine the value of the meteorite that I was already in possession of.

If I could learn to mine the value of my ADHD and use it to find ways to burn brighter and not burn out, now would that not be a great story worth sharing?

But I knew that to build this fancy machine, I would have to work extremely hard not only to bring Oh back into my life but also make him a key factor in it as well. I would have to get to know Oh intimately and find ways to make my life interesting enough so that Oh would forever hang around with me going forward.

At this very point, the first of many game changers in my life popped out. It was the concept that I had within myself a fantasy machine, my personal Smile Making Machine, and its algorithm Oh. This algorithm, Oh, magically uses the ingredients or Ex-Factor I feed it, to churn out either smiles or grimaces. Oh, after entertaining me and my loved ones with my smiles, I was producing more grimaces than smiles, and this was burning me out. Could this be, I wondered, because he was grimacing himself because he was not enjoying my Ex-Factor anymore? A grimacing Oh was surely turning me into a Smileless Pauper. I was faced with the question: How can I change this situation?

The next few adventures on the odyssey now slowly began to get clear in my mind, and I set out to paint a big picture of what I wanted to achieve through it. I knew, as part of these adventures, I would need a maverick process to invent Oh and bring him to life, as, till now, he was just a figment of my imagination. Then I needed a great team to help me in Ohism. Then I would need tools to measure and monitor my progress, to check if the changes I made in my life as I worked with Ohism, make me smile more and grimace less.

In short, the big picture of what of what I wanted to achieve on my odyssey was:

1. Energize myself to invent Oh.
2. Build a team to help me in Ohism.
3. Monitor and Measure my smiles.

Before I pushed on, I said to myself, "Okay, now I've invented the concept of Oh and it's time to have a solemn naming ceremony."

To honor the selfless and unrecognized role ADHD and Oh have played in my life for over five decades, until I was careless and lost Oh, and as a constant reminder that I alone would be responsible for using ADHD and Oh wisely, I presented myself with a new title: Kiran Vas, ADHD, Founder of Oh Landia, the home of all the Ohs. Simultaneously, I made a commitment that I would enjoy the odyssey for the rest of my life wherever it may lead me.

If you have made it so far, congratulations. Let's enjoy a time out.

Remember if you return to the book, you are plugging into my odyssey, which is full of adventures to bring Oh back into my life. When you return, please strap on your hyperfocus talent. A talent that in addition to your unique ability of attention deficiency and hyperactivity will be of great use to get through this book. What follows is how I, along with my heroes, villains, helpers, pixies, leaders, entrepreneurs, magicians, philosophers, rebels, and more, get nerdy, quirky, serious, and deep. My words will be a mix – tangible, intangible, structured, unstructured, realistic and unrealistic, and, in some sections, you may feel it's hard to get a grip on what I'm trying to say. But, remember, I am "Perfectly Imperfect," so skip them, and hopefully you'll return to them because it could be that I found some inspiration to invent Oh in these sections. What follows is a series of adventures where through a real-life or fictional story, I unravel the concepts and tools that helped me in pursuit of Ohism. As I created and wrote this book, I was always accompanied by my trademark mischievous smile, for it keeps me flourishing despite a fair share of grimaces. It is now created by Oh, and just keeps getting bigger and bigger and more contiguous to the circle of people I interact with daily. Lastly but just as importantly, within each adventure lie pools of value. I hope you can find in them the inspiration to plan and execute your own odyssey.

CHAPTER 3

THE POWER OF VELCRO

Unfortunately, before I could jump right in and begin sharing my adventures with you, I had to spend some serious time planning the odyssey.

For this, I turned toward the rich cocktail of entrepreneurial and leadership experiences that I had garnered over three decades in such roles. I accepted that my odyssey was going to be complex – a lifelong mission, in fact, and that Ohism would be the key factor in helping me smile again. I would have to work extremely hard not only to bring Oh back into my life, but I would have to get to know him intimately and find ways to make my life interesting enough for him to hang around with me and enjoy life together. It required that I approached inventing Oh, not as a hobby but as if I were starting a new entrepreneurial venture, an "ADHD Venture."

Reflecting on some of my best years in the corporate world, made me realize that Oh helped me smile the most when I was in an organization that was excellent in creating energy, working with a world-class team, and using effective and efficient methods to continuously measure how well we all were faring as individuals, a team, and the organization.

Well, this time around, to invent Oh, I had no energy, no team, and no organization to support me. This was a one-man show. I became a virtual organization! I knew I was capable of creating energy, and that on my odyssey along the way I would inspire a world class team to help me. Further, I would figure out maverick concepts and toys to calculate how profitable, in terms of smiles, my investment in inventing Oh has been.

Now that my mission was clear, to enjoy the odyssey to find, free, bring back, and keep Oh in my life, I got out a blank piece of paper to figure out how to plan for it. Despite over two decades of project management experience, I was a novice at planning an odyssey. But help was at hand when "Somebody" told me that to start creating energy, I should have a clear purpose, an answer to "Why do I need Ohism in my life?" A purpose would help me remain focused on fixing imperfections in the attention deficiency part of my ADHD. The word sounded intimidating, and as I researched different methods to find my purpose, I found that each bit of mumbo jumbo used to glorify the word appeared even more complicated than the previous one. So, I used the genius of my disorder and found a purpose that fit me perfectly: Focus my attention on trying to smile more and grimace less! As simple as it may sound, I just loved it. Smiling comes naturally to me, almost without an effort. I just love to smile, and I knew that when I smiled, it has always been so contagious that those whose lives I touched smiled with me as well.

So, with that, the Mission and Purpose box was ticked. Somebody also told me that finding a hobby or doing something I love will help in fixing imperfections related to my hyperactivity. A hobby sounded like fun. But I found it tough, for my only hobby over the last three decades had been to spend most of my time working hard for a corporation that helped me pay my bills. And now that hobby was burning me out.

Once again, the genius of my disorder came to the rescue. Instead of spending time and money to find new hobbies, it helped me find an easier way: put the label of hobby on something that comes naturally to me. The choice fell on my love for cooking, eating, and smiling, and before my mind wandered off to something more exotic, these three were quickly labeled my hobbies. As I love using mnemonics to help me remember things, I nicknamed them my Guts as cooking, eating, and smiling all are connected with my gut . They're fun to be with. They're my natural aphrodisiac. They're my inspiration for impulsivity. They're my best friends that have been by my side through thick and thin.

I was now the proud owner of a mission, purpose, and hobby. But Somebody was still not satisfied that I was doing enough to plan my odyssey. They suggested that I needed to discover my passion as the process of discovering it would help me enjoy Ohism. Well, this Somebody was becoming really irritating. So, to get them off my back, I figured that for five decades, I have passionately enjoyed my own crude version of leadership, and entrepreneurship. In my latest fad, I was now passionate about experimenting with the intricacies of the perfections and imperfections of my brand of ADHD. So, I labeled ADHD, Leadership, and Entrepreneurship as my passions and chose to nickname them ALES (while eating good food, I enjoy drinking a good ale). It also occurred to me that all three are individually and collectively like an ale. Each of them, with their combination of perfections and imperfections, make me who I am. Like ales, they can be sweet, bitter, frothy, or flat, depending on their mood when I need their help to perform an action in my life. Like a good ale, they keep me smiling when I enjoy their company in moderation. When I overindulge in them, they entangle me in a grimace as I endure an awful hangover.

I knew, deep down in me, the Ales hold an important secret: they know how to make me smile and grimace. But the challenge ahead was to get the Ales interested in Oh and helping me in Ohism. I knew I had to find a way to always be in charge of them if they chose to help me in Ohism. If I let them take over, they would try to do things their way and they would surely make me grimace.

I was thrilled that I had found my own way to invent Oh: a fun mission, a simple purpose, with hobbies and passions that were already part of my daily life, and came naturally to me, things I enjoyed and knew a lot about. This combination of four things, though quirky, was perfect for me to further plan and execute my odyssey. Before Somebody asked me to do one more complicated thing. I had already declared to the world that:

My Mission is:
To enjoy the odyssey to find, free, bring, and keep Oh in my life.

My Purpose is:
Focus my attention on trying to smile more and grimace less!

My Goals:
I decided that I would have three interconnected goals:

1. **Ohism** - This was a personal goal for me - Find ways how Oh can help me burn brighter and not burn out.

2. **Pioneer the Art of Extrapreneurship and become an Extrapreneur** - This is my platform to share relevant parts of Ohism to inspire people like me.

3. **Become a Smiling Billionaire** - This is my platform to share the power of Oh with the world and create a billion smiles.

Somebody asked when he heard this statement, "And, how are you going to do that?"

"Well," I replied smiling, "I'm going to go on an odyssey with my Ales and Guts. The odyssey will have a number of adventures, and during each of them, I will find out more about how to invent Oh and how he uses my Ex-Factor. I think my undiagnosed ADHD caused an imbalance in my Ex-Factor, which is why Oh is making me grimace more than I smile.

"To rectify this imbalance, on my odyssey, I'll redesign my Ex-Factor. I'll include the new knowledge of my perfect and imperfect qualities of my brand of ADHD, Leadership and Entrepreneurship that can help me make my Ex-Factor powerful again. Then, Oh will be able to enjoy it again and use it to make me smile more and grimace less."

Somebody queried again, "And, how are you going to do that?"

"I'm going to learn how to be in charge of my Ales and learn to use the perfections in their qualities more, the ones that make me smile more. I can then add them to my Ex-Factor. But, to achieve this, I will learn to train my emotional muscles that make me smile. I'm also going to learn how to not let them be in control of me. For this, I have to tone down the impact of the imperfections in my Ales, the qualities that make me grimace. I will have to learn to train my emotional muscles, the ones that make me grimace and reduce the impact they have on my Ex-Factor. As I progress through the adventures, I will develop a powerful Ex-Factor that will help me to find, free, bring, and keep Oh in my life forever. That is the essence of my odyssey and Ohism, my dear friend," I said.

Somebody quipped, "I understand why you want to burn brighter and stop burning out. What is Extrapreneur and Extrapreneurship?"

and, looking even more worried, he queried, "What is a Smiling Billionaire?"

"Extrapreneurship is a tribute to my Ale qualities. Extrapreneurship is a collection of stories, concepts, and toys to help me find input to strengthen my Ex-Factor. As I learn the art of Extrapreneurship, I become an Extrapreneur, and as my skills in Extrapreneurship increase, I'll share Extrapreneurship with the world. I hope others will be inspired by them to plan and execute their own odyssey.

"But finding and freeing Oh from his captors is not enough, and to ensure that I never lose him again, I have to convince him that I'll make my life interesting enough so I can attract him back into my life and work hard to keep him there forever. Only then will I enjoy the beauty of Oh to make me smile more. And I want the world to smile along with me, which is why I have set a goal to create a billion smiles every day and become a Smiling Billionaire."

If you have not yet disappeared to find your own mission, purpose, hobby, passion, and goals and have 107 ideas for discovering your own Oh, you might be wondering who "Somebody" is. He is me, and I hope you hang in here for a while.

Authoring *Perfectly Imperfect* turned into powerful therapy for me to analyze my imperfect life and plan my future with ADHD. Writing helped me process the chaotic thoughts, feelings, actions, and words of the monologues I had with myself. Those had revolved around whether the factors behind my successes and failures in my personal and professional life could help me find ways to burn brighter. As I documented my monologues, it was clear that I was unconsciously doing many cool things at the personal as well as professional levels, but remained unaware of the value they were adding in my life. As I read and reread my monologues, I found fantastic input I could use to inspire me to reach my three goals.

A word of caution, I use acronyms, mnemonics and metaphors linked to well-known concepts in personal and professional life in my writing as I have a lot of fun creating them. They stick like Velcro in my brain and help me remember to use them actively. They also inspire me to formulate my stories, concepts, toys and visual games that serve as cornerstones in my writing. They also help me to engage with a world-class team that works alongside me and ensures that I remain steadfast on the path to achieve my three goals. They give me innovative ways to explore complex emotions by giving me the opportunity to view them through the lens of things I love - cooking, eating, leadership, entrepreneurship, and more.

PART 2

FERTILE IMAGINATION

My fertile imagination helped me develop these collections of stories and concepts. I used them to process the new information and experiences that I now was more conscious of, in my changing world. I have organized them into hierarchies with each story and concept playing a pivotal role in helping me smile more and grimace less.

EAST MEETS WEST

When I was diagnosed with ADHD, what was truly amazing was to learn to accept that, henceforth, many actions and reactions of mine would be different from those of the Kiran I knew for five decades. Luckily, there is one thing that makes this transition less stormy; for almost exactly half my life I lived in the East and the other half in the West. I've enjoyed figuring out the spoken and unspoken values of these cultures as well as the skills each requires, since my situations often required me to transition seamlessly between them. I also learned how to survive what it feels like being in the right front quadrant of the hurricane when the differences of these two cultures clash, often many times a day. So, acceptance of the new turn in my road was easier when I used the East meets West analogy; when I thought of ADHD as a new culture that I would be living with for the rest of my life. I knew making my transition to my new culture could be tough, but it would also help me achieve my three goals.

Copenhagen is home, a beautiful city that I enjoy and where I have lived with my wife for 26 years, Marianne and our children Kristian and Kia.

23 January 1967, Bangalore, now Bengaluru. On what I imagine was a marvelous day, I came shouting and kicking into this world. For the first three decades sporting a "Made in India" tag, I roamed her middle-class streets, imbibing her rich culture, and living a privileged life. On 17 February 1996, a glorious sunny day in Bengaluru, I hit the jackpot when Marianne, "Made in Denmark" agreed to be my life partner. We had a cozy and small Indian theme wedding of about 150 guests, and instead of a formal reception, we had a picnic.

After close to two and a half decades in Copenhagen, I claim to be "Maturing in Denmark," the fairytale land of Hans Christian Andersen. As I mature, I enjoy learning the intricacies of a Western culture while fighting to hold on to my Eastern one. The potent cocktail of these two cultures, with their conflicting perfections and imperfections, has given me qualities that I've used to rack up an impressive scorecard of personal and professional successes and failures.

I enjoy my successes in my roles as husband, father, son, brother, uncle, in-law, and friend. I also love my secondary role as a maverick chef, storyteller, clown, go-to guy to get things done, peace breaker, and peacemaker. My standout success is that Marianne and I have raised two wonderful children Kristian and Kia who, today, are responsible adults.

To pay my bills, I've worked for corporations of all sizes and bravely crawled up and slid down their craftily designed corporate ladders. My career checklist has signs of adventurous years as a merchant marine, a project manager navigating challenging projects, a technologist, a management consultant, and a small business owner.

My standout failures were the years I was a live-at-work dad and the few times I tried to climb the corporate ladder on what I thought was my wall only to realize that I had placed it against the wall of somebody else who used me as a rung on their own way up.

Well, I'm perfectly imperfect, and, in 2021, when I was at the highest point of my financial security and lowest point in my mental security, I found myself becoming a helpless spectator as ADHD disrupted my charmed life and began burning me out. Before all was lost, I turned to my own stories, the ones that I had been scripting for five decades, as my source of inspiration. I needed to unearth ideas on how I could start achieving my first goal: find ways to burn brighter and stop burning out.

The value I extracted from this rewind of my past life, setting the stage for the rest of the book is the concept of Oh Yes Stories and Oh No Stories – the fountain of my smiles and grimaces. Each set of Oh Yes and Oh No Stories is a collection of Oh Yes and Oh No Emotions, and each of these stories and their emotions are valuable sources of information for me to understand the changes I needed to make to bring Oh back into my life again.

THE SMILELESS PAUPER

The concept of a smileless pauper symbolizes the horrid transition before my ADHD label arrived, and one that continued for many months before I was comfortable adorning it. The concept helps me accept that life often gets harder before it gets better. I used the term smileless pauper during the days when I was creating an overdose of Oh No Stories. I hated every moment of being a smileless pauper, so remaining one for the rest of my life was clearly not an option!.

I thought getting hit by a meteor wasn't fair, and, often, I felt that I also had a series of hurricanes raging inside me that slowly drained me of energy. I could trace back the start of my hurricane season to 2018, and by 2020, I was mentally and physically drained. If my life at that point had been measured in smiles, I would be Kiran, the Smileless Pauper.

My gloomy demeanor as a smileless pauper wasn't fair to me, my family, or my friends, though my foes loved it. To remain forever in such a state wasn't an option. I knew that being hit by ADHD-powered meteors and hurricanes will be part and parcel of my life going forward. I also knew they're going to happen regularly and come without warning. I realized I would need to learn how to predict them and also survive and thrive amidst them to the best of my ability.

Thankfully, I found a way to move beyond my smileless pauper status. My time with the medical professionals led me to the 5th of January 2021, when they diagnosed me with ADHD and I was brought to the portal of a new world in which I was told I had to learn ways to survive and thrive with ADHD.

Fair enough, I accepted that I had to undergo a transition to enter this new world. But to facilitate this transition, I needed a safe environment where I could first learn to survive and then thrive with ADHD. My fertile imagination came to my aid and suggested that to simulate this new world, I should create, in a corner of my crater, a parallel universe that I decided was an ethereal world Oh Landia, the home of all my mysterious forces and Ohs.

Thus, Oh Landia was founded as my safe environment away from prying eyes, where I could simulate my ADHD meteors and hurricanes and experiment with ways to first learn to survive and then thrive with ADHD. In the process I learned more about my Oh Yes and Oh No Emotions and the value that ADHD brings to my life, while always remaining focused on my three goals.

Even though I loved the concept of Oh Landia, I could only stare at it from a distance. I gazed at the portal protecting Oh Landia, not daring to approach it. Every time I wanted to move toward it, I felt powerless, as I was still caught in the right front quadrant of a hurricane that I called "The Hurricane that captured Oh."

For six months, the hurricanes continued to blow with regular frequency with a force that paralyzed me. Occasionally, I gazed longingly at the portal but dared not move closer to it even when there was no hurricane. In these calmer periods, I felt I was on an ADHD obstacle course with a regular stream of new obstacles, trying to learn to navigate them, I learned how to handle quite a few of the hurdles by myself, but now I was faced with many new and more complex ones that came with ADHD. I needed professional medical help to learn how to navigate those.

It took me six months of sweat and tears along with the medical professionals to learn this new art. As I acquired these new abilities, the forces of the hurricanes seemed less furious and didn't paralyze me as much. All this while my Oh Yes and Oh No Emotions recycled between relief, shock, anger, hope, acceptance, and back again. It was hard for me to acknowledge that I had ADHD and it was disrupting my perfect life. We monitored my progress both during the hurricanes and on the ADHD obstacle course and when I was energized, ready to take back most of the control of my life to try to survive by myself, they wished me good fortune. I was now ready to venture toward the portal beyond which lay Oh Landia to continue my odyssey.

Alone but energized, I rebooted my Smile Making Machine and Oh, but there was still no sign of my smiles. Disappointed that he was not yet back in my life, as much as to calm my bruised ego that was still not able to deal positively with being linked to ADHD, I jokingly commented that a mysterious force may have taken Oh captive. However, the ADHD diagnosis had also set free my fiery temperament and the never-give-up attitude that also had been taken captive by the same force for the last few years.

Bootstrapped with these qualities, I finally mustered up the courage to approach Oh Landia. As I cautiously moved toward the portal, I was hit by a severe hurricane. This time, instead of being paralyzed by it, I dived straight into it, determined to discover which of my Oh No Emotions had kept drawing me into them.

As I tossed and turned in the hurricane, I discovered that the key to surviving its blows was to identify, isolate, and eradicate a few of my Oh No Emotions, especially the types that kept attracting me into the right front quadrant. These emotions needed hurricanes to flourish and make me chronically grumpy. They had killed off my smiles.

The way to get out of the hurricane, I learned, was to identify and learn to unleash the energy I can create with a few of my most powerful Oh Yes Emotions, the ones that will energize me and release me from the shackles of the Oh No ones. That would, in turn, eject me from the hurricane, beyond my ADHD obstacle course, into the calm world of Oh Landia. Once I reached Oh Landia, I could begin to slowly start discovering the camouflaged value of my ADHD and how to use it to invent Oh and achieve my three goals. I had a plan to approach Oh Landia, and I started to execute it.

I had no clue about how to identify and unleash the energy of my Oh Yes Emotions. There was one thing I was sure about – that with hard work and my never give up attitude, I would understand the value that ADHD brings to my life and learn to use it wisely. But for this, I would have to learn more about ADHD in greater depth and grasp the potential value it held for me.

I'm a compulsive knowledge seeker, and I browsed the internet for anything that had the word ADHD. Buried in the millions of bytes of juicy tidbits, there were two that got my attention. The first: ADHD is hereditary, which meant that if Kristian and Kia ever had their share of hurricanes, a possible cause could be ADHD. The next was that many famous leaders and entrepreneurs also have been diagnosed with ADHD. This meant that I still had a huge potential of leadership and entrepreneurship qualities waiting to be unleashed in my life.

There was a definite value in this. Clearly, remaining a Smileless Pauper was not an option. On the other hand, the leadership and entrepreneurship tidbit was so thought provoking, it appeared like another potential game changer. It set free my next set of invisible friends, my leadership and entrepreneurship talents that I now realized had been subdued within me for many years. With them by my side, I knew on the odyssey, I had a powerful combination of talents and experiences that would enable me to design a way to navigate the obstacles that came with ADHD. They would also enable me to find ways to unleash the most powerful Oh Yes Emotions that would energize me and eject me from its turbulence into the calm world of Oh Landia.

By the end of 2021, with my physical and mental health strengthened, my energy level more stable, and hating every moment of being a Smileless Pauper, I was ready to take responsibility to find how to work with my perfections and imperfections linked to my brand of ADHD. I was determined to do whatever it took to work toward achieving my three goals and to start gathering my smiles that would lead me away from my Smileless Pauper status. Strapping on the last of my weakest of smiles, I found myself eager to move on to the next adventure, to enter Oh Landia, simulate my ADHD meteors and hurricanes, and experiment with ways to learn more about my thirty Oh Yes and Oh No Emotions and the value that ADHD brought to my life.

CONCEPT 3

THE EXTRAPRENEUR LADDER

The concept of the Extrapreneur Ladder is a spin on Corporate Ladder. I use it actively in my life as an analogy to help me monitor how I'm faring on the odyssey. The more energy I use on creating Oh Yes Stories, the more I will tone the emotional muscles that help me strengthen my Ex-Factor, and the higher I climb up my Extrapreneur Ladder. Each step will take me one step closer to an aspect of Ohism. The reverse is also true; if I'm creating an overdose of Oh No Stories, the power of my emotional muscles and strength of my Ex-Factor diminishes, and I can fall a step or more down the ladder too.

As a child, and even often today, I always thought that the grass was greener on the other side of the wall. The higher the wall the greener the grass. I was curious, so there was no wall too high to climb to explore if this were really so.

The same analogy was true now, so before I entered Oh Landia, I wanted to take a peek through the portal to see what lay on the other side. But I was reluctant to peek because I felt that Oh Landia would disrupt my life forever.

To prepare myself to enter Oh Landia, as there was no book *A Traveler's Guide to Visit Oh Landia*, I had to rely on my disruption experience from the corporate world.

As a management consultant I've used the word "disruption" to sell projects to clients while trying to guide them on how they can turn their corporation's woes around. But this time was different. I was trying to sell myself a project to enter Oh Landia, daring to disrupt my own life, to develop into this unknown persona – an Extrapreneur.

I was nervous. So, to pep myself up before teleporting myself out of the hurricane, taking a peep through the portal, I turned to my bragging gene. I told anyone who was willing to listen that "I'm going to Oh Landia where I want to become an Extrapreneur." As my confidence grew, I began throwing the words Extrapreneur and Extrapreneurship around in conversations; however, behind the confident veil of the words was a meek whisper that I attributed to a scared Oh, "Kiran, the process you're about to enter of becoming an Extrapreneur is an irreversible one. It is not for the fainthearted. Are you ready to turn your back on the privileged life you have now and continue on your odyssey in his new mysterious world, Oh Landia?"

"Yes," I told the meek whisper, "I am ready!" With my leadership and entrepreneurship spirit for company, there was now nothing that could hold me back from entering Oh Landia.

To gain more confidence before I was ready to take my first peek at Oh Landia, in the depths of my imagination, I pictured myself as a fearless hero, wandering bravely in Oh Landia, with my invisible friends, Leadership and Entrepreneurship on my shoulder, navigating around obstacles, volunteering to take on years of strife with only the vague promise of becoming an Extrapreneur leading a marvelous life hanging somewhere far away on the fuzzy horizon.

I was all excited and getting ready to teleport myself out of the hurricane and start my next adventure in Oh Landia, when a new whisper started buzzing in my ear: "Kiran, what is Extrapreneurship, Extrapreneurs, and Ex-Factor?"

I myself was still in doubt about these three terms, so this was my chance to sort things out. I replied "Extrapreneurs are people like me, gifted with the extra qualities of ADHD, Leadership, and Entrepreneurship. To become an Extrapreneur, I must learn the craft of Extrapreneurship. It's a learning-by-doing craft, one that will help me achieve my three goals and become a Smiling Billionaire. When I commit to learning Extrapreneurship, I also commit to strengthening my Ex-Factor, my recipe for the ideal cocktail of my perfect and imperfect ADHD, Leadership, and Entrepreneurship qualities, the ones I use to improve the way I communicate, coordinate, and connect with the world.

As the hurricane brought me closer to the portal, I got more and more nervous and the whisper got a bit more frenetic: "How are you going to monitor that you're strengthening your Ex-Factor and improving the way you communicate, coordinate, and connect with the world?"

The meek whisper was irritating, and I wanted to turn back and run deeper into the hurricane. But the fear of being stuck forever in it egged me on to build my Extrapreneur Ladder, the one I would scale into Oh Landia.

When I had finally built it, despite being tossed and turned about by the hurricane, it had six steps and between each step was a recommended list of talents and skills I would have to develop to strengthen my Ex-Factor. When I looked closely at it, I knew deep down that this was the perfect thing to bring out each time I start a new adventure or have an obstacle to overcome. Using the Extrapreneur Ladder, I can crawl up to the highest step my Ex-Factor has the power to bring me to. Then I can stand on it and only when I enjoy the view or appreciate the complexity of the obstacle course ahead of me, can I decide if I'm equipped with the right configuration of my Ex-Factor to succeed in the adventure or navigate the obstacle ahead.

I loved my Extrapreneur Ladder and was ready to use it. To conclude, I answered those whispered questions, saying, "Extrapreneurship is a set of interrelated stories, concepts, and toys that I learn on my odyssey. They will help me to understand the plethora of new possibilities ahead. Now that I'm aware that my Ales have many other qualities that I never knew of, I can document them so I understand the risks and rewards that lie ahead of me, and monitor my progress as I strengthen my Ex-Factor to achieve my three goals."

Once I realized that I was getting more comfortable with grasping the concepts of Extrapreneurship, I put on the last of my smiles, and thus energized, I let out a loud cry, "Oh, Why not?" and teleported myself out of the hurricane. I landed on my feet in front of the portal, got up, and clutching my Extrapreneur Ladder, I peeped through the portal and got my first glimpse of Oh Landia.

The value I extracted from this concept is that, at regular intervals, before making a decision about how to proceed in a complex situation in life, I should sit on my Extrapreneur Ladder and enjoy the view ahead of me and behind me, and determine whether or not I'm ready to undertake the adventure ahead of me.

WELCOME TO 'OH LANDIA'

Oh Landia is my ethereal playground for my odyssey and my safe place where I can train to be who I want to be. Oh Landia exists in those last few millimeters of my mind and body that are uncorrupted by five decades of life on Planet Earth. In Oh Landia, I will declutter my life and free up space in my mind and body to let the magical boundaries of this new land spread in my imagination.

As I peeked through the portal in awe, what I saw was hazy. I realized that it would play out across two worlds: a material world of Planet Earth, the one I live on and Oh Landia, an ethereal world of pixies that is home to all my Ohs and to which I can teleport myself at will. Journeying between these two worlds – to learn to become a Smiling Billionaire would surely throw up many obstacles at first, but, over time, I would learn to navigate seamlessly between them and practice all that I'm learning in Oh Landia on Planet Earth. There, I will find the final proof that I'm achieving my three goals and becoming a Smiling Billionaire.

I was still nervous; so, to boost my self-confidence, I dreamt up a new word called DontDoNation, a name of Planet Earth, in which a much-used phrase that's directed at me is:

> *"Don't you dare....bite your nails, sit with your legs on the sofa, run, talk back, mumble, swim in the dirty water, wear those dirty socks.*

Or,

> *Why don't you ever ...listen, follow the rules, sit still, stop fidgeting, pay attention, and more."*

I loved my life on DontDoNation, but knew it was about to become much more exciting. Now as counter to DontDoNation, my ethereal world Oh Landia had taken shape. In it, if I were met by the words "Kiran, do you dare......." and if I were up to the challenge, then, in line with my three goals, I could discover ways to become the Kiran I wanted to be.

As the view through the portal to Oh Landia was clearing up, I visualized Oh Landia as a virtual independent country founded by me in 2021. It is a figment of my imagination. So, like a chameleon, depending on my mood and the place I want to learn Extrapreneurship, it can one day be Goa, or a coffee plantation, or the Swiss Alps, or a cold gray winter day in Copenhagen, or a hot day in a desert in the Middle East.

Oh Landia is not found on any map, but I decided that the map of Oh Landia would look like my life's puzzle, the one that I am trying to solve on the odyssey. As I drew the map it became clear that the Ales were the three main pieces of the puzzle. Are they working together in harmony or are they in conflict? This has a significant impact on the Oh Yes and Oh No Stories I create.

Visually, the role the Ales played in my life was best depicted by a set of capes on the map. So I decided that the significant geographic features of Oh Landia would be three capes. At each cape there was a confluence of these three mighty oceans, each a symbol for one of the Ales. If they were all in a good mood, my life was in harmony, and I churned out Oh Yes Stories. If any of them were at odds with me or one or both of the others, my life was filled with conflict and I churned out Oh No Stories.

Further, I realized that just as the weather at a cape is unpredictable and can swing from glorious to extreme in quick time, I would have to always remember that on my odyssey I would have to juggle the predictable and unpredictable, known and unknown perfect and imperfect qualities in my life.

As I finished drawing the map of Oh Landia, I nicknamed the capes The Cape of Oh Yes, a metaphor of a beautiful place that I lived in for five decades and enjoyed a life filled largely with smiles, with just a few occasional grimaces; The Cape of Oh No, a metaphor for the place I am living in the hardest period of my life filled overwhelmingly with grimaces; and the last cape was called The Cape of Oh.

I had no clue what life in Cape of Oh looked like. But I dreamed that it would be a safe place in which I could learn to live a life of harmony with the Ales and embrace all our perfections and imperfections. Like an explorer ready for my next adventure, I was apprehensive as I gazed in trepidation at the mysterious and enticing horizon I had sketched on the map and marked as the final destination of my odyssey. I was confident that on the odyssey I would discover amazing insights about living with the Ales as well as engage in some epic battles with them. I decided that the natives of Oh Landia are eagerly awaiting my arrival. They are wise people who will mentor me in the art of Ohism and the infrastructure of Oh Landia and help me learn ways to bring Oh back into my life.

Oh Landia is my celebration of the title of ADHD. I had the audacity to appoint myself as its founding father. What will happen when I enter Oh Landia? I knew I could create a plan, as I'm surrounded by infinite ethereal things that are the source of my maverick ideas and, thereby, smiles. To keep my life simple, I decided that for each maverick idea that created Oh Yes Stories, I would fix a must-share-before date by which I should spread it to the world. A failure to do so is an opportunity lost to create some of my billion smiles. Sharing this book with the world is an example of a maverick idea.

In Oh Landia, an Extrapreneur will never stop searching for meaningful things that can inspire us to increase our fluency in the field. I decided that just as I had scaled walls as a child in search of new exciting experiences, here too, as my fluency in Extrapreneurship increases, I can climb up or fall down my own Extrapreneur Ladder, placed on my wall of choice, at my pace.

Historically, the best way to learn anything new for me has always been through stories. I'm blessed with a fertile imagination and knew I had access to a lot of my own stories. Clearly, this was the place to start the search for inputs to strengthen my Ex-Factor. Once I realized that I was getting more comfortable with grasping the concepts of learning about Ohism and Extrapreneurship in Oh Landia, I put on the last of my smiles, and thus energized, with a loud cry "Oh, Why not? jumped through the portal and into Oh Landia. Now began my next adventure – to relive my stories and discover the emotional muscles to strengthen my Ex-Factor.

The value I extracted from this concept is how important it is for me to have a safe space away from the prying eyes of people as I try out quirky things that make me smile but may make me seem ridiculous in the eyes of others.

THE STORY ARCHIVES

I am eagerly seeking a way to bring Oh back into my life. There are so many options to do this, but as I investigate them, I realize that I have a built-in database of millions of my own stories archived within me. Stories in which I've been the hero, the villain, the rebel, the leader, the entrepreneur, the magician, the romantic, the clown. I have to find an elegant way to access the valuable information in these stories. As I do this, the concept of the Story Archives is born to help me always remember that the solutions to my problems are, more often than not, within me and not outside me.

My first contact with Oh Landia was my head: I landed on it and got a well-deserved bump. I was now ready to venture further into this new wonderland. The first sign that greeted me read,

"ADHD is your life partner, to have and to hold, for better, for worse, for richer, for poorer, in sickness and in health, to love and to cherish."

When I had gathered my wits, I spotted a sign that said "The Story Archives", with a catch phrase below "You are your stories." I picked up a brochure on the Story Archives and found these sections very relevant for the odyssey ahead – Analyzing your past stories to understand the value they bring to your life and How to use this value to help you create the future you dream of."

I opened the door and got my first view of an Oh Landian. Boy, she was a serious pixie.

She came up and in a serene voice said, "I am Mrs. Bolt, the librarian. Welcome to the Story Archives of my Library. Feel free to wander around, and, if you need any help to bolt your nuts, you know where to find me." And, in a puff she was gone.

Meet
Mrs. Bolt

I scratched my head at her last comment, "Weird," I said aloud. As I wandered through the archives, I came across a shelf labeled Kiran's Incredible Collection of Oh Yes and Oh No Stories. I was thrilled. Neatly stacked in boxes, were many artifacts of my past. As I browsed through them, I found handwritten notes of key moments in my life; letters; report cards; certificates of achievement; pictures; recordings; conversations with family, friends, and foes. The list went on and on. I skimmed through them and started day dreaming about the past with a small smile on my face. When I reached a few artifacts that documented some of the most pivotal moments in my life, I soon realized just how enormous an effort I would have to put in to analyze these stories, for in them lay the secret of what my Ex-Factor was!

When my leadership gene sensed my energy levels drop, and a grimace coming on, it suggested, "Kiran, you shouldn't be disheartened. Before we start analyzing the stories, let's sort through your stories strategically. I suggest that we use the 80/20 formula. That is, 80% of our best Oh Yes Stories or worst Oh No Stories are created by 20% of our perfections or imperfections." I loved Leadership's suggestion.

He continued, "Let's also make a list of your perfections and imperfections, specifically linked to your Ale qualities. With this formula and list, we have an effective way to browse through what felt like millions of stories and find a pattern in the root cause and the unifying element behind your Oh Yes and Oh No Stories."

With a sigh of relief, I said, "Let the spring cleaning of my stories begin."

Leadership whispered, "Remember to add an Oh Yes and Oh No label and a 'Do more of It' or 'Don't do it anymore' date to each of them."

When he saw me looking confused, he guessed it was about the dates; so, he explained, "A 'Don't do it anymore' date is for stories that make you grimace; we should find out how to stop creating them. On the other hand, a 'Do more of it' date is for those that make you smile, the ones you are not creating enough of currently. The date for 'Do more of it' will lay down a timeline to start creating Oh Yes Stories regularly. Once our spring cleaning is done, we can analyze all these stories. That will help us to understand the role your ADHD, Leadership, and Entrepreneurship as well as your perfect and imperfect qualities have as villains or heroes in creating the Oh Yes and On No Emotions of these stories. This analysis will help you to learn more about your Ex-Factor."

In earnest, I started the spring cleaning, though it's something I normally hate. After a few months, despair set in. The last of my smiles was exhausted. Tired and disheartened, my entrepreneur gene started buzzing in my ear, "Kiran, let's get out of this creepy place. There must be a hundred easier ways to become an Extrapreneur."

"Hell no," said my leadership gene. "Kiran, we must complete the spring cleaning. I know it brings a grimace to your face, but it's vital for you to become an Extrapreneur. Have faith in your attitude and continue to find the key to unlock the value in these stories."

Fortified with these words of encouragement, I pushed ahead with the spring cleaning. The grimace on my face remained prominent. For months, relentlessly, I sorted through literally thousands of stories, reliving many of them in my future avatar of Kiran, The Extrapreneur, The Smiling Billionaire.

When I was done with spring cleaning 'Kiran's Incredible Collection of Oh Yes and Oh No Stories' archive, I appreciated the power of 80/20. Here, before me in badly written notes, lay the key to unlock the value of the Oh Yes Stories I need more of, and the Oh No Stories I need to reduce if I wished to strengthen my Ex-Factor.

Over the next few months, I spent many hours analyzing each to discover my obvious as well as hidden values. I painstakingly mapped them and filtered the list down to thirty Oh Yes and Oh No Stories that I imagined were brewed by my Ales. Each story is brewed using a combination of the Ale Emotional Muscles that either make me smile or grimace.

With this piece of wisdom garnered from the Story Archives, the task ahead of me on the odyssey to achieve my purpose, smile more and grimace less, was now clearer: enjoy these thirty Oh Yes and Oh No Stories; find out how their emotional muscles individually or in combinations, make me smile and grimace; and discover the inspiration to train each of their emotional muscles so they can help me strengthen my Ex-Factor. In the end, that will make me achieve my three goals and become a Smiling Billionaire.

Using the concept of the Story Archives and the 80/20 formula, I drew up a map of my analysis of my Oh Yes and Oh No Stories and the Oh Yes and Oh No Emotions linked to the countless combinations. The result of this analysis highlights that my undiagnosed ADHD is a probable cause that weakens my Ex-Factor, and, as a result, Oh makes me grimace more than I smile. As my Ex-Factor weakens, Oh is deprived of what he enjoys the most i.e. to make me smile, so he shrivels up and becomes the weakest version of himself. He becomes so ashamed of losing this power to make me smile that he goes into hiding. Here he is found by my Oh No Emotions behind my grimaces. As a few of these Oh No Emotions thrive by keeping me in my miserable situation, they love the imbalance in my Ex-Factor. As Oh uses this to make me grimace more than I smile, they have taken him captive and do all that they can to make me grimace. Soon Oh who thrives from my smiles, becomes even more frail and can no longer play an active role in making me smile.

To rectify this imbalance in my Ex-Factor, and free Oh from his frail existence, on my odyssey I must redesign my Ex-Factor to include the new knowledge of the perfect and imperfect qualities of my brand of ADHD, Leadership, and Entrepreneurship so Oh can enjoy a good smile and become strong again. To refine my Ex-Factor to become powerful again, so that Oh can once more be active and make me smile, I map thirty Oh Yes and Oh No Emotions that seem to impact my perfect and imperfect ADHD, Leadership, and Entrepreneurship qualities. Fifteen of these Oh Yes Emotions help Oh make me smile and fifteen of these Oh No Emotions help Oh make me grimace. These are the thirty Emotions I will have to train so that they can dynamically work with each other and not against each other or in isolation to make my Ex-Factor powerful again. They are what Oh will use from now on to make me smile more and grimace less.

The map of my Oh Yes and Oh No Stories and Emotions looked like this:

*To help me create more **Oh Yes Stories** in which **I am more:***

Alert, Confident, Courageous, Competitive, Diligent, Enthusiastic, Energetic, Focused, Friendly, Funny, Grateful, Humble, Heroic, Playful, and Thoughtful,

*I need to train the muscles behind these **fifteen Oh Yes Emotions** so I can **create emotions** linked to*

Admiration, Adoration, Amusement, Appreciation, Awe, Calmness, Excitement, Interest, Joy, Nostalgia, Relief, Romance, Satisfaction, Surprise, and Sympathy

*To help me create less **Oh No Stories** in which **I am less:***

> Aggressive, Argumentative, Chaotic, Egoistic, Envious, Greedy, Materialistic, Helpless, Impatient, Irritated, Forgetful, Frustrated, Guilty, Lethargic, and Restless,

*I need to train the muscles behind these **fifteen Oh No Emotions** that **create emotions** linked to*

> Anger, Anxious, Awkwardness, Boredom, Contempt, Confusion, Craving, Embarrassment, Disgust, Disappointment, Distress, Fear, Horror, Pain, and Sadness

Wow! That's a mouthful.

⌒

Before I move on to the next adventure, a word of caution. Emotions and emotional muscles being fluffy expressions, and inspired by Mrs. Bolt's comment, "If you need any help to bolt your nuts," I decided one way to work with emotion was to view it as an object that I enjoy, in this case nuts. So I often refer to them as Nuts. If you're wondering why, let me clarify: a Nut encapsulates a set of interconnected thoughts, feelings, actions, and words linked to a particular emotion. On the odyssey, with time and patience by my side and in the serenity of Oh Landia away from my chaotic life on DontDoNation, I can enjoy the immense value of each nut that symbolizes a set of emotions I want to work with. I have the luxury to unpack and analyze the thoughts, feelings, actions, and words of each of these emotions and understand the impact they have on my smiles and grimaces. And as I exited the Story Archives, I bid adieu to Mrs. Bolt and whistled my Oh Ditty that I had also composed to cheer me up as I was spring cleaning my stories.

Kiran,

I am mostly naughty,

I seem to be a natural leader and a maverick entrepreneur,

I can't be bothered with attention to detail,

I make careless mistakes,

I love to daydream, especially when I'm bored,

I do not like to study,

I love to be late,

I love to irritate people,

I love to play pranks and tease others,

I enjoy being defiant of authority, and deliberately annoying people,

I believe in myself,

I rarely give up when things get tough,

I am honest, faithful, trustworthy and charming,

I love to break invisible boundaries, and

I love to chase my daydreams.

The Story Archives is a great concept. It helped me remember the vast number of stories I could call on to search for solutions to many of my problems. It forced me to remember to take the harder and more painful route to look inward for solutions than the easier route to look outward for solutions to my problems. I frequently visit the Archive of Stories when I feel a bad case of Stress, Anxiety, Depression, and Sleeplessness (SADS) coming on, so instead of being helpless and indulging in navel gazing, I force myself to get lost in The Story Archive and relive the stories stored there to cheer me up with a few smiles.

COOL AND UNCOOL MOVES

I need to find ways to refine my Ex-Factor to meet the three goals in my life. I know that I need to be active to create the energy for this purpose. I know that just sitting on the couch and identifying my goals will not produce any results, and I need to make a move on and start doing new things. These needs triggered the concept of Cool and Uncool Moves. From now on, every investment I make in Ohism to move towards achieving my three goals must be a Cool Move, one of my everyday actions that creates energy. Moreover, I always need to be sure that I focus on doing more Cool Moves than Uncool Moves to maintain a surplus of energy to help me achieve my three goals.

The adventure to complete the spring cleaning of my Story Archive was a success. But it also gave me a glimpse of how challenging the odyssey would be. For, if each adventure were as tedious, I risked the possibility that my last few smiles would run out too soon, forcing my odyssey to come to an abrupt halt.

To mitigate this risk, I needed to find a way to maintain a healthy balance between my smiles and my grimaces, and this search led me to develop the concept of Cool and Uncool Moves. Cool Moves are simple everyday actions that I've learned from people and content that I admire, slightly tweaked to suit my brand of ADHD, leadership, and entrepreneurship. They help me burn brighter and smile more. Uncool Moves are actions that make me grimace and drain me of energy. Having a love for playing games, I realized that I could view the adventures as a series of intertwined games played in Oh Landia. If I played these just by myself on my playground and with my rules, it would be easier to monitor the amount I smile or grimace each time. In Extrapreneurship, I called each of these games a Cool Move, one that helps me train my emotional muscles. As I learned to play and master each particular Cool Move, I found that I could understand the emotions I experienced better and thus identify the tweaks that were needed to ensure that they strengthened my Ex-Factor.

Training my emotional muscles to excel in mastering Cool Moves was not simple. I realized that I needed to approach this with the mindset of a professional Athlete. Athletes have a superior Ex-Factor, which is finely tuned to enable them to excel in their chosen sport. But to make this Ex-Factor count, and scale great heights, they also need a team of professionals to train and manage their careers. These professionals continuously introduce them to state-of-the-art methods to develop the particular Ex-Factor which helps them edge past their closest competitors. In order to understand the mindset of such athletes, I did some quick research into the methods of my favorite heroes. Behind each visible success, there were hours and hours of hard work that one doesn't see. Along with their team of chosen professionals, they design and follow a process to train, manage, and continuously sharpen their Ex-Factor. In the process, they are exposed to intense physical and mental stress; they usually shed tears, tear one or more muscles, or even break a bone or two. But they also learn to stay positive during good times as well as bad, to play for the team, and to pick themselves or a teammate up every time they go through a torrid patch.

It may take many years to find your ideal team of professionals. But, when that happens, the team will help you focus on what I define in Extrapreneurship as Nut Worth, the four pillars of wealth: physical, mental, financial, and social. It's clear that an athlete who doesn't manage any of these pillars properly can, at any stage of their career, suddenly lose balance and face a high risk of their career totally burning out. However, if they manage these pillars well, and have the controls for them firmly in their hands, they can develop the power to burn brighter and extend their careers for many more years.

If I wanted to excel in Extrapreneurship, I had to onboard a team of professionals who would first help me understand the components of my Ex-factor and then support me further in designing and diligently following a process that will train, manage, and continuously tune my Ex-factor to increase the four pillars of my wealth.

Learning Extrapreneurship was now getting exciting! But I still heard a nagging whisper, "Kiran, all this sounds like hard work. Are you really willing to give up the comfortable life you've built for yourself, to start changing your lifestyle and embark on this airy-fairy-sounding odyssey?"

With an irritated look (though the question was very relevant), I answered, "Yes. I have no intention of remaining a spectator in my own life and watching helplessly as ADHD continues to disrupt it. I have always been a disruptor, so, I will, instead, use ADHD as my change agent, one that would inspire me to burn brighter and stop burning out."

The nagging whisper continued prodding, "But, what actually are Cool Moves, Kiran?"

I replied promptly, "Cool Moves are simple everyday actions that help build perfect qualities to create energy. There are both Old Cool Moves and New Cool Moves. Old Cool Moves are good actions based on positive qualities that I've learned since I was a child and a dependable source of my Oh Yes Stories. Unfortunately, over the years, I've taken many of these Old Cool Moves for granted and stopped using them regularly in my daily life. New Cool Moves are actions that will awaken good new qualities that I must develop to become an Extrapreneur that will help me in the future to create many Oh Yes Stories.

"Uncool Moves is the evil twin of Cool Moves. They are actions that I have developed over the years which unleash bad qualities and are the source of many Oh No Stories. I'm human and will always be attracted to both Old and New Uncool Moves. I imagine that getting rid of them will be the biggest challenge in my future to becoming an Extrapreneur.

"The greatest source of Uncool Moves is when I try to copy the bad qualities displayed by anti-heroes. I know that Uncool Moves are detrimental to my health. Unfortunately, because I think that they're so valuable in my life and I can't live without them, it's very difficult for me to stop doing them, so they continue to create many Oh No Stories in my life.

"While learning and integrating Cool Moves and unlearning Uncool Moves, any progress I make in climbing the Extrapreneur ladder, big or small, is valuable. As a minimum, a Cool Move stimulates my four pillars of wealth, has no bad side effects and can be applied to many aspects of my life. The most important thing about Cool Moves is that they should cost me as little money as possible to master them. On the other hand, they will require me to invest a lot of time and energy to master them."

I was pleased with my reply since it silenced that whisper. I was now ready for my next adventure to identify the team of professionals (I dubbed them my Miners and Millers), the ones who would mold, guide, and direct me in Extrapreneurship and provide the support system I needed to survive and then thrive on my odyssey.

∽

For me, Cool or Uncool Moves is a great concept. At times, when I feel I'm not smiling enough or grimacing too much, I can revisit this collection, and select the few of them that I'm confident will boost my energy levels.

MINERS AND MILLERS

When my undiagnosed ADHD was burning me out, I reached out to many professionals, family, friends, and a few foes whom I respected to help me get through these tough periods. The complication was how to filter the quality, quantity, and often conflicting advice I was getting from them to stop burning out. This filtering task wasn't easy, but after my diagnosis, I realized that I was dependent for my survival on a few good souls who stuck with me through my darkest moments and my gloomy demeanor. Standing on the shoulders of these great people, I created the concept of Miners and Millers, a spin on a board of directors, to showcase how important it is to find a good balance between being an entrepreneur and leader to achieve your wildest goals.

It was somewhere between 2018 and 2021, as I reflected on my Oh No Stories, that I realized that I could categorize my advisors and supporters into two groups, based on the nature of the guidance and direction they were giving me on how to survive my hurricanes. I called these groups Miners and Millers. The people who fell into the group of Miners generally had an entrepreneurial mindset and encouraged me to work hard to find the hidden value in my hurricanes and meteors and to discover innovative ways to extract this value, as it would help me achieve my three goals. On the other hand, the Millers generally seemed to have a leadership mindset and encouraged me to be more patient so as to better understand the long-term impact ADHD would have in my life and gradually build a robust and sustainable process to survive and thrive with it.

Both categories of advice, though contrasting, were valuable. As my deep conversations with both Miners and Millers continued, I was gathering a vast amount of information based on their diverse life experiences. Now, I really needed to process these in a structured way so as to filter the relevant inputs required to reach my goal.

That was how the concept of "Mining and Milling" was formed. Mining and Milling are the processes that Miners and Millers use in their professions to find solutions to my answers. I imagined this to be an information processing filter, though it was really just a solo interview technique in which I would ask myself why, what, how, where, and when questions pertaining to the problem I was trying to solve using the information I was gathering from the Miners and Millers. I visualized the process as if I were first taking explorative bites into pieces of the information, to see if I liked it. If I liked it, I stored it to be chewed on at leisure to go deeper and uncover the solutions I was seeking. After hours of Mining and Milling, usually all by myself, I was gradually able to filter out a list of possible answers! The first couple of times I tried Mining and Milling were tough. I needed to probe deep into my soul and find honest answers. At the start, I cheated a bit and found the perfect answers that would pacify my ego. But, in hindsight, I realized I was only fooling myself and slowly learned to embrace honesty whenever I practiced Mining and Milling.

Though Miners and Millers are separate professions, in Extrapreneurship I define Mining and Milling as two separate but interconnected processes. Together, they're like the symbol of infinity, seamless with no start and no end. When I apply them to process my stories and find my Oh Yes and Oh No Emotions, I go into biting mode, often with a Miner. I revisit the story and find the courage to dig deeper. I must be prepared to have sweat on my brow and accept the personal consequences of discovering the impact each of them has. I can't stop there, either. I have to bravely design each of the Cool and Uncool Moves that I need to master to help me smile more. When I find a Cool/Uncool Move that I think has a role to play in strengthening my Ex-Factor, I go into chewing mode with a Miller with the skill to help me analyze it. With their help, I'll be able to zero in on actions that can help me master the Move, extract maximum value out of it, and show myself how to integrate it into my daily life.

Mining and Milling sounds simple, but it's all the more complex for someone like me with ADHD to practice. Because of my brand of ADHD, mining my stories for opportunities is my passion; it comes naturally to me and makes me smile. But the analytical and diligent work required to mill the opportunities that will strengthen and tune my Ex-Factor into my daily life, often makes me grimace.

A valuable toy that I got from Mining and Milling was the "Bored Map." This map helps me pinpoint a chain of emotions that usually bring on boredom, and when I get bored, I usually get restless and trigger a series of Oh No Emotions. These lead to grimaces that I could easily have avoided and indicate that I need to break this series of Oh No Emotions by performing a few Cool Moves that will make me smile.

It was now clear that in order to learn Extrapreneurship, I would have to learn to be both a Miner and a Miller and strike a proper balance between their qualities. THAT would help me strengthen my Ex-Factor! Any failure to achieve a balance, on the other hand, would mean I cannot benefit from all my perfect Ale qualities! Thus, my Miners and Millers became my professional team who would mold, guide, and direct me in Extrapreneurship and support me to survive and thrive on my odyssey.

Once I had formalized the concept of Miners and Millers, I began the process of identifying them. They included my immediate family, a couple of rare friends, respected foes and teachers, my team of medical professionals, and my cocker spaniel, Charlie. Working with them, I analyzed my pre- and post-ADHD diagnosis stories and found a number of Cool Moves to help me bring Oh back into my life.

This concept was immensely valuable; it helped me identify my Miners and Millers, with whom I interact with as my personal board of directors. They all are committed to giving me strategic guidance and support to achieve my mission, purpose and goals. I consult with them one on one at regular intervals and share my progress on my odyssey and I value their advice regarding course corrections I need to make to reach my goals.

Equipped with one more powerful concept that would help bring Oh back into my life, I realized I had made definite progress in climbing up the Extrapreneur Ladder. I was now ready for the next adventure to learn more about Oh.

My Smile-Making Machine

If I wanted to create a billion smiles every day, I had to run my life like a business. The user story for me to do this led me to create another concept: I was a businessperson with a product called the Smile-Making Machine whose most impressive feature was Oh the algorithm, the secret behind my contagious smile. But now as the quality, quantity and brilliance of my smiles decreased, I was losing all my customers and heading toward becoming a Smileless Pauper. I desperately needed a way to turn my failing business around, and the way to do this was to reinvent the Smile-Making Machine and invent a more powerful version of Oh.

One day, while in the shower, I let out a sudden shout "Oh!" The reason? I had been thinking of one of my favorite gadgets: an ice-cream-making machine, the type in which all I have to do is follow a recipe, add all the wonderful ingredients in, and just press a button to create the ice cream of my choice. I had just found one more concept: that I have my very own Smile-Making Machine deep within me. The one that has been the true source of my smiles. I imagined my Smile-Making Machine with an algorithm Oh, that takes the information I feed it with to produce my smiles.

But the situation I faced now was The Smile-Making Machine and its algorithm Oh, after performing well for five decades, is burnt out. Puzzled as to why the machine had burnt out, trying to find an answer, I returned to my Miners and Millers and shared the concept of my Smile-Making Machine and Oh and the probable role he plays in my life. Most of them grinned at the absurdity of my Smile-Making Machine, but I had fallen deeply in love with the concept. After hours of Mining and Milling on the role Oh plays in my life, we drew a conclusion that Oh has for five decades led a perfect life living in a beautiful place called Cape of Oh Yes. Here, Oh, using my powerful Ex-Factor made by doing things I love and that come naturally to me, has churned out millions of smiles that come in three sizes: Oh Yes, Ooh Yes, and Oooh Yes.

But life in Cape of Oh Yes did not last forever. My Ex-Factor gradually lost its zing, as my undiagnosed ADHD makes my life miserable. This is followed by a horrid period in a cold, dark place called the Cape of Oh No. There, Oh, the power of my Ex-Factor, diminishes, and the quality and quantity of my smiles diminish too. Now, Oh can only churn out a stream of grimaces as I struggle to tackle new obstacles that ADHD brought into my life. These grimaces also come in three sizes: Oh No, Ooh No, and Oooh No, and as my grimaces accumulate, I am burning out. In my miserable state, thankfully some mysterious forces had taken Oh captive and prevented him burning out completely alongside me. I convinced myself that if I could bring Oh back into my life and train him to work with my most powerful Ex-Factor, this new version of Oh would play a crucial role in helping me create a billion smiles and become a Smiling Billionaire.

I knew this seemed like a wild dream.

Until that point, I had 107 exciting ideas on how to become a smiling billionaire bubbling in my mind. But, by the next morning, 106 of them had lost their bubbles, the only exception being the idea of Oh as the algorithm of my Smile-Making Machine. All this while I had been dreaming about Oh. But I knew that my now famous whisper would return once again to question the validity of the concepts that had been churning around in my mind. Sure enough, in an irritating voice, it said, "Kiran, you don't have the creativity, courage, and ability to find and free Oh."

No matter how much I tried to convince myself that Oh was just a gimmick and I would soon get bored of him, my Miners and Millers had noticed a spark in my smile and shored me up with these words: "Kiran, we have absolutely no doubt that you possess the qualities needed to find and free Oh. But you need help to free something as maverick, intangible, and formidable as Oh. We know nothing about fixing broken Smile-Making Machines, but let's all think about who you can ask for help to achieve this."

We struggled for a few days and finally reached a conclusion that was simple yet unconventional. The Miners and Millers concluded, "Kiran, you have three incredible partners in crime: your Ale qualities. They could be the right ones to help find and free Oh. The challenge is that they have strong individual, often contrasting qualities.

To get the partnership to work, we have to find a way to bring all of them into play. Only as a team will you be able to bring together all the qualities to find and free Oh.

"The question you need to answer before you enter into a partnership with the Ales is do you have the courage to get to know each of them closely, understand the role they play in creating your smiles and grimaces, and convince them to help you to find and free Oh? We agree that once you've freed and retrained Oh, he'll help you script some of the most powerful and meaningful Oh Yes Stories in your life."

Boy, I knew that my Miners and Millers were right. A well-trained Oh could help me reach my goal of becoming a Smiling Billionaire.

The value of my Smile-Making Machine and Oh was that they gave me something tangible to keep my fertile imagination occupied. I think it's amazing that a simple concept like Oh is all it takes to make me smile, and it also gives me something that others, who may otherwise find my odyssey too complex to follow, can easily relate to.

MISSING OH REPORT

If I wanted to bring Oh back into my life, I needed to be able to identify what he looked like. But as I now knew I had a lot of variants of Oh in me, I needed to be sure that I freed the right Oh from his captors. As I figured this out, I stumbled upon the concept of a Missing Oh Report, which is a spin on a Missing Person's Report that creative human resources officers make to attract new employees, a description of the type of person they feel is presently missing from their organization. The Missing Oh Report helped me describe what Oh looks like and share this description with my loved ones, so when they see flashes of him in my smile, they can point this out to me, and I would be a step closer to bringing Oh back into my life.

I found a Missing Person's Report template and filled it to the best of my ability with details of all the traits I thought Oh had. But I had no clue what Oh looked like and the impact he had on my life. I knew that he made me smile but had no clue about which actions of mine made him smile. I also had no clue as to why, how, when, and where he had been taken captive.

To help me write the Missing Oh Report I decided to sketch him. I was sure it would help me to understand what he looked like and what made him smile and grimace. Of course, that was easier said than done. In no time I was all confused, having conjured up a hundred images of what Oh might look like. Perhaps the irritating whisper was right about not having the qualities, courage, and ability to bring Oh back into my life.

So, to silence the whisper, back to the design board, I went but this time with a blank piece of paper and a printout of my thirty Oh Yes and Oh No Stories. One day, as I was chilling in front of a bonfire with a few Miners and Millers, I poured myself a glass of cold Ale. I watched contentedly as the glass first filled up with froth and then slowly settled down into a rich brown color still topped with a lovely, vibrant froth. As I took a sip, the cold ale made me warm and bubbly inside. As we watched the fire gracefully dance in the wind and discussed design options to build the sketch of Oh. And, suddenly, it all fell into place.

With the Ale and fire as a prop, the Miners and Millers helped me visualize Oh as an Ale and as the flames of a fire burning inside me. Both the Ale and the fire, in their own way, could either make me smile, or by raging uncontrollably inside me, make me grimace. As I visualized these scenarios, they helped me analyze the impact of an Ale and fire in my life. Oh, like an ale, keeps me smiling as long as I enjoy it in moderation. But, when I overindulge, they entangle me in a grimace as I endure an awful hangover.

From watching the fire, I felt Oh was like a matchstick. If I used its flame well, it could create sparks and start something as powerful as a fire. If I looked after the fire well and applied its energy intelligently, it would make my everyday life comfortable. I could enjoy doing what I love and comes naturally to me as I go about creating my Oh Yes Stories. On the other hand, if used unintelligently, the match stick had the power to create a destructive fire. It was these types of fires that had created my most powerful Oh No Emotions, the ones that I encountered in the Cape of Oh No and never wanted to face ever again in my life. With a smile on my lips and a shaky hand on the Mission Oh Report, I sketched the six shades of what Oh could look like.

Meet
Oh Yes

Meet
Ooh Yes

Meet
Oooh Yes

Meet
Oh No

Meet
Ooh No

Meet
Oooh No

This analogy of Oh as an Ale or the flames of fire was really cool. If I could find, free, and retrain Oh with the right process and intentions, he would help me release more of my perfect Ale qualities to make me burn brightly. If I freed and trained him with the wrong process and intentions, he would use my imperfect Ale qualities, I would be sent back to the upper right quadrant of my hurricane, and I would burn out.

⸎

The value of the Missing Oh Report was that it helped me document the reasons I smile and the reasons I grimace. I had some of the input I needed to mount what I jokingly called an Oh Search and Rescue Operation. It also taught me how I must include a team of competent advisors and ask for their help if I wished to bring Oh back into my life.

Fast forward to August 2021. As I now worried less about ADHD and more about Oh, I told myself, "ADHD may have knocked the stuffing out of me, but it has opened the amazing world of Oh Landia for me to discover my favorite Ohs."

I knew I was ready to test my hypothesis to bring back my smile. If I find the ideal combination of my perfect and imperfect qualities that come with my brand of ADHD, Leadership, and Entrepreneurship to develop a powerful Ex-factor, and learn to use my Ex-Factor effectively, I can do more of what I love, that is, smile, and by example, inspire others to smile too and support me in creating a billion new smiles every day!

MY ETHEREAL UMBILICAL CORD

In my Ales, I have three passions within me that would all play a powerful role in bringing Oh back into my life. I viewed them as holistic parts of myself with each, in their own way, giving me energy to burn brighter. To use their qualities effectively, I needed a way for all of us to bond closely together. This is where the ethereal umbilical cord concept came as a godsend, as I visualized it as an umbilical cord that unites me with the Ales.

I started to spend a lot of time with the Ales, and we had a number of heart-to-heart conversations. We spoke about how we probably were quadruplets and been separated from each other at birth and it would be cool to attach all of us back to my "ethereal umbilical cord" so we could connect, communicate, and coordinate seamlessly in the way we interact with the world.

They also loved the story of why I invented Oh, and how I lost him and was now on my odyssey to bring him back into my life. When I asked them to join me on the odyssey to find and free Oh, they all agreed, though a trifle reluctantly. With a sheepish smile they said they were ready to be attached to my ethereal umbilical cord so we could work together toward this goal. As we got to know each other, our ethereal family of four blossomed. We enjoyed sharing my stories and identifying which of us was the hero or villain. As we adjusted to our new roles in our family situation, we had a fair share of smiles and grimaces. While we had many common qualities and enjoyed our time together, we also had many contradictory ones that caused friction and unhealthy and unnecessary competition. When we interacted with each other using our contradictory qualities, we were foes and undid some of our bonding. This made me grimace.

One day, sitting around a bonfire, I explained the entire concept of Oh to them and the role Oh played in my life. They were silent when, in a sad voice, I explained about a missing smile and that I thought Oh was the reason behind my smiles and grimaces. I felt their concern as I explained how Oh gets data from my Ex-Factor, which is an ideal combination of the perfect and imperfect qualities that come with my brand of ADHD, Leadership, and Entrepreneurship. I also told them how he used to make me smile and grimace. As I was missing Oh, I needed their support to find the ideal combination of my Ex-Factor and learn to use my Ex-Factor effectively, so I can do more of what I love, that is smile, and by example, inspire others to smile too and support me to create a billion new smiles every day!

They digested what I told them in silence, and we shared what we thought was the role Oh played in our lives. As I heard each of them express their thoughts, I began to realize that each of us had a vested interest in bringing back Oh into my life, as we all wanted to burn brighter.

We took turns sharing our vision of how we can find and free Oh. The entrepreneur blabbered about his ideas to find, free, and retrain Oh, then commercialize him, selling copies of him to others for bucket loads of money. When I retorted, "It's not about money but smiles," he countered sarcastically, "You can't live only on smiles, Kiran." To drive his point home, he commented, "We already have an abundance of qualities to find and free Oh. We should get moving and start creating a billion-smile empire."

When Leadership's turn came, he said, "Kiran, while money and smiles are great, but if you could choose only one to enrich your life what would you prefer? A life with a lot of money but without a smile or a life with a lot of smiles without money?"

These questions irritated me, and I sarcastically replied, "A life with a lot of smiles and a lot of money."

Leadership shrugged his shoulders. "If you can dream it, you can achieve it. Please never forget that your responsibility as the world's first Extrapreneur is to design and follow a process that will help you attain the mission that we know you're capable of. As you enjoy the process, you'll come to lead a life of smiles that attracts money."

Through these wise words and wisecracks, my ADHD soon got lost in his own fantasy world, pondering how Oh would help him burn brighter. As he didn't care about buzzwords, he got up and left. I joked that he had probably gone off on his own odyssey to find

Oh. By the time we discovered he wasn't coming back, he was quite a distance away.

We tried hard to catch up with him, but he was too fast for us. We begged him to slow down. Reluctantly, he stopped, and we returned to the bonfire and collected our thoughts. When we all were in a good mood, we concluded that we were all in this odyssey together and needed Oh In our lives for our own selfish reasons.

Sitting around the bonfire, watching it burn warmly, in the spirit of true partnership, we committed to being equal partners, in good times and in bad.. We agreed that for our partnership to be successful, all must be winners from the start and committed to investing our perfect and imperfect qualities and regulating our roughest qualities to help me become an Extrapreneur. When the Ales asked me what my latest vision of Extrapreneurship was, I replied, "Extrapreneurship is my freedom to design a lifestyle that celebrates my ADHD. Extrapreneurship inspires me to appreciate my perfections and imperfections and learn how to strengthen my Ex-Factor." With these words, they all put up their hands to partner with me to bring back Oh in my life. As we signed our partnership agreement, I was amused when I read the names they had signed the agreement with. ADHD's scrawl read, Nut Cracker, Leadership's beautiful script said P Leader, and Entrepreneurship had inked Spark Plug.

⌐

The value of the Ethereal Umbilical Cord has meaning on two levels. The first level is how I must always be connected to my ADHD, leadership, and entrepreneurship qualities, as the old adage "United we stand, divided we fall" seems so true. At the other level, it taught me it could take months to find, free, and bring Oh back into my life. But that was just the beginning, for then, the really hard work would start: to keep him with me for the rest of my life. It also made me realize that getting rid of Uncool Moves is not easy, as the Ales will not give them up so easily. I was happy to have the Ales as my partners and it was time to move on to my next adventure to make some sort of a plan for our odyssey.

NUTS AS EMOTIONS

I have a hard time dealing openly with my emotions. I needed to overcome this barrier. "Leaders and Entrepreneurs are hard nuts to crack," led me to the concept of Nuts as an analogy to help me understand more about my thirty Oh Yes and Oh No Emotions. A nut is also a perfect symbol of an emotion that also has a source of energy stored in its core. This source of energy is protected by many layers, each with its own function. I have to be highly effective and efficient in Mining and Milling my nuts to enjoy their energy.

As soon as our adventure to draw up a plan started, I was met with immediate resistance. Nut Cracker couldn't understand why we needed to plan our odyssey and Spark Plug agreed with him. Nut Cracker said, "We're all optimists, we don't need a plan. Let's all be heroes and get cracking to hunt down the captors and free Oh from their clutches." But Leadership said, "All heroes have a plan, or they end up being zeros. Let's build a master plan for the odyssey together." Finally, we all agreed on the importance of a plan on the condition that all of us will be the heroes on the odyssey and will bring all our qualities to it. The first task on our master plan was for me to share a history of Oh with the Ales. Luckily, I had a Missing Oh report and it went along these lines: "Oh, is the word that I mumble unconsciously when I get obsessed with doing 'something.' It's the trigger that sets many actions in my life into motion. It's followed by a series of Oh Yes and Oh No, those are among the most heard and used words in my life. This 'something' makes me come alive. Very often, I know nothing about this 'something' and have no clue of the final outcome..."

I paused to see if the Ales were getting a hang of Oh. When they nodded in agreement, I continued. "Oh is also a word I often hear from a family member, friend, or foe in our interactions as they express their Oh Yes and Oh No Emotions in response to my thoughts, words and deeds. I know, by the tone of their Oh that the outcome of my thoughts, words and deeds will land me in trouble or they think I am about to do something amazing. The latter is mostly on rare occasions!"

I explained further, "Every day, I collect my share of Oh Yes and Oh No Emotions. I appreciate the depth in the word emotions, but as I like to be tangible when solving life's puzzles, I have shortlisted thirty Stories and thirty Emotions that we will have to train to develop our Ex-Factor."

At once I saw that they were confused about Ex-Factor. I patiently took them through the concept, explaining that it stood for the ideal personalized combination, or the best confluence, of my Ale qualities that would give us the power to find and free Oh and bring him back to our life.

When they began to grasp the concept of Ex-factor, I continued, "I have a hard time dealing openly with my emotions, so I chose the analogy of Nuts for the simple reason that I love eating nuts. But a nut is also a perfect symbol of an emotion that also has a source of energy stored in its core. This source of energy is protected by many layers, each with its own function. I have to be highly effective and efficient in mining and milling my nuts to enjoy their energy."

I paused and when I was met with no objections, I continued, "My thirty Oh Yes and Oh No Emotions each have their own thirty Oh Yes and Oh No Nuts." When I saw the look of disbelief on their face, I said, "Yes, I have identified thirty nuts that we will enjoy on the odyssey together. Each nut has distinct tastes: a sweet one brings a smile on faces and a bitter one brings a grimace. I smile like a baby when I enjoy Oh Yes nuts because of the pleasurable sensation they give me. The Oh Yes nuts, like my Oh Yes Emotions, come in three sizes: Oh, Ooh, and Oooh." I feel I'm losing them, but they seemed hooked and keen to hear more. "The flavor of an Oh Yes nut can last a few minutes to an hour. Some examples are when I'm enjoying a finger-licking good curry with the Guts. Ooh Yes nut can last a few days and can also add flavor to other lives. Some examples are doing well in an exam or project, or when someone I care about achieves their goal. The flavor of an Oooh Yes nut is the premium version of Oh Yes, and I'm in a smiling trance for weeks. My smiles are contagious and spread to my family, friends, and may also make my respected foes smile. The birth of my children, or discovering that if I use my ADHD qualities wisely I can lead the life I dream of are two examples…" I paused but they were now eager for more.

I continued, "Flip the coin. The Oh No nuts like my Oh Yes Emotions come in three sizes: Oh No, Ooh No, and Oooh No. The flavor of an Oh No nut makes me grimace for a few minutes, but I can get over it quickly. The grimace lasts for as long as I do something that makes me feel discouraged, worried, or apprehensive. Examples of Oh No nuts are when I lose my cool on something trivial, misplace my house keys, lock myself out of the house. The reason behind my grimace is something I have control over, and if I focus and get a system in place, I can reduce the frequency of this grimace.

"The flavor of an Ooh No is when I do something that makes me feel terrible and makes me grimace for a few days. In an argument, for example, I might say something nasty that I later regret, or I might be concerned about something in the future that's beyond my control. The price volatility of Bitcoin is an example. The grimace caused by an Ooh No nut can last for days. It reflects inner feelings of being deeply disappointed, worried, apprehensive, and melancholy. But the good news is that many of the underlying reasons behind my grimaces are things I can control. If I focus and get a system in place, I can reduce the frequency and impact of this grimace. The worst is the flavor of an Oooh No nut. I experience it very rarely; it's when something tragic happens in my life that makes me feel terrible for months. An example is when a loved one passes away."

We took a break and refreshed ourselves then I shared my Mission, Purpose, and Goals of the odyssey ahead with them. I accepted that my odyssey is complex. It was going to be a lifelong mission and that Ohism would be the key factor to make me smile again. We would have to work extremely hard to not only bring back Oh in my life but also get to know him intimately and find ways to make my life interesting enough for him to hang around with me and enjoy life together. They all agreed to be part of the odyssey, and they were on board when I suggested replacing the My with Our in my Mission, Purpose, and Goals.

Our Mission is:
To enjoy the odyssey to find, free, bring, and keep Oh in our life.

Our Purpose is:
Focus our attention on trying to smile more and grimace less!

Our Goals:

1. **Ohism** - This was a personal goal for me - Find ways how Oh can help us burn brighter and not burn out.
2. **Pioneer the Art of Entrepreneurship and become an Extrapreneur** - This is our platform to share relevant parts of Ohism to inspire people like me.
3. **Become a Smiling Billionaire** - This is our platform to share the power of Oh with the world and create a billion smiles.

We took a break and refreshed ourselves, then discussed the three goals in detail. All of them agreed that they bought into the meaning behind the word Oh. Now that we had a description of Oh, we agreed on the importance of the odyssey so we could turn up the smiles created by my Oh Yes Emotions and turn down the impact of my grimaces created by my Oh No Emotions.

When all of us had a background of the mission, purpose, and goals of the odyssey, I was ready to dive deeper into the more complex adventures that will take us forward toward bringing Oh back into our life.

The value of the Nuts concept is that it has so many meanings, but the most important one, I feel, is that it helps me to deep dive to explore many strong emotions in a creative way.

STRATEGIC TIME OUT 1

Wannabe Extrapreneurs, before you get lost in my odyssey, a word of caution. I admit, for my odyssey, I had to learn to equip myself with new qualities and unlearn many of my rough qualities. More importantly, my victories and defeats during it were all my own and not measured in money but in the intangible currency of smiles and grimaces.

My odyssey is hard, and, every day, part of me wants to escape to the good old days to continue to be a sidekick in somebody else's story. But the other part wants me to stay and discover ways to reach my three goals, the ones that focus on helping me burn brighter and not burn out. I was ready for the next adventure to introduce Extrapreneurship to the Ales.

CHAPTER 4

STORIES FROM THE CAPE OF OH YES

This chapter is a collection of Oh Yes Stories I am proud to call my own. They are from the real world, help me reflect on my life and have a profound impact on understanding my past and using it to prepare myself for my changing world. I have organized the stories into hierarchies with each story playing a pivotal role in helping me smile more and grimace less.

> *The Entrepreneur in me is aggressive.*
> *The Leader in me is confident.*
> *My ADHD is invisible.*
> *But what you see in me*
> *Is often just only a small part of the whole.*

I had my mission, purpose, goals, hobbies, and passions, and it was time now to Mine and Mill a selection of incredible Oh Yes Stories to understand how I could strengthen my Ex-Factor.

I had a head start Mining and Milling my stories thanks to my children. Over the last few years, they had encouraged me to document them for posterity, so, I had already handwritten a large number, covering somewhere close to 500 pages. What I didn't know as I wrote them was the role my Ales had played in each; nor did I know they would become the source of inspiration for me to find my Ex-Factor.

As I relive these stories, I enjoy this visual of me as a pearl hunter enjoying the good life and glorious weather on Cape of Oh Yes. These few stories are my tribute to the privileged life I had led mostly till now. When I'm on Cape of Oh Yes, I smile like a million dollars as I collect my pearls, surf the waves of life, relish good food, and smile in the company of an endless number of well-wishers.

Let's take a walk down memory lane with the Ales and try to get a handle on my Ex-Factor.

NUMBER 25 SERPENTINE STREET

Even though my present situation was miserable, I had a foundation of stories, Miners and Millers, families and friends to help me bring Oh back into my life again. The question was where to start. The answer came in a roundabout way: why not start at the place in my life where Oh first helped me burn the brightest. This was at Number 25 Serpentine Street, my ancestral home in which I have experienced different shades of all my thirty Oh Yes and Oh No Emotions surrounded by love and security created by my dad and mom. They were my first Miners and Millers who ensured that the values of the family that were now critical to helping me bring Oh back into my life were passed down through generations.

Kiran (Don't You Dare) Vas was born on the 23$^{rd\ of}$ January, 1967, in the town of Bengaluru in India. I was the only son of my parents Kevin and Blanche, born between my sisters Anita and Maya.

As a child and teenager, I was skinny, athletic, injury prone, a chatterbox, very distracted, and captain of my one-man daydreaming team. But I was blessed with broad shoulders and nerves of steel that could absorb the punches that I regularly seemed to attract from both friends and foes.

We lived in a charming bungalow built on 25 Serpentine Street, and here I enjoyed an ordinary, happy, and secure family life. Number 25 is mommy Blanche's pride in which she, with love, raised her family and anything the four of us dragged in. It was a quaint bungalow, a paradise of beautiful flowers and fruit trees on which I spent a lot of my time, climbing as high as I could, to daydream.

Dad and Mom were the best examples of Miners and Millers. They shaped many aspects of my life as I evolved from a clumsy, injury-prone child to a spicy teenager, a reluctant student, a career-focused young man, and a proud husband and father. The grace they conducted themselves with as they navigated their own struggles helped me appreciate them all the more as I experienced dark days during my own hurricanes.

Dad was a disciplinarian from whom I learned the basics of leadership. He was self-made. He carried himself with the grace of a military general proud of his troops. Structure, determination, cleanliness, being well-groomed, and no procrastination were his buzzwords, the ones he inculcated in us from birth, mostly gently but, when needed, with the firmness of a drill sergeant. From the time he got up, the house ran like clockwork but could play out different genres. One day, it could resemble an action movie set, the next day turn into a comedy set, and, on the third day, be full of drama.

Daddy was the producer and director. His three children were the cast, and with a booming voice, legendary temper, and smoking like a chimney, he directed each of us to dream and work hard to make it happen.

Dad was frugal. The rubber hose with which we watered the garden was about 20 meters long and about 20 years old. Every time it sprung a leak, dad would patch up the hole by binding old cycle tubes around it. When sections of the hose were too fragile to fix, he would cut the fragile parts off and join them together with a connector. Over the years it remained 20 meters long (though only about 10 meters of the original hose were left) and very colorful with all the patchwork. Every morning, before one of us started to water the garden, Daddy would remind us to pressure test the hose for leaks, and only when it was certified leak free could we start the watering. The lessons in frugality paid rich dividends as it ingrained in me the concept of waste not want not, which is a core principle in Extrapreneurship.

Mommy Blanche was gentle, elegant, kind, and caring and would never hurt a fly. She was the youngest of 17 children and had this amazing family of 380-plus members which spanned 5 generations. From Mommy, I learned the basics of entrepreneurship. I guess you have to learn to be mean, lean, and tough as nails to hold your own against 16 elder siblings. She also taught by example – she ran a successful home business keeping paying guests to support Daddy's meager income. Mom was always elegantly dressed, loved her food and sweets and a good laugh. She was a fabulous storyteller and I learned from her the art of storytelling, the pun, and that ice cream can cure almost any pain in a few minutes.

The kitchen was the heartbeat of Number 25. It had a lovely old-fashioned fireplace where we had the luxury of having cooks who prepared our meals and treats of the day on a wood or charcoal fire. As we grew up, the warmth and smell of the fireplace was replaced by the modern conveniences of electricity and gas, but the heartbeat of Number 25 remained essentially the same.

Cooking is a passion in our family, and I learned this basic art from many fabulous chefs in it. Dad's cooking skills started and stopped with making peanut butter. But he was a master shopper who loved to go to the market and buy the ingredients for his favorite curries. Unfortunately, he loved the spare parts of an animal more than any of us and would come home with one chicken that somehow seemed to have four heads and eight feet, all of which went into his favorite dish, chicken vindaloo. These quirks, he said, made the difference between him enjoying a good curry and a great curry.

Number 25 was the center stage on which I was the main act. I constantly sought to improve my nascent leadership and entrepreneurship skills as I led my friends to perform several boyish pranks to show off our prowess. Many of these thrills were so hazardous that it's a wonder that I got through my teens with just a few broken bones and scars.

On the flip side, in the days before computers, I could also spend a lot of time alone entertaining myself in novel ways. I enjoyed playing cricket all by myself in the backyard. For hours on end, I would simply throw a ball on a wall and whack the rebound, mimicking my cricket hero of the week, playing the match of my life against 11 of my foes. This one-man cricket game now appears to be a fantastic cure for solving my attention deficiency by using my hyperactivity disorder.

⌇

All said and done, Number 25 shaped me. Here, I learned to enjoy the sunny outdoors, chase a ball, play the fool, eat and smile, all while surrounded by loved ones.

As I relived these stories, the songs 'Papa' by Paul Anka and 'Mother of Mine' by Neil Reid provided a source of reflection. I was fortunate indeed to have a world-class leader and an entrepreneur at home to mold, guide, and direct me to develop the basic qualities in my Ex- Factor almost from my first breath. I also worked on my personal principles and values, the ones that, today, adorn the walls of my bedroom where I can read and appreciate them every day.

OUTSTANDING

I was privileged to study in St. Joseph's Boys High School, a school that had the reputation of developing students who excelled in academics and sports. While we were ultracompetitive on and off the field, it's another ecosystem from which I had a fount of stories to help bring Oh back into my life. At St. Joseph's, through a diverse set of disciplines covering academics, sports, drama, and friendships, I had a fantastic opportunity to train many of my emotional muscles, and in its hallowed halls, my leadership skills began to form.

"You're an outstanding student, I say!" This was a frequent comment from my teachers, who would then promptly banish me from the class for some incident for which I was generally deemed guilty of.

I was privileged to attend a reputable Catholic school. For the seven years during which I roamed its hallowed halls, I enjoyed the time I spent outside the classroom more than that inside it. I had a self-diagnosed allergy to school books. In the classroom, I was the class clown, the back bencher, and did just enough to get a passing grade in my exams. I was too distracted and hyperactive to focus on anything being taught, as I definitely enjoyed my clown act far more than listening to anything the teacher had to say.

I was a nearly-permanent fixture in the detention room. I became an expert in writing "I won't talk loudly anymore in class" on the blackboard. As if such a punishment would have helped stop me anyway!

I went to school to play. Time in the classroom was a necessary obstacle I had to face before I could chase a ball around a field with my classmates. I dreaded the sound of the school bell ordering us to come back to class. The sports field was my battlefield and winning was a matter of life or death. I was highly competitive and passionate. I shouted, screamed, fell, got hurt, broke bones, got into major fights, and made many friends and a lot of foes.

In my final year of school, to the envy of all other athletes and to the disbelief of many, without any plan or training, I won the 800m event and, with it, the largest sports trophy that day. I ran without a care in the world, oblivious of others, and before they knew it, I had crossed the finish line.

What a feeling it was when I breasted the tape, and later when I ran home from school with this huge cup to proudly show off. How much I must have bragged about how I won that cup! I was so reluctant to return it to school that it almost had to be pried out from under my blanket, as I slept with it every night. I can still relive all the emotions on that day. This victory is one of my greatest stories. I still look fondly back on it and get inspiration when I need a reality check on my present levels of self-confidence, self-understanding, and self-control. Sports, no doubt, played an important role in defining my Ex-Factor throughout my life.

"Ring out the battle call of duty, unfurl the flag of faith and toil" was the school anthem we sang before the start of a school day. Okay, this may seem like they were training us to go into battle, but the structure and the quality of the education and sports we got there proved to be a major contribution to developing the good qualities I have in my Ex-Factor.

One of my greatest teachers was my Hindi tutor Jill. She had polio and used a wheelchair for over 53 years. Jill was also an early inspiration to entrepreneurship. Against all odds, she made a living teaching and knitting with no show of pain. I will always remain grateful to Jill, because without her mentoring and discipline, I would not have been able to create the structure that helped me find my passion to pursue an academic career after my teens.

When away from school, I was often in trouble with my neighbors who, whenever they saw me, seemed to be whispering, "Oh Dear, not him again," So, I nicknamed them The OhDears.

The family of OhDears is the stereotype of DontDoNation, whom I like to stay a mile away from, as they rub me the wrong way. I'm sure the reverse is also true. They represent the dream family in TV commercials. The father Jack is as fit as a fiddle, well groomed, and Mom Jane is dressed fabulously and wears shining high-heel shoes. They live in a neat bungalow with a beautiful lawn and shining cars in the garage. Their two kids, Master Prim and Miss Proper, are well behaved, always at the top of the class and seem to have jumped out of a glossy magazine. Even worse is they have a cute puppy, Snowy, who cleans up after himself.

The OhDears were the prime target of my pranks. The list was endless, but they all revolved around finding new ways to tease Master Prim and Miss Proper or by jumping over their wall to play a prank or two. When things went wrong, Jack and Jane were quick to come over to Number 25 and complain to Dad. I got my fair share of punishment, but this didn't deter me from continuing to be a thorn in many OhDears' sides.

My penchant for being the leader of the "naughty boys' team" flourished both at school and in the neighborhood as I led a group of boys and girls from one hairbrained scheme to another. It seems, however, that I must have pushed the line too far. Much to my chagrin, after I finished school in 1983, my application to a reputable college was rejected. The feedback given for the rejection was that a teacher who bore the brunt of my pranks had informed the college authorities that I was the ringleader of a group of troublemakers. This left my dad quite amused; he said it was the first time he had come across an applicant being rejected for demonstrating leadership skills.

⌒

For me, Pink Floyd's 'Another Brick in the Wall' was a song that had tremendous meaning; I fondly recalled it even as I wrote this story. I was fortunate to have Jill and my love for sports to mold, guide, and direct me in my formative years. Even though in school I prioritized sports over education, and was rewarded with a few broken bones, I built lifelong relationships I can still count on when the chips are down. I was fortunate to have world-class teachers and classmates and look back at those glory days every time I need to become a warrior and defend what is rightly mine.

THE SAILOR

To understand the rough qualities associated with ADHD, I revisited my career as a merchant marine, which I believe, over a period of 7 years, exponentially developed many of the finest qualities in my Ex-Factor. I matured from a bubbly boy to a responsible man as I sailed across the seven seas and discovered the beauty of nature and people on DontDoNation. More importantly, unconsciously, life at sea pressure-tested many of my rough ADHD qualities, especially attention deficit. If I had exhibited signs of ADHD in my sailing days, it indicated that I had the willpower to overcome many more rough qualities, as even a moment of lack of concentration by a merchant marine officer with navigation and cargo-handling responsibilities could cause an environmental disaster.

After my pre-University, in the mid-1980s, I had limited opportunities in India to pursue my audacious dreams. When every young Indian wanted to be a doctor or an engineer, I wanted to be a sailor. I didn't know how to go about pursuing this dream, but that didn't hold me back.

Even though Bengaluru is more than 300 kilometers away from the coast, my childhood dream was to sail the seven seas. I loved water so much that if I saw a body of water, no matter how clean or dirty it was, I had to jump into it and splash around.

My love for the sea began when I was about seven, as the merchant marine seamen I met all appeared to me like heroes. Good looking, happy and prosperous, they sported swanky clothes and possessed the latest gadgets. They also shared with me the most amazing stories of their adventures at sea. But in 1985, when it was time for me to find an apprenticeship, the shipping industry was in a crisis. I was forced to abandon my dream of a career in the merchant navy and reluctantly pursue my Bachelor's in Science. So, as I messed around experimenting in the world of physics, math, and electronics, these years in college were mostly party time. In addition to being the class clown, I became the captain of the party team. The joy of chasing a ball around a field for hours was replaced by the thrill of hanging out with girls on the dance floor for hours.

After getting my bachelor's in 1988, I was forced to focus on finding a job to pay my bills, as the shipping industry was still in a crisis. So, I dreamt of joining a multinational corporation. Using my gift of the gab, I talked my way through a series of tough campus interviews, to attain a much-coveted management training position in a reputable company in India that offered me a job in Mumbai, the "city of dreams."

At 21, I was ready for a new adventure. I packed all my belongings into my dad's 25-year-old suitcase tied with string and, with a few rupees in my pocket, moved from the small town of Bengaluru to the big city of Mumbai to start the first of many of my corporate dramas.

With the fancy corporate title of Area Account Manager, I learned to sell fans, sewing machines, furniture, and kitchen appliances on the streets of Mumbai. Here, I got a crash course in sales from the experts and realized that in Mumbai, everybody had the gift of the gab. I learned how hard it was to sell commodities, but later in my career, those years of roaming the streets of Mumbai with a kitchen appliance under my arm, learning the art of selling, helped me in countless ways.

The dream corporate job was exciting to begin with. But after a few months, I figured out that corporate life consisted of the same handful of scenes of a movie being replayed six days a week. One day, I was witness to a romance in the corner room of the office, the next day an action film in the sales department, the third day a Wall Street crime movie in the finance department as someone has probably used just a bit too much of somebody else's money. After binge watching these corporate movies, I got bored and decided to once again turn to my dream of joining the merchant navy.

In 1989, opportunities to join the merchant navy, though still scarce, started to emerge. To land them, however, you needed connections. I called, pestered, and visited people who could help me open the cracks in the door of a shipping company looking to hire apprentices. Tough as this was, I created a network of people who were willing to give of their time to help somebody else's dreams come true.

In 1990, after many months of banging doors and hanging outside shipping companies' offices, I finally got selected as an apprentice.

My joy knew no bounds. I borrowed money from my dad to get into navigation college and started living the dream of the tall, dark, handsome sailor with a repertoire of raunchy sailor stories to share.

The merchant navy was perfect for me. It offered me the full pallet of guts and glory, thrills, ego boosting and boasting, adventure, and risks, and on the other side, hours of peace and quiet. However glamorous being a merchant navy apprentice may sound, life at sea is actually quite tough. One must learn to cope with the loneliness, being away from family and friends and making sacrifices like missing out on so many key family milestones. A significant one for me was when I missed the wedding of my elder sister Anita, the first wedding in our family, by two days, as I had to join a ship.

The lessons I learned while sailing were many. The one that left an indelible impression on me, and which I particularly cherish, was my first interaction with the chief officer. When I walked into his office with my million-dollar smile, I was welcomed by these words: "You're the new sheep on the ship to be sacrificed on the altar of success. On board, keep your eyes and ears open and your mouth shut. This is the way you'll learn the skills needed to be a good apprentice and later become a truly good officer."

The ships I sailed on were oil and gas tankers, literally sailing bombs, which had every element of the excitement I craved for. I visited most parts of the world and shouldered the responsibility of leading people in thrilling environments, including sailing through storms, navigating the vessel in congested waters, and loading and discharging millions of dollars of oil and gas that, if handled carelessly, could cause an environmental disaster. The counterweight to this thrill was enduring many lonely hours on the bridge where I learned to appreciate nature, how her elements change with little warning, watching the beauty of the sun rise and set, and marveling at the star-filled night sky with only the wind and sea breeze for company.

I enjoyed every aspect of sailing, except being sea sick. I became so skilled at my job as an apprentice, that within a year, I was promoted to Pumpman, a technically skilled member of the deck crew. In this role, I got my first taste of serious responsibility, as I was now in charge of the liquid cargo transfer system that handled millions of dollars of oil. A small glitch in my plan could have huge environmental, financial, and personal consequences. I embraced this responsibility and learned how important it was to grasp the nitty gritty details of every aspect of the task you're responsible for, how to make a detailed plan, communicate it to the crew, and follow up on it so that we, as a team, could all execute it with precision.

After 16 months on the ship, the captain advised me to sign off, as I was ready to become a deck officer. I had to go back to Mumbai and return to college to focus well and study really hard. The exams I had to pass were tough and there were other challenges too. As a young man in a big city with money in my pocket, temptations to get distracted could be found at every corner.

Failure was not an option. If I wanted to go after the big bucks that officers in the merchant navy make, I had to pass my exams in the quickest possible time. I cut out all distractions and used what I later learned is an ADHD trait – hyperfocus – to do exactly that.

At the start of my sailing career, I sailed on ships called "rust buckets." One beautiful morning in 1993, in the Singapore Straits, I saw a magnificent blue ship sailing by with a white star on its funnel. I was fascinated by its beauty and elegance, and I fell for the ship, hook, line, and sinker. I decided then and there that I had to join the company Maersk, which owned the ship.

When I was back in Mumbai, I had a huge slice of good fortune; my network introduced me to the recruiting team of Maersk. After a strenuous selection process in 1993, I qualified and joined the company. Working with the Danes, who seemed to come from a world as far away from India as you can ever imagine, was a nightmare at first. But as I got to know them, I was led down a new, unexpected path.

A life at sea showed me that if something interested me and if I focused on finding out what I need to achieve it, I would succeed. I also learned that I could be responsible for lives and material things of great value. The learning I cherish the most is the importance of building a network of people who could help me to achieve my dreams.

I have always needed to dream the impossible, to dare to be different as this helps me come out of my comfort zone. When I succeed, I have a source of smiles for many years that never runs out.

Marriages are Made at Sea

As I transitioned from being a bachelor to a husband and father, many of my weakest emotional muscles that I required to be the joint head of a family, started getting trained for the new role. I began to shift from being carefree to being responsible for providing my family with a foundation to continue to learn, live, and further refine our family values. Once again, many more of my rough ADHD qualities were pressure tested. At the same time, some of my finest ADHD qualities attracted the love of my life and wife for 27 years and counting. Together, we've been partners in establishing the foundation for a happy, safe and secure family life.

Mr. Sunshine is among the first words I hear every morning for 27 years. But I need to roll back to 1994, the year it all started. One evening, in Bengaluru, I had a serious motorcycle accident on the highway. Lying with vehicles whizzing around me, those few minutes had a huge impact on my carefree life. In that short span, I realized how fragile life could be and clearly understood that I had to take it more seriously, invest in myself, and settle down.

I was probably distracted when I crashed into a car, flew into the air, landed on my helmet in the middle of the highway with vehicles speeding by. I looked into the eye of death, but fortunately, it didn't welcome me home. With a broken hip, I was chained to the bed for six weeks as part of my recovery.

The feeling of freedom as I was able to walk again was just amazing, but the significance of the accident was that it made me realize how fortunate I'd been in life, how fragile my life can be and that it's not only your neighbors who have serious accidents.

After a year spent in recuperation and with a dodgy hip as a memento, I joined a new merchant ship, now as the First Officer. Here, once again, good fortune and opportunity worked in my favor. Out of the blue, I fell in love, hook, line, and sinker, with a beautiful Scandinavian apprentice Marianne. Surprisingly, Marianne too fell in love with me. When we signed off the ship, we holidayed in India to meet my family and experience Number 25 as well as the streets of India I spoke so much of. She had many questions she wanted answered before she decided how our relationship would develop. I had decided that I wanted to marry Marianne within the first month of meeting her. Once she had most of her answers, she proposed to me on New Year's Eve, December 31, 1995. Yes, you read that right. Marianne proposed to me. With marriage, I became what my friends in India lovingly called a Danish Pastry; that was our favorite pastry, the one we usually bought as kids when we pooled our money at the local bakery.

Over the years, when I asked Marianne why she married me, much to my dismay, Marianne would say "definitely not your looks," but she fell in love with my mind, my mystery and unpredictability, and my smile. Marianne always said that I bring sunshine into her life and that was how 'Mr. Sunshine' was born .

After our wedding day on the 17 February 1996,we sailed one last honeymoon voyage on the merchant ship as officer and wife. On that trip, Marianne got pregnant. We moved to Denmark to see if we could set up a family there. This was a long shot and really hard, as I didn't know the Danish language and the weather was the opposite of sunny Bengaluru. We had the privilege of staying at Marianne's parents' house for a few months, but it drove all of us crazy. So, we packed our bags and went back to my safe and secure Number 25 to get ready for the birth of our first child.

Kristian was born in June 1997 and because of some life-threatening birth complications, we got our first taste of turbulent family life. We were shaken, but the turbulence passed with no long-term damage. Every problem throws up new opportunities, and with a young child, I realized that being a sailor and having a growing family wasn't an option. I had to find a new career path.

Marianne went back to Denmark to raise Kristian, and I went to the United Kingdom where I used all our savings to study International Logistics, a degree that nobody had even heard of in 1997. The decision to invest in myself and a futuristic education turned out to be one of the best I've made in my life. Logistics was a new field, and studying it meant taking a huge risk, but fortune favors the brave, and in just a few years, everybody was clamoring for employees who had a logistics background.

I enjoyed my time at University. I found out that I actually loved to study and was quite intelligent. I pitted my brain against a lot of very talented and ambitious youngsters from all over the world. The fun fact was I could be a nerd in stuff that interested me, and I could compete with all these brilliant youngsters academically.

The investment paid off and I was soon well set for a land-based career. In this new avatar of an intellectual with a degree, I moved to Wonderful Copenhagen to start on my adventure in the cross section of corporate life and fatherhood.

⌒

I was fortunate to have a world-class Miller in Marianne who compliments me in so many ways. We epitomize my Miner and Miller concept. We discuss how we complement each other in that where one is strong the other is weak, but however much we deviate from this harmony and balance, we must be robust enough to bounce back.

My Mistress

As I transitioned from being a boy from the East to a husband and father of the West, I preferred to call myself a global citizen. However difficult this transition was, my leadership and entrepreneurial qualities started blooming in parallel with the aches and pains of a family with little children, demanding managers, corporate targets to meet and a mad rush to climb up the corporate ladder. I became what I call a "stay-at-work father" and many of my beloved qualities that helped me climb the ladder of private and professional life rebelled and slowly started burning me out.

1998, Copenhagen Denmark

With a million-dollar smile on my face and a dream, we moved to Copenhagen. Three decades of hard work and dreams began paying off. I was on top of the world, and nothing could stop me from seeing how high I could go from here.

Marianne got a job to make sure we had a roof over our heads, and I went out to test my charm and my gift of the gab to try and land my dream job. After a lot of trial and error, fine tuning my CV and working my interview charm, I finally got a chance to start working afresh. The emotions when I received the appointment letter were really mind-blowing. I had made it across the bridge from the sea to the shore and into the global corporate kingdom. My job was to work with Information Technology, though I had no clue what it was about.

After our induction training that lasted three months, we had to do the catwalk for various department managers to select us. I wondered, what chance did a young man who didn't know computers, spoke a different language, and looked lost in the world of OhDears swarming the corporate world, have?

Thankfully, my first boss recognized my passion for entrepreneurship and leadership. He was quick to notice the smile, charm, and energy as well as the lightness in my footsteps when my mind was on fire. Under his tutelage, I overcame the struggle to learn a new language, learned to program computers, and navigate the dangers of the corporate kingdom. His invaluable advice to me was that in life always try to retain 20% of your energy reserves for unknown future opportunities in the corporate kingdom. He stressed that this 20% of energy would be so valuable that it could help when one got the next corporate venture; an opportunity that could be worth millions of dollars. He was spot on, and with this formula, I did deliver, for him and my employers, millions in revenue over the years. Competing in the corporate playground and raising a family, added a new dimension of responsibility that I enjoyed. I was fiercely competitive, success oriented, and overfocused on work. Our daughter Kia was born in 2001 and lived a happy secure family life. I was fortunate that I had the support of Marianne who gave our young family the structure to function smoothly so I could immerse myself in the challenges of the corporate kingdom, which excited me no end.

I enjoyed leadership development programs, where I could sit for hours in rapturous attention, listening to visionary speakers sharing their wisdom and figuring out ways on how to bring futuristic ideas to life. I enjoyed large business transformation programs and leading people, processes, and technology into the digital age.

On the other hand, I detested "useless meetings" where any smart corporate suit camouflaged a lack of knowledge behind PowerPoint slides filled with buzzwords. After a few years, when I had achieved sufficient seniority, whenever I could take no more of their buzzwords, I would hijack the meeting and find more interesting ways to challenge the speaker on the idea they were pitching.

In the corporate kingdom, because of my attitude and aptitude, project management, intrapreneurship, entrepreneurship, and consulting came naturally to me. It also made me a talented corporate fireman and I was often called to put out fires that started because of the ineptitude of a person on a rung above me and extinguished by the skills of the people a few rungs below me. The life of a firefighter took its toll on the amount of quality time I could spend with the family. I began to devote more and more time to my mistress, Corporate Life. In her company I was regularly seduced to go above and beyond the call of duty at work. This inevitably put a great deal of pressure on me, which, at that time, I was able to absorb with my broad shoulders.

Even though I kept racking up an impressive list of achievements, I often felt that I was underperforming compared to the OhDears. I continued to push myself as hard as I could to prove (mostly to myself) that I could achieve even more.

At home, I thrived in my roles as a husband and father. Marianne became the rock-solid foundation in our lives. Honey, I forgot… the kids, …to do shopping, …my keys, …my purse, these became phrases I commonly uttered most days of my life. Fortunately, I had Marianne to help me out of these recurring faux pas situations.

My family's main complaint was that even though I may have been physically present at home, I was mentally absent. And it was very difficult for them to reach me at work. To them, it seemed that work was more important to me than they were. A glaring example was that while in the company of my mistress Corporate Life, I didn't allow myself the luxury of picking up the phone when they called. Soon, they abandoned all their efforts to reach me at work.

Everything was not as hunky dory as I make it seem. We were a young family and had our fair share of drama. Fortunately, despite having Corporate Life as my ultra demanding mistress , I managed to secure a supporting lead role in the family. I was tasked with providing the family with security and being the fountain of energy that would enable us to experience new things in our life. The strange part about my years in the cross section of corporate life and fatherhood was that at work, I was conscientious, neat, tidy, and hardworking, but I was completely different at home where distraction, carelessness, untidiness, and, later, irritability were my hallmarks.

The counterweight to my being mentally absent at home while I engaged on the corporate battleground collecting an impressive collection of scars was Marianne running more and more of the house singlehandedly. In the end, she paid a heavy price, leading a stress-filled life with work/mommy/wife burnout. Later on, we came to know that being married to someone with ADHD takes a toll on the whole family. My ADHD didn't help her to burn brighter but made her burn out. But we fought the good fight together, rekindled her spirit, got her and the family back on our feet, and the burden of running the house was now shared by all of us.

Older and wiser, my love to be a pioneer continued, and I enjoyed starting new projects and business. I enjoyed staying ahead of the pack where I could experience the thrill of building new corporate kingdoms. I learned that being a pioneer meant that I always needed to be faster than the rest. But this also meant I usually had my back to the pack; so, I had to develop my own arrow-proof vest to shield myself from the arrows shot at me by disgruntled members within the pack, each of whom was determined to pull me down. I also discovered that I was a people person. I had a natural protective instinct for the younger and weaker members of my pack. I also slowly learned that to inspire them, I needed to be a good leader and communicator and learn to be a connector of the right people.

I also learned that it was best for me to move away once I felt that my job in one particular area of the corporate kingdom was done, to move on while still on the top. I generally found new challenging opportunities to grow my corporate strengths. I saved many frustrating hours by making a conscious decision to stay far away from office politics. A cool trick I learned to prevent me from being forced to do things the way other people wanted was the niche leadership art of how to get other people to enjoy doing things my way.

The higher I crawled up the corporate ladder, the greater the number of toxic people, whom I called leeches and chattering monkeys, I had to deal with. How I hated them! A leech, without you knowing, latches on to you and sucks your knowledge and energy out without giving anything back. When they're done with you, they quietly drop you and move on to their next victim. A chattering monkey, unlike the leech, is always hovering around, chattering constantly in one's ear, "See me," "Do my work for me," "I'm better than you."

These leeches and chattering monkeys seem so charming. You indulge them for your own reasons, but after a while, you wake up to the fact that you've let them suck the knowledge and energy out of you without giving anything in return. When they're done with you, they quietly drop you and move on to their next victim. Despite the leeches and chattering monkeys, my career progressed fabulously, as I moved from working with large global corporations, to start-up companies, to being an independent consultant. During three decades in the corporate world, my ability to choose a career that drove my passion and leadership has been a great source of smiles or grimaces. But, ultimately, these sources of smiles ran out.

CHAPTER 5

STORIES FROM THE CAPE OF OH NO

This chapter is a collection of some undeniable Oh No Stories that I cannot disown. I am proud to call them my own. They are from the real world, helped me reflect on my life and had a profound impact on the process of understanding my past and using it to prepare myself for my changing world. I have organized the stories into hierarchies with each story playing a pivotal role in helping me understand why I was grimacing more and smiling less.

The Entrepreneur in me is shattered.
The Leader in me is stunned.
My ADHD is thinking,
my time to show them my destructive power is nigh.
But what you see in me now is once again
only a small part of me.

As I relive these stories, I tremble at this visual of me sitting shell-shocked on the cold, windy, and stony beach in the Cape of Oh No.

These few stories are my tribute to the worst years of my life till now and how I survived them.

STORY 6

THE PEAK

I am at the peak of my private and professional life, and, gradually, the slide down from the peak starts, slowly but surely, without me being aware of it.

What Cape of Oh Yes didn't prepare me for is what happens when the pearl-bearing oysters disappear. This unimaginable scenario occurred in 2018, when the glorious weather on Cape of Oh Yes was gradually replaced by violent hurricanes. Unfortunately, unlike the oysters that moved on to better places, I was caught in the right front quadrant of the hurricane, and landed in a place I called Cape of Oh No. I was transformed into a Smileless Pauper.

I can trace my story back to approximately when my pearl-bearing oysters first started to disappear. I believe this was possibly as early as 2010 when I started suffering from excruciating pain in my shoulders and neck. Scans showed that my shoulder joints were so badly damaged that they looked like the shoulders of a stone quarry worker who had spent years breaking stones with a hammer. I had both my shoulders operated on but even after this, the mobility of my shoulder movement remained restricted and I was told that I would have to continue to do physical therapy for many years to keep them in reasonable condition. The advice from well-meaning medical professionals was that the shoulders will only get worse with time; learn to live with them. With my hips, knees, shoulders, and neck already shaky and getting weaker by the day, my physical wealth seemed to be decreasing rapidly.

As my hands and brain are the tools I use at work, I worried about how I was going to continue to make a lucrative living. I feared that more of my body parts would start to go on strike or break down, and I wouldn't be able to find sufficient spare parts to fix them. I was afraid that my good fortune was running out, so I did what seemed the most rational thing at that time: I immersed myself in work and tried to increase my skills in the corporate kingdom. I became even more serious about my job and learned to be hyperfocused with no stone left unturned to deliver outcomes of the highest quality. All this took a toll on me, and inevitably, after years of burning bright, I started burning out.

In 2012, when I was at the peak of my financial security, I had my first bout of insomnia, triggered by anxiety. For a year, I tried to cure my insomnia by myself, till one day, my children convinced me to seek professional help. I worked with a therapist for a few weeks, and he delivered wonders. Soon enough, I was cured and began sleeping like a baby again. The problem was that I had developed such a rigid presleeping routine, I feared I would slip back into insomnia again if it were broken. The result: I became overdependent on my presleeping routine and placed such unreasonable demands on myself and my family to enable me to get a good night's sleep that it drove them crazy.

Cape of Oh No symbolizes how hard, frustrating, and annoying life can be when it doesn't go my way. It also shows me that I have developed a portfolio of unhealthy, undesirable qualities that have also made me the man that I'm not so proud of today. It also symbolizes how privileged I am, as my desire to get away from the Cape of Oh No, though complex, is in my hands. It just takes a lot of patience and the struggle of an odyssey to get away from there.

JUMPING OFF

It takes a lot of courage to say stop and jump off the corporate ladder!

As I started burning out, life became complicated, as, even though I was afraid, I had no option but to put on a brave face and learn to reduce the pace at which I was burning out. What life has since made obvious to me, was that if I didn't get off the corporate ladder voluntarily, I ran the risk of falling down from it and doing irreparable damage to myself. As burning out wasn't an option for me, I learned the hard way that it takes a lot of courage to say stop and jump off the corporate ladder! As I had the support system around me to prepare and support me for the jump, I accepted the risks of an uncertain future and jumped.

2018, Copenhagen Denmark

The competition was fierce in the corporate kingdom. But, with my ever-increasing corporate skills, I managed to tick off a few more of my personal and professional dreams.

Now I realize that when I searched for the meaning of the word "success", I looked up the wrong dictionary. I understood it as "excess." For some strange reason to satisfy my bulging ego, I was determined to compete with the OhDears and, like them, kept on acquiring more and more material things only to keep my ego happy.

For the first time in my life, I had spare money to spend on the luxurious things in life. We never lived a lavish lifestyle, and always lived within our means, but when you have money, the temptation to acquire more material goods is addictive. We acquired trinkets and gadgets and traveled as if there were no tomorrow. Soon, parts of my life resembled a vault.

Worse still, as my financial wealth increased, my mental wealth started diminishing. I developed tunnel vision to blend in with the OhDears. I had everything I dreamed of, but I forgot all about my love for the sunny outdoors, or how to chase a ball, play pranks, gather pearls, and all the other things I had always enjoyed on the Cape of Oh Yes.

A permanent frown replaced my smile. I became self-absorbed. My levels of self-confidence, self-understanding, and self-control were low. Looking at myself in the mirror, I couldn't recognize the Kiran I loved. The smile, the charm, the quick wit, the love to party, the love to play pranks, the drive to work hard, manage high levels of stress, all became a distant memory.

Adding to the inner conflicts were the external ones, like being caught in corporate mind games. This sucked the last bit of energy out of me. I had everything I could dream of, except my smile. Like other OhDears, Viagra and buying a shiny 2-seater red BMW sports car seemed like the best options to bring a few smiles back. But hell no, this was not the right answer. In 2018, the pressures of the corporate world burnt me out and I started having severe anxiety attacks for the first time in my life. I was forced to take a few weeks off to recover from stress, and during that time, I took the decision that from January 2020, I would quit my present job and find one that was less stressful. I needed to find a way to stay at all costs in the Cape of Oh Yes.

I followed up on this decision and restarted my independent consulting career, with the hope that it would help to reduce my stress levels. But at that precise moment, the force of the hurricanes hit an all-time high in Cape of Oh Yes. I was sucked into the right front quadrant of the hurricane.

My World Falls Apart

My secure world finally fell apart and I was forced to muster all the help I could to survive what I consider the bleakest and most lonely days of my life. I was blessed to have a fantastic team of Miners and Millers whose shoulders, love, and compassion I relied heavily on as I attempted to survive those scary days. Memories of my serious motorcycle accident on the highway in 1994 came pouring back. This time it was not just a few minutes during which I had vehicles whizzing around my head. Now, the darkest of thoughts in my head, ones that I had little control over, made me realize how fragile life could be. I clearly understood that I had to take it more seriously, invest in myself, and settle down. I was determined to use this opportunity to rethink and redesign my life to learn to survive and thrive with ADHD, but to do this, I needed to dig deep, focus, and stay strong.

Marianne and I were at a beach house outside Copenhagen. We had just gone for a lovely walk, and I was making our favorite comfort dishes of rice, a spicy Indian soup called rasam, and crisply fried slices of beef steaks.

Marianne had always complimented me on my cooking skills and said that I'm like an artist in the kitchen, with a specialty called designer cooking. By this, she meant that my process of making food is messy, but the output is amazing, and the dish can never be recreated the same way.

I have a degree in multitasking that gives me the license to muck up many things at the same time. With too many pots boiling, I got distracted and, lo and behold, the rasam took on a life of its own. It bubbled out of my cooking pot and was crawling its way to freedom all over the kitchen table. The stove was a mess. While cleaning up the rasam, I found a strange looking spice that I had never used before in my cooking. It seemed to be frothing and foaming and the leader of the pack of spices trying to crawl out of the pot to their freedom. I picked him up, and with a dirty look, threw him back into the pot again and closed the lid. I was totally stressed out with the disobedient rasam. To cool down, I went for a walk on the beach. I was angry at the world and myself, and I blamed it all on the rasam. I spent an hour fuming and then came back and picked a fight with Marianne, something which I rarely do. After sharing a few unpleasant words about my recent intolerable and unacceptable behavior, many of which should have been said by one of us a long time ago, we kissed and made up.

That night, the fight I had with Marianne plagued my mind with the worst Oh No Emotions imaginable. These emotions triggered high levels of anxiety that kept me awake the whole night. As I tossed and turned, I imagined all the worst possible scenarios of my life falling apart and relived the trauma of my previous years of suffering from insomnia. My sleepless nights continued for a few weeks, and in a disturbed state of mind, my old friend, Mr. Fonges (fear of not getting enough sleep), whom I met in 2012, and who later visited me every few years for a few days, came to stay permanently. These were unwelcome visits, as in his constant company, I became a dreaded version of myself. Usually, with self-medication and therapy, I managed to get rid of him after a few weeks. This time, however, Mr. Fonges had come to stay. His presence irritated and frustrated me. Soon, I was bone-tired of him and wished for him to go away. Within a few weeks, I was a total mess.

Ouch! is all I can say. But yes, sometimes it takes an outsider disguised as Fonges to hold up a mirror for one to see the truth. On the 13th of March 2020, when the global pandemic became another one of my hurricanes, I awoke to find that I had been washed ashore on the Cape of Oh No. Sitting shell-shocked on the cold, windy, and stony beach, I hastily constructed a hurricane shelter. From there, weak and weary, I watched helplessly as the hurricanes arrived with a force I had never encountered before. I rode each hurricane out more by chance than plan. I choose not to describe my pain in these moments as we all have different definitions of pain, but there were a few days when I barely got by, and I credit my Miners and Millers and Cognitive Behavior Therapy for getting me through those.

In April 2020, it didn't require too much arm-twisting from Marianne to get me to seek medical help.

I started a consultation with my family physician. The diagnosis, after answering a few questions, was, "Kiran you have a bad case of SAD," my acronym for Stress, Anxiety, and Depression. The pills he gave me had a nasty reaction and I was soon in a state worse than the one I was in before the visit to him. Over the next few months, using a different medicine, he shored up my physical and mental wealth. But I was still a Smileless pauper, and he recommended the next step should be consultation with a psychiatrist.

⌇

My years wandering the Cape of Oh No from 2018, helped me experience my roughest ADHD qualities. I was fortunate to survive the hurricanes and it showed me how volatile the swing of the pendulum of Oh Yes and Oh No Emotions can be. But I also learned that neither a smile nor a grimace is permanent, and I continued on my next quest to find ways to energize my weak smile.

SHRINK WRAPPED

I realize that my ADHD gift came to me shrink-wrapped. As I opened it, I had a lot of conflicting emotions about psychiatric help. I was afraid of the stigma attached to it. I was afraid of the consequences it would have in my interactions with friends, foes, and even the insurance companies. But with nothing to lose, I decided to meet the psychiatrist. To my relief, she helped me slowly dismantle all my false notions about getting psychiatric help. At the end of the first meeting, she told me quite firmly that whatever problems I was facing, if I put in the effort, I could get back to being the Kiran I dreamt of.

Oct 2020

After a few sessions, the psychiatrist asked me to spell out my goals, so we could be sure once I had achieved them. The answer was prompt: To sleep well and find my mischievous smile again. After a few more consultations, she said she would like to diagnose me for ADHD. If her diagnosis proved to be right, I would have the keys to achieving my goals in my own time, with my own effort, and in my own way.

"What is ADHD?" I asked her. "Impossible, whatever it is I cannot have it."

I had no previous knowledge of ADHD, so I browsed the internet for anything that had the word ADHD in it. The books, research papers, and online content I found highlighted what a life with ADHD would look like. My future life looked scary. I prayed that I didn't have ADHD.

Committed to this ADHD path, I agreed to move forward with the diagnosis. To prepare for it, Marianne, I, and a few Miners and Millers spent hours on self-reflection and answering questionnaires to trace my life back as far as I could go. When we were done with our homework, I was convinced I didn't have ADHD.

On the 15 of Jan 2021, when I left the last of my diagnosis sessions with the psychiatrist, I had my medical record stamped for life, Kiran Vas, ADHD. I was shattered. But soon, I realized that all was not lost. Over the next few sessions, the psychiatrist told me that now, equipped with my ADHD title, I could reach levels of fulfillment that I only could have dreamt of till now if I chose to learn the right moves to help get me there.

First, however, I had to accept my ADHD and make peace with the new Kiran. I had to stop trying to change ADHD and force fit it into my present life. Instead, I had to change my life and align it with both the perfect and imperfect qualities of ADHD.

Initially, I was shattered to think that I wasn't normal, that I was fragile. But, in a sense, I was also relieved. Now I had greater clarity about myself and my special qualities; I knew why I would never be an OhDear. I knew now that ADHD was one of the root causes of my missing smile. I can only wonder how different my life would have been if someone had made this diagnosis earlier, say when I was a teenager. But that doesn't change anything.

Over the next eight months, in the company of my Miners and Millers and medical professionals, slowly, day by day, amazing things started to happen. As my physical and mental health improved, I started crawling my way back to the Cape of Oh Yes, the place I missed so much and was desperate to return to. With each step in that direction, a new dread emerged. "Was I just going to go back to the life I had been leading earlier?" I asked myself, "Wait a minute, Kiran; do you really want to go back there?" "Hell no!" Somebody whispered inside me. "Let's sit down for a bit and think this through."

In the silence of No-man's-land, with the dread of being dragged back to Cape of Oh No always lurking around even as Cape of Oh Yes kept enticing me back, I caught a glimpse of a new exciting horizon that I called The Cape of Oh. I knew that THAT was where I wanted to go! I had no idea what it would take to get there, but, one thing I was absolutely clear about: THIS was where I wanted to reach. With nothing more than a weak smile to invest in my odyssey, I took my first steps in that direction even as I continued with even greater focus on my odyssey to find and free Oh. I was ready to learn more about my Ales and chose to spend time with Nut Cracker to try to decipher the treasure he brings to my life.

MY BUGGY LIFE

It dawns on me that Nut Cracker and I have unconsciously lived together for 54 years. I use the analogy of Nut Cracker being like a bug from the software world that causes me at times to display erratic behavior. To find and fix the bugs in me, I need to analyze Nut Cracker's likes and dislikes, strengths and weaknesses, so I can identify which perfect qualities of his make me burn brighter and which imperfect qualities of his make me burn out. If I have to learn to live in harmony with Nut Cracker. I need to learn to never to be cowered down by Nut Cracker, to look him in the eye and learn to say, "We're in this together, for better or for worse, so let's make the most of the time we have together."

Hanging out with Nut Cracker, who has always been in me, was weird.

Even though I grew up with Nut Cracker, I assumed we knew each other well. In reality, we are unique individuals and knew very little about each other. He lived within me, so he knew very little of my outside world, and I knew very little of what strings within me he pulled in my everyday life. We started our relationship with healthy curiosity, rivalry, conflicts, and many blame games for who is responsible for all our Oh Yes and No stories. We soon grew comfortable with each other and began to enjoy each other's company. We found we are similar in so many ways and complement one another in many ways too. One day, in a melancholy mood, Nut Cracker said, "The difference between you and me is that you have a gift of ADHD, while I'm the gift."

Puzzled, I asked him what he meant. He said a gift makes someone happy or feel special. On the other hand, as he was "the gift," however exclusive he may be, he was just something that I could use, neglect, or reject as per my whim and fancy. I was blown away. I respected his sentiment and vowed not to make it come true.

As I did a lot of Mining and Milling of the information I was gathering about Nut Cracker, I sometimes wondered whether I would be able to compute the potential value of what Nut Cracker brings to my life beyond what I'm slowly appreciating through understanding his role in my present Ex-Factor. As I learn about Nut Cracker, I find out he's so formidable, and with the new knowledge I'm gathering about him, I know we have the potential to be an awesome team.

One evening, as we were chilling in front of a cozy bonfire, and I typed my day's journal on my computer, my lifelong relationship with Nut Cracker fell into place. Using my computer as a metaphor, I told him my hypothesis about why he caused so many Oh No stories.

"Imagine my Smile-Making Machine has an operating system that is programmed with you and Oh at birth. The Smile-Making Machine is Indian; remember it is a symbol of me. But the operating system, on which you were installed by mistake, was Danish. I did not know you were Danish. At birth, the manufacturer, by mistake, gave ME an English keyboard to communicate with YOU. So by default I used the English language to communicate with you. But as you only know Danish, you struggled to understand what I was telling you to do. This miscommunication causes you to make me grimace."

Nut Cracker grumbles, "Okay! Doesn't make sense, but it happens!"

Unfazed, I blabber on, "Through the keyboard, I communicate with my brain, which includes you, to guide the rest of my body on what I want it to do. But as I was typing away in English and my brain was communicating to the rest of my body in English, it couldn't communicate properly with you, as you didn't know English."

Hurt, Nut Cracker snarls, "Okay."

I can see I have hurt his feelings, so I tread carefully. "There are a lot of similarities between the English and Danish alphabets. But the English language has 26 letters and the Danish language 29."

Nut Cracker looks up with a frown, "Twenty-nine letters?"

"Yes," I reply, "Twenty-six of the letters, that is the letters A - Z are the same. They have the same script but are pronounced differently in Danish. In addition, Danish has three extra vowels: Æ, Ø, Å. So, after I came to know about you, I realized that I had always used an English keyboard when I communicated with you, and, as you never knew much English, this could be the reason you couldn't understand what I was trying to say to you to make me smile."

I can hear Nut Cracker bubbling as he says, "Spot on! The way you explain it makes sense to me. When you communicate with me, you use English to communicate with me, so I struggle to understand what you're saying to me. So, the cause of my being irritated with you is that sometimes I don't understand what you say, and I do the opposite of what you're asking me to do. When I communicate with you, I do the exact opposite. I think you're Danish, so I use my command of the 29 Danish letters when I communicate with you. But, your understanding of Danish is poor; you don't understand me and we miscommunicate. Gobbledygook! That is why we have miscommunicated for so long."

As I felt the joy radiating on my face and Nut Cracker bubbling inside me, I fell hook, line, and sinker in love with him. I've found out that my Smile-Making Machine has a malfunction, but as there is no return to manufacturer option, I have to live with him for the rest of my life.

To understand more about the impact of Nut Cracker in my life, I hummed "We are the Champions" by Queen. I was ready to start the process to accept Nut Cracker in my life and believed he would help me find and free Oh. But to do this I had to stop trying to change Nut Cracker's qualities to fit in my present life and, instead, change my life to include Nut Cracker qualities.

In the company of Nut Cracker, slowly each day, my physical and mental health improved. I could feel myself crawling toward the Cape of Oh. I didn't know what it would take to get there. But this was where I wanted to go. I invested a few more smiles that I had just earned with Nut Cracker in my odyssey, I took my second step toward the Cape of Oh and increased my focus to find and free Oh.

CHAPTER 6

MISSING OH

"We are in this together," I tell the Ales, and I dream up a few more concepts that will help us all work as equal partners to bring Oh back into my life with each concept playing a pivotal role in helping me smile more and grimace less.

THE PARTNERSHIP VOWS

In a partnership, everybody must be a winner

I find myself in a situation where, suddenly, I have three new partners in my life whom I knew very little about. From the corporate world and from 25 years of marriage, I knew that building a strong partnership takes time, often years, and very rarely happens overnight. To kickstart building our partnership, I needed to get to know each of the Ales independently and collectively. A comical way to do this, I decided, was that my next adventure would focus on accepting the newest and probably most difficult partner Nut Cracker as my life partner. The symbolic event I chose mainly to comfort my still bruised ego struggling to accept that I had ADHD, was to picture myself as the groom in a movie. I settle to be the tall handsome sailor in a Bollywood love story of a modern-day Indian arranged marriage.

As I didn't have the luxury to court Nut Cracker (I assumed I'd be wearing the pants in this partnership) before taking our partnership vows in this adventure, I cut out the romantic scenes of falling in love, everybody telling us we were a match made in heaven and so on, and directly zoomed in on our partnership ceremony.

I visualized Nut Cracker as a nervous bundle of energy that encapsulated the perfections and imperfections that come with my brand of ADHD. On our special day, I stood in a daze inside Oh Landia's famous Temple of Doom, with a fuzzy notion of how my partner Nut Cracker looked. With backing out no longer an option, I reluctantly muttered the partnership vows, "We are in this together, for better or for worse, so let's make the most of the time we have together."

At the reception that followed, still dejected about my label of ADHD, with my eyes focusing on my navel, I sat frustrated through numerous sugary speeches from family, friends, and respected foes, who tried to sugarcoat my new life. They shared one well-meaning tale of how someone they knew was battling bravely with ADHD. As they saw the size of my growing grimace, and as this was my special day, they were quick to remark that a higher power told them that I was different from these other poor souls and would enjoy a happy partnership with Nut Cracker.

Finally, when they all ran out of words, it was time to enjoy the scariest part of the ceremony, the wedding dance. For some unknown reason, I unconsciously chose that the dance should be an elegant waltz instead of a more flamboyant Indian dance. With Nut Cracker in my embrace, we began to dance. But I must have looked like my dad's chicken with four heads and eight feet. I was stiff, the waltz was painful, and my usually cocky self deserted me. As we waltzed on, tripping on each other's toes, I assumed a leadership role and bravely tried to lead Nut Cracker. A few kicks in the shin and bruised toes later, it dawned on me that Nut Cracker wanted to lead. But, transitioning to new roles did nothing to decrease the blows on my shins and toes. We got through the waltz and when all the guests had departed, in the confines of the honeymoon suite, I added an extra paragraph to our partner vows that "we both will do whatever it takes to learn to waltz and live our lives in harmony."

During our honeymoon, we practiced our waltz; we were in constant conflict about who was the leader and who was the follower. By the end of the honeymoon, unable to handle one more conflict with Nut Cracker, I knew that to live in peace with Nut Cracker, I had to stop trying to lead ADHD to fit in my present life. I buried my bruised leadership ego and, for a change, learned to be a follower in the partnership and requested Nut Cracker from now on to lead me.

The decision to be a follower for once in my life paid rich dividends. From Nut Cracker, I learned a lot of ADHD-friendly best practices: Cool Moves on how to waltz in harmony with ADHD. Most of these moves were based on the advice of medical professionals working with ADHD on what I should do to change my life to include the finest and roughest qualities of ADHD. Move by move, to the monotonous tune of "Don't do that; Do this; Don't do that, Do this; Don't do that, Do this", I learned to waltz with ADHD and my bruised shins, toes, and ego all made a remarkable recovery as we waltzed further into Oh Landia.

To understand why I needed to make Nut Cracker my partner, I enjoyed humming 'Just the Two of Us,' a song by Grover Washington, Jr., and Bill Withers.

⌒

The value I extracted from this adventure is that I accepted that I must follow the "How to ADHD Handbook" I got from the medical professionals to learn to survive and thrive with ADHD. There was no quick fix by which I could get access to learn to do this. I had to put in the long hard miles and develop my emotional muscles that would make me a "marathon man" and not a "sprinter." Becoming a marathon man is a challenge for somebody with ADHD who, probably with hyperactivity as a trait, wants to sprint to everything that looks exciting and sprint away from everything that looks boring, but fortunately, we had the patience of P Leader to help us through this challenge.

MR. SPECTACLES

I needed to find a way for Nut Cracker to be my equal in our partnership with the Ales. But this was easier said than done, as Nut Cracker came with a broader spectrum of qualities that are a bit more complicated than Spark Plug and P Leader. I do not have the choice to dim Nut Cracker's rough qualities that are burning me out, I follow the advice of the medical professionals and also start to educate myself on my assets and liabilities that come with my ADHD title and can be regulated by medicine. As I had never used medication for lengthy periods, it was a challenge accepting that it could help make my life with ADHD easier. But not taking it was also not an option. So, I had to find a maverick way to tackle my apprehension over taking ADHD medication.

As I continued to go deeper into Oh Landia, I recalled that in contrast to all my previous titles that I had consciously worked hard to earn, for my ADHD title, I had worked hard too, but unknowingly! I achieved a higher score on the ADHD diagnosis questionnaire than on the thousands of other academic exams I have crammed for. On January 5th, 2021, when I received my ADHD title, I didn't celebrate as per the usual template of family, friends, and respected foes, guzzling copious amounts of alcohol, high fives, dancing and letting our hair down. Instead, the day and weeks that followed were spent in sharing my ADHD title with my Miners and Millers, debating how to live with this title and the shame I would have to overcome as I shared my title with the world.

After the mandatory period of drowning in my pity, I indulged in the sofa-bound academic pursuit of learning more about ADHD on the internet. Day by day, the more I surfed the internet, the more scary the stories I read appeared. As I got afraid, confused, and worried, the quantity of my grimaces increased, and I developed an unhealthy passion in a new sport called "navel gazing."

To help me find a way to accept that I needed medication, someone gave me an analogy, comparing taking medication for ADHD with having new spectacles that let me see the world around me with fresh eyes after years of struggling to see it clearly. The ADHD medication would help me "see" with greater clarity. I loved this analogy.

I reused the trick of visualizing Nut Cracker as a source to help me deal with my ADHD and thought of my medication as Mr. Spectacles. If Mr. Spectacles, like Nut Cracker, was to play a pivotal role in making me smile again, I had to make him and the other members of his family who managed my ADHD and SAD medications, my best friends.

Slowly, as my relationship with Mr. Spectacles improved, I started to smile more and grimace less. I credit Mr. Spectacles for the crucial role he played in ejecting me out of the hurricane. A few more months in the company of Mr. Spectacles helped me see the world with fresh eyes. They gave me the much-needed energy that helped me keep the unwanted visitors, SAD and FONGES away. With Mr. Spectacles' help, as I started sleeping better and the impact of my SAD diminished, my physical and mental wealth grew, and I started living a stable life with ADHD. In due course, while on my odyssey, I bid adieu to many of my medications, fondly recalling that they had played a crucial role when I needed them in my life,

However, in time, even as Mr. Spectacles moved from a leader role to a support role in my odyssey, the curious entrepreneur in me could not stop searching every nook and corner of the internet to learn more about ADHD and how I could find and free Oh. In no time, I got frustrated filtering through the millions of "wise words on ADHD," on how to deal with this and that, hacks on this and that, and other get-rich schemes. I decided I needed a "Crappy Alarm" to retain my sanity. I quickly constructed a virtual "Crappy Alarm." With this marvelous button in my hand, I learned to slowly turn the de-energizing power of the internet down one less search at a time. Time away from searching the internet for useless information led me to discover that in the tangible and intangible value of my millions of stories, especially my thirty Oh Yes and Oh No Stories, I had the foundation of my own "innernet." What I needed was an internal search engine to search for solutions within my own Oh Yes and Oh No Stories to develop my Ex-Factor.

The more I surfed my innernet, I realized I was gifted ADHD by chance and not by choice. In contrast to the other impressive collection of titles conferred on me only after spending hours mastering the qualities that come with the title, my ADHD title was conferred without any training. Fortunately, I found a number of handbooks on how to turn my roughest ADHD qualities to my advantage and began to see my gift of ADHD more clearly with fresh eyes. I started to share my ADHD title with family, friends, and respected foes. In time, I got used to saying Kiran Vas, ADHD with a smile on my lips and not a grimace.

~

The value I got from this adventure befriending Mr. Spectacles was the importance of making minor but consistently meaningful medicine and behavior adjustments almost daily to survive with ADHD. There was no doubt that Mr. Spectacles helped me move further away from Cape of Oh No. Even though I complain about the possible long-term impact of Mr. Spectacles in my life, he gives me the energy to see the bigger picture. He showed me that I had, through my millions of stories, the basic information and tools that I could learn from already in my innernet, and these could get me further away from the Cape of Oh No. If I continuously refined these, they would be useful throughout the odyssey.

The further I wandered away from Cape of Oh No, my weak smile began to gradually seep through my veil of grimaces. I imagined I could feel my Smile-Making Machine trying to kickstart Oh with all the information I was collecting on ADHD. I was ready to wonder more and worry less about how ADHD can inspire me to burn brighter.

With Oh, Nut Cracker, Spark Plug, P Leader and Mr. Spectacles, I now defined two of the three themes of my big picture of what I wanted to achieve on my odyssey.

1. Energize myself to invent Oh.
2. Build a team to help me in Ohism.

It was now time for me to focus on the third theme – How to Monitor and Measure my smiles.

NUT WORTH

Measuring and monitoring smiles and grimaces is fluffy and tricky. To solve this problem, I asked myself, "If health is my wealth, will I manage it just as effectively?" This was a tricky question to answer, and I pondered over it for a considerable amount of time. It led me to the concept of Nut Worth that is a twist on the financial term Net Worth, which puts a tangible value on my financial assets and liabilities. This is when I started viewing my ADHD perfections and imperfections as my assets and liabilities. What a wonderful story it would be if I had an equation that could use my emotions or Nuts as variables to calculate the value of the hard work I was investing to smile more and grimace less!

My odyssey started with no grand plan. I assumed that with all my life's experiences, I had all the Cool Moves to find and free Oh. But did I?

By the autumn of 2021, I could feel a few smiles that felt as if they were being created by Oh. In the warm sun and long days, I felt like a happy farmer as I went about harvesting my Oh Yes Stories for their value and weeding out a few Oh No Stories from my life. Basking in the glory of my harvest, I still felt a bit gloomy, however. Something in me was saying that for my next harvest of smiles, if I only sowed seeds from Mr. Spectacles or relied on the harvest from my ADHD perks, it would be difficult to create a billion of them! My gloom was rooted in the fear that when I faced my next hurricane, I wouldn't be robust enough with just the help of Mr. Spectacles and a few ADHD perks to survive it. I had no wish to be teleported back to Cape of Oh No.

As I worried about future imaginary hurricanes, I tried out various solutions. These mostly pivoted around optimizing the way I used Mr. Spectacles to smile more and grimace less. I suspected that if I worked only with Mr. Spectacles in optimizing my ADHD assets and liabilities, it would definitely make me smile more. But my path to a billion smiles would then be linear, and, in a worst case, if I got bored with optimizing my ADHD assets and liabilities, would start to taper away. What a horrific thought this was! Imagine if, in the future, my smile that I had worked hard to bring back into my life was once again replaced by grimaces. That would certainly frighten Oh and drive him away from my life again.

I realized the smiles that I was getting from Mr. Spectacles, was like smile hacking. Though this was extremely useful in the here and now and would definitely improve my smiles in the short term, what

I really needed was a sustainable and exponential way to grow my smiles.

So, back I went to Mining and Milling. I churned through a number of stories searching for maverick ways to grow my smiles. Many days later, tired and happy, I concluded that my Leadership and Entrepreneur perfections and imperfections or assets and liabilities that had taken me far in life were still underutilized. I had to find ways to make them equal partners and heroes in my odyssey. If I could discover a process to release the untapped potential value of Ales, this could be an exponential way to strengthen my Ex-Factor and bring and keep Oh permanently back into my life.

Well, smiling is easy when things are going your way. But when you're a Smileless Pauper, facing the battle of your life, you realize the full value of each smile and it's hard to put a dollar sign on how much you'll pay to bring it back. I knew I needed a way to measure that value of my smiles and grimaces, and I convinced myself that the success of my odyssey lay in the value of my smiles measured in a corny term called "Nut Worth."

To figure what lay behind the buzzword Nut Worth, required more Mining and Milling. The secret behind the Nut Worth concept is, as an entrepreneur, I always knew my net worth, so as an Extrapreneur, I should always know "what my nut worth is."

I define Nut Worth as an aggregation of four mutually exclusive, collectively exhaustible yet integrated sources of the four pillars, Physical, Mental, Financial, and Social wealth. When they're in balance, they ensure I smile more than I grimace.

My Nut Worth represented by the four nuts that I love the most

Peanuts - Physical Wealth

I love peanuts. They are affordable, easily available, and so versatile that they can be enjoyed in many ways. Peanuts is a perfect symbol of my physical wealth, which includes all the actions I do to stay healthy, how physically active I am, my diet, my weight, sleep routines, and more. I have control to develop and maintain my Physical Wealth until genetics or another Nut Worth pillar takes over and then I need the help of medical professionals to manage this wealth.

Cashew nut - Financial Wealth

I can eat cashew nuts every day, but that would be expensive. A cashew nut for me is a symbol of prosperity. A cashew tree has so many uses but the crown jewel of the cashew tree is the cashew nut and a perfect symbol of my financial wealth. My financial wealth includes all the actions in terms of money I need to earn to live a good life and the extra money I invest in my tangible and intangible financial assets. I have a lot of control to develop and maintain my Financial Wealth until one of the other pillars takes over and then I need the help of professionals to manage this pillar of wealth.

Walnut - Mental Wealth

A walnut resembles a brain, and, therefore, I chose it as a symbol of my mental wealth that includes all actions that I do to nurture my emotional and psychological well-being. I have a lot of control to develop and maintain my Mental Wealth until one of the other pillars takes over and then I need the help of professionals to manage this wealth.

Hazelnut - Social Wealth

The hazelnut is a perfect symbol to help me nourish my social wealth and includes all the actions that I do to build and nourish my relationships with family, friends, colleagues, and, to some extent, my foes. It also rhymes nicely with the hassle I'm faced with from my leeches and chattering monkeys. I have a lot of control to develop and maintain my Social Wealth until one of the other pillars takes over and then I need the help of professionals to manage this wealth. The adventure I embarked on was to find a way to start accumulating a well-balanced Nut Worth. With unwavering focus, I once again analyzed my thirty Oh Yes and Oh No Emotions from different angles, from distinct roles and perspectives in life. It became obvious to me that I had more than enough Ex-Factor in me to bring Oh back into my life. All my thirty Emotions impacted each of the four pillars of my Nut Worth in a unique way. So, I concluded that if Cool Moves could train my thirty emotional muscles to develop my Ex-Factor, I would be on track to build a robust Nut Worth. A bigger relief was that I didn't need to reinvent any parts of my life or invest a huge amount of money in developing my Nut Worth. I just need myself, my innernet, my ability to hyperfocus, and my gift to consume a vast amount of knowledge and personalize it for my situation in life. The actions I will use to develop my Nut Worth are old techniques and no big secret. For me to succeed in this, I had to turn up every day, put in the hard miles and keep repeating the meaningful Cool Moves I was learning consistently, till they became a valuable routine in my daily life.

⌒

The value I got from this adventure deciphering the Nut Worth concept is that it gives me the ability to calculate the positive or negative impact of future Oh Yes and Oh No Stories I accumulate in my life. Nut Worth is the cornerstone of my three goals. If I can keep it well founded for the rest of my life, it can help me bravely face the fiercest hurricanes and meteors that I encounter. As I perfect the art of having a well-balanced Nut Worth, I will develop a process that helps me find the ideal balance between the four pillars of wealth as I make the transition to become an Extrapreneur. My Nut Worth is also a tangible metric to baseline whether I'm squandering any pillars of wealth and to help ensure that I always have a reserve of Oh Yes nuts for hurricane days. I also realized that for many years when I was in the Cape of Oh No, I felt shameful about my vulnerabilities and did not easily accept them. I kept showing the world a fake version of a healthy Nut Worth, but in reality it was a farce to mask the truth that my Nut Worth, like Oh, was frail.

A fun way to measure our Nut Worth is every now and then, I sit in a quiet place with any or all of the four nuts. I then process a few that I'm wondering or worrying about. As I process the stories, I carefully peel the layers of the nut, feel the textures, taste it, and eat it to see how the pillar of wealth I'm worrying about is shaping up.

As I finalized the Nut Worth concept, I could feel that Oh loved the concept and I thought I could hear him purring softly in my belly.

How to Build a Pixie

Since I would be spending a lot of time with my imaginary partners the Ales on the odyssey, I decided that if I could imagine what they look like, it would be easier for me to have serious conversations with them on how to bring Oh back into my life. But most of the images of leaders and entrepreneurs I admired were extremely formal or ridiculously informal. I need an in-between image that would make me smile every time I saw them irrespective of whether we were chilling together or at loggerheads with each other. As I was beginning to accept that the Ales are my gifts, treasures, superpowers, and other similar buzzwords, my logic told me that the Ales must be immortal, extraterrestrial, or supernatural, as my odyssey unfolds in an ethereal world. I opted to go for a dash of the supernatural with a generous dash of the frivolous and decided that each of them would be a "pixie."

I decided that my next adventure would be to see how I design real-life pixies to get to know them better and how their perfect and imperfect qualities could help me create some more Oh Yes Stories to get Oh to purr more.

To visualize my pixies and their individual Ex-Factors, I thought there could be some inspirational leaders and entrepreneurs in DontDoNation that I could model my Ales' Ex-Factor after. If I could train them to be like these inspirational leaders and entrepreneurs, it would be just a question of time before I could create a billion smiles every day!

I went straight to the internet and, in a blink of an eye, I managed to find gigabytes of information on people like P Leader and Spark Plug. I was thrilled. I thought to myself, "How lovely it would be to find a few whose lives fascinate me. I could analyze their personal and professional successes to discover their Ex-Factor and a few of their greatest Cool Moves that make people smile." I compiled a list of the perfections and imperfections of these exceptional people that would help me identify what qualities to model my pixies behavior on. Such a checklist of perfections and imperfections could help us improve our understanding of each other and grow as a team over time. It could also be used as well to measure and monitor our smiles and grimace.

Click by click as each page came to life my brain was swirling in confusion with literally loads of crappy information on the so-called amazing qualities of entrepreneurs and leaders. The way they showcased their perfections on social media made it all appear easy to practice in real life. I began to wonder, "If it were really so easy, how come there were so few amazing leaders and entrepreneurs whom I actually know?"

Before I got carried away and started training the Ales with these what I called "social media qualities," I immediately redesigned a "Crappy Alarm" button, which I now visualized as a button on Nut Cracker's head, that jumped up and down like a nervous bundle of energy. When I got overexcited by a Cool Move suggested by a leader or entrepreneur, Nut Cracker sensing my excitement, bounced up and down with me and begged me to try it out. At this point, the Crappy Alarm would go off, indicating that I may be going off on a crappy tangent to my odyssey. To stop me trying these social media qualities, the Crappy Alarm gave a shrill noise. To stop it and bring back my focus to the three goals of my odyssey, I had to bang Nut Cracker on the head. This sounded painful, but it was effective, as each alarm helped me reduce the time spent searching the internet for crappy leaders and entrepreneurs and their hyped Cool Moves. Over time, I realized that trying to follow many of the overhyped actions of people I found online and recommended by other smart-looking people, was adding only superficial value to my life, actually making me grimace more than smile. These were not qualities I needed in my Ales.

My next sources of inspiration were the wise words of gurus who lived in the most exotic corners of the world. As I studied their wisdom, handed down over generations, I picked up inspiration from many exceptional people whose good qualities and Cool Moves didn't set off the Crappy Alarm. Analyzing their lives and under-standing the theory behind their Cool Moves gave me inspiration on how to train the Ales and my emotional muscles to make me smile more and grimace less.

The source of inspiration for Cool Moves was "It works only for millionaires." I followed the advice on how to lead a successful life from quite a few millionaires on their social platforms. Many were really inspirational, but an equal number used every marketing trick in the book to showcase how easy it was to make a few hundred thousand dollars in a few days. We just had to send them some money and if we followed their advice, they would guarantee our success; if not, we would get our money back. I soon started referring to them as mind manipulators. In the most convincing words, they shared wisdom about leadership, entrepreneurship, and more as they cruised around the world in private jets. I picked up a lot of good Cool Moves from them. But soon, their eloquent use of the English language and glittering self-help solutions showed me how inadequate I was not only as a leader and entrepreneur but also as a human in their fancy model of the world. In time I found my smile being replaced by a grimace, so I stopped following them. With the mind manipulators out of my life, I realized that quite often, their advice required me to invest a lot of money on their magic gadgets, which often came with huge discounts. Fortunately, before I bought any of them, the Crappy Alarm went off and I realized investing in gadgets was against my "best things in life are free" rule. I eventually turned off this source of inspiration for Cool Moves, too.

Once again in the throes of Mining and Milling, I found an amazing source of information for Cool Moves that has always been right in front of me. This source of Cool Moves required the least amount of internet time. All it required was for me to learn the art of observing exceptional normal people solving the toughest challenges in their lives or for others. Observing them without judging was tough for me, but the inspiration I got from spending time with social workers, charity organizations, the aged, addicts in recovery, people whose lives have been impacted by life-threatening diseases, and others has been mind-blowing. Many of them shared their experiences with me, and I absorbed them happily like a sponge. At the same time, I also realized that other than being inspired and appreciating their ability to smile in their dark moments, it would be years before I became brave enough to use their coping mechanisms as a source of inspiration for Cool Moves.

Stumped as to how to go about searching for inspiration to model my Ales after, I had no other option but to surf my innernet.

⌣

The value I got from this adventure on the Pixie concept was it made me realize that my fertile imagination was going to be a continuous asset on the path to becoming a Smiling Billionaire. The value I got from the Crappy Alarm concept was it forced me to take responsibility to find most of my own Cool Moves to bring Oh back into my life.

Strategic Time Out 2

As I had gotten to know my Ales a bit more, I shared with a few family and friends my experiences and understanding of how I was faring on the odyssey so far and the roles I envisaged the Ales would have in helping me bring Oh back into my life. Many appreciated my mission, purpose, and three goals, and I got lots of encouragement from them. I also got a lot of negative feedback. The negative feedback was fair but harsh. It often hurt. The Miners and Millers told me if I were going to use this feedback in a consistent, meaningful way to become an Extrapreneur, I needed to develop hippopotamus skin, accept the feedback, and then put the inputs that mattered into action to achieve my three goals.

Learning to accept the feedback was a nerve-wracking experience. There were many counterintuitive points of view on why, what, how, and when ADHD and Oh brought smiles and grimaces into my life. My initial romantic view of ADHD was challenged. I still didn't know what I had to do that would bring Oh back into my life again. On the bright side, I learned to appreciate how easy it was for my Oh Yes Stories to brighten lives.

I am thankful for my ADHD label, as it helped me open my eyes even more and observe the world through the eyes of a leader and entrepreneur with ADHD. The ADHD label also helped me try out new adventure types that I would never have dared to while I was living a comfortable life on the Cape of Oh Yes. The label also helped me pivot to embracing a new career, one that would allow me to use my talent to hyperfocus on creating a useful body of knowledge. Through my three goals, it would also help me inspire others to find their own ways to smile more and grimace less.

But for the free-spirited souls among us, a qualitative measure to confirm my feeling that my Ex-Factor is being strengthened is to sit in silence in the dark and place my hand on my tummy. I close my eyes and I imagine with all the new information I was gathering about the Ales and training my emotional muscles, I can hear Oh purring silently in the background. For the data driven souls among us, I don't as yet have a quantitative measure that I'm smiling more and grimacing less, but I am sure I will design one soon. It seemed it was time to move on to my next adventures where I could start experimenting on how to thrive with ADHD. But, before I was ready to cross over the invisible Cape of Oh No border line to the Cape of Oh, I took a selfie of my emotional muscle that looked like this.

Punch lines of my new stories

I'm more:

Alert, Confident, Courageous, Enthusiastic, Energetic, Focused, Playful, Thoughtful

> *I'm less:*
>
> Aggressive, Argumentative, Chaotic, Helpless, Impatient, Irritated, Lethargic, Restless

My Emotions

> *The Oh Yes Emotions I enjoy:*
>
> Amusement, Appreciation, Awe, Calmness, Excitement, Interest, Joy, Nostalgia, Romance,

> *The Oh No Emotions I am better at managing:*
>
> Anger, Anxiety, Awkwardness, Boredom, Confusion, Embarrassment, Disappointment, Sadness

With a few of my emotional muscles in the best shape of their lives, I was ready for the next adventure to go deeper into Oh Landia and start exploring my Innernet with the Ales to bring Oh back into my life.

PART 3

CLUMSY CREATIVITY

My fertile imagination gave me my first collection of stories and concepts. My creativity that is my least used talent in the ICE pack, is clumsy at its best. But after I found out how to use my creativity, it took over and helped me convert my collections of stories and concepts into toys. My first collection of toys further enhanced my ability to process the new information and experiences that I was more conscious of in my changing world. I have organized toys into hierarchies with each toy playing a pivotal role in helping me smile more and grimace less.

CHAPTER 7

How I found my Oh

My imagination allows me to develop concepts and process new information to understand my changing world. My stories helped me reflect on my life and prepare myself for my changing world. My creativity then takes over and helps me turn my concepts and stories into creative solutions that I call Toys to live in my changed world. As I imagined and created these toys, I enjoyed a load of smiles. These are a collection of my favorite toys that I will use on the odyssey to measure, monitor, and refine the impact of my Cool Moves on helping me attain my three goals.

> *What I measure is what I can change. And if I don't measure,*
> *I often find it difficult to grasp what I must change.*

RED COOKING POT

As I started surfing deeper and deeper into my Innernet, I needed an easy way to browse through the millions of stories there and find an interesting way to rerun those with punch lines that would help me smile more and grimace less. Though the high technology, and largely online world I live in was filled with shiny gadgets, it was my humble Red Cooking Pot and my hobbies of Cooking, Eating, and Smiling (all things I can operate offline) that turned out to be my biggest allies and confidants at this time. The Red Cooking Pot I use became a symbol of my mind and body. It served as a portal for me to access what was going on in my innernet. As I reran and analyzed my stories, each of the characters that I looked at closely to see how they impact my emotions, got magically converted into the spices that combine to make the curry.

With my eyes open wider and my ears as sharp as they've ever been, I wander deeper into Oh Landia and reach the part where I can see that I'm on an exquisitely beautiful island, with mountains, jungles, a breathtaking coastline, exotic animals, and flora and fauna of all kinds. It's a treasure trove of nuts of every kind. Surrounded by such beauty, I appreciate the need for Oh Landians to live off the Grid with no access to the DontDoNation. As I wandered around, I spotted a sign:

> Dr. Eye Can
> Clinic Stop Tuning Yourself
> Creative Ways to Discover your Oh

I read the sign outside and as I browsed through my innernet, I learned that the doctor is a virtual encyclopedia of knowledge and has used old wives' tales mastered from the University of ICanDoItMyself to earn his home-made doctor's degree. He seems to be an expert in Ohism. So, I decided to visit the doctor to ask him to help me find the inspiration to bring Oh back into my life.

When Dr. Eye Can opens the door, I step in and see an image of myself in the mirror. He welcomes me and after I introduce myself and my mission to bring Oh back into my life, he offers me a glass of water and we settle down. He grasps my predicament quickly and tells me he's a savant, and his specialty is helping people like me who one day get up and find that their Oh is missing in action. At ease in his presence, I share my Missing Oh Report and my dream to burn brighter. He seems amused at my dream but asks curiously, "Kiran, what are your goals?"

In a jiffy I puff my chest out and reply, "I have three goals, and before you ask, yes, they are achievable and measurable. They're based on how Oh can help me: Burn brighter and not burn out; Pioneer the Art of Extrapreneurship and become an Extrapreneur; Become a Smiling Billionaire."

He smiled at my passion as I mouthed these words and replied, "I can help you bring Oh back into your life, but I am neither an artist, management consultant, nor finance guru; so, I can't help you in those areas. I have a creative way for you to experiment with your perfect and imperfect qualities to find your Ex-Factor and put them all to great use." Soon, we're engrossed, discussing classic creative scenarios like dancing, sketching, learning languages, new hobbies, and more to bring Oh back into my life. Nothing really tickled my fancy, and we agree to have a few more Mining and Milling sessions together.

One day, as we were discussing Ohism in front of a majestic waterfall, and we discussed its immense beauty that covered up the immense power it has, Dr. Eye Can admitted, "Mrs. Bolt has told me about your impressive collection of stories, and I've read a few of them. I love them. What a fertile imagination you have." I thanked him, and he said, "Let's see if we can train your underdeveloped writing muscle with your overdeveloped visualizing muscle, to see if a combination of these two creative muscles could help bring Oh back into your life. Try your hand at writing what you visualize and let's catch up again.

With no clue about what habits and skills went into writing about whatever I visualized, I tried many different techniques. Finding stories to train on wasn't a problem for my fertile mind and there were tons of them in the vault. Getting them down on a piece of paper as a poem, memoir, song, essay, fiction novel, drama, nonfiction novel was the hardest task for someone like me with ADHD. But my funny and visualization bones refused to give up and kept pushing me to draft stories of my life humorously. The words that poured out as I scripted one comical scene after another invigorated me, and I found myself smiling more. The best aspect of my writing and visualizing was that the Crappy Alarm still went off continuously, warning that I may be going off on an unrealistic story line tangent. But I was having tremendous fun writing what I was visualizing, so I learned to ignore it. Initially, as I binged on my writing, my fertile imagination was on overdrive and my thoughts gushed out like the majestic waterfall that I had learned to appreciate for its beauty and immense power. With more determination than interest, I documented most of these thoughts with a pen on old notebooks. Writing was refreshing and helped me sort through the myriad rambling thoughts streaming through my mind. As I studied the words, I couldn't make heads or tails about what they were trying to tell me. With no tools to process these rambling thoughts for their value, especially as they were often packed with raw information, I was soon frustrated, buried deep in information and struggling to find any meaningful inspiration on how to bring Oh back into my life.

Okay, I had a problem. But I soon found a solution to my frustration in the many epics about learning the power of breathing. Learning to breathe in any systematic way is tough for me, as well as at least two of the three Ales who are restless by nature. As my Crappy Alarm went off constantly, I forced myself to take a writing break, sat back, and for the first time in my life tried to learn how to breathe deeply.

In time, deep breathing taught me the real meaning of the word "patience", something that many brave teachers had unsuccessfully tried to teach me for five decades. Still at odds with finding meaningful information in my writing to help me learn Ohism, I called on Dr. Eye Can and shared my predicament.

"Not a problem, Kiran; follow me." We walked and walked and finally reached the same spot with a majestic waterfall that I use for my Mining and Milling sessions. As I once again took in its beauty and raw power, Dr. Eye Can asked me to breathe deeply and follow the waterfall. This was tough but I tried my best. My eyes were glued to the main body of the majestic waterfall, but Dr. Eye Can guided me to observe a few gentle streams flowing away from the main body of the waterfall. When I started doing this, I relaxed a lot more and he told me that my written words consisted of both the main body of the waterfall and the gentle streams. It was a brilliant analogy!

I started reflecting on his words and began to appreciate that an infinite source of inspiration for bringing Oh back into my life could be found in the delicate words that were so very like those gentle streams. I knew that if I learned the technique of how to follow these gentle streams without getting lost in the power of the waterfall, it would lead me to find Cool Moves that I could master and use to bring Oh back into my life.

Dr. Eye Can was pleased that I had grasped this and commented, "Isn't it similar to when we pour a glass of Ale? Initially, more often than not, our eyes are drawn to the mesmerizing froth that forms on the top of a glass, rather than the main body of an Ale. Yet, in reality, the latter has the largest impact on how much we enjoy an Ale."

I must admit, I really love this analogy and use it in many aspects of my life.

From then on, I started studying and even had conversations with the gentle streams. Very often, as I gazed at my reflection in the water, I didn't enjoy the stories that the reflections were throwing back at me. Soon, as I had been growing a lot of hippopotamus skin lately, I was brave enough to follow a few of them as long as I dared to. In time, I liked the stories they were sharing with me.

In May 2021, I replaced paper with a computer, and started to describe what I saw in a few of these meandering streams. Within a few days, many of these words provoked something deep inside me, so deep, that I really couldn't immediately put a finger on what they were trying to communicate.

I continued to write with no clear aim. But the more I wrote, the more I realized that my underdeveloped writing muscle would help me document observations from the stories in my innernet and where I would discover the most meaningful inputs for the Cool Moves I needed to find and free Oh.

Of course, all portals need a search engine, and as I discussed this need with Dr. Eye Can, through gentle poking and prodding, he made me realize that the simplest search engine to my innernet is my humble Red Cooking Pot, in front of which I have spent hours in the kitchen, creating my favorite curries. I explain to the doctor how I have an unconscious habit of turning to cooking whenever I have a problem that I need a solution for. I've always turned to my Red Cooking Pot to make my favorite curries in which all the stakeholders in my problems are mapped to spices that go into my curry. As I curate the curry, the spices I add seem to communicate with each other and solutions to my problems just seem to appear.

Dr. Eye Can loved how I use my Red Cooking Pot to turn my stakeholders into spices as a trusted problem-resolving method. We agreed I would use the Red Cooking Pot and the curries being curated in it to consciously analyze the impact my new Stories, Concepts, Cool Moves, and Toys were having on my odyssey.

I brought my Red Cooking Pot out and showed it to Dr. Eye Can. He admired it and appreciated that it was round and made of iron with a matching red lid, explaining, "I love the pot, especially since as we cook we can seal it tight and trap the juices that are being released by the ingredients bubbling inside. Once in a while, we will have to lift the lid, so like you, it can blow some steam off. This is just what we need to find inspiration to bring Oh back into your life."

I was so impressed with Dr. Eye Can's selection of the Red Cooking pot as the search engine to my Innernet.

⌐

Dr. Eye Can, sitting in his Clinic Stop Tuning Yourself, is a constant reminder of the fallacy that I have the knowledge to treat myself to overcome any turbulence of my life. What I learned the hard way is that it's better to go to professionals when I have issues with any of the pillars of my Nut Worth and not try to fix them myself. I also find solace in the analogy of the froth in an Ale as this helps remind me that whatever may be the size of my Oh Yes and Oh No Emotions, I should remember that with my ADHD, Leadership, and Entrepreneurship qualities, I have a steady foundation to smile more and grimace less. The liveliness or dullness of the froth is representative of whether the Ales are in concert with or at war with each other at any given moment. It also reminds me that, in time, like the froth, they'll also settle down and once again be in harmony with the main body of the Ale and with each other.

TOY 2

THE SMILEOSCOPE

Now that I have the Red Cooking Pot as a portal to access my inner-net, I need a few toys to help me track and trace where Oh is being held captive. This toy is The Smileoscope, inspired by the stethoscope that Dr. Eye Can uses to listen to the source of the smiles and grimaces that the Ales are creating inside me and to determine their quantity and quality. The Smileoscope also helps Dr. Eye Can follow the footprints of the smiles or grimaces with the hope that they will lead him to the place where Oh is being held captive.

Winter 2021

After a few months on my odyssey, doing all I could to find Oh, one morning, slouching over the kitchen table, I took stock of my Nut Worth. As I reflected on my progress, I admitted that for the last few weeks, I was more restless and could feel I was heading toward a new hurricane season. I was anxious that despite all the effort I was putting into Ohism, I still had no clue where Oh was being held captive. Fair enough, I had a mission, purpose, goals, and a fluid plan of where I hoped the odyssey would take me. But, like Daddy's hose pipe, my plan was full of holes. This plan had gotten me far, but now I was frustrated by a lack of progress after a few good months. Even though I had crossed the border and was well on my way to the Cape of Oh, I felt lonely and lost. Even though I knew my smile was back, often over the last few weeks, when looking into the mirror, I found myself sporting a Cookie Cutter Smile, the type where all my smiles seemed stiff and look the same. Most of them lacked the sparkle of the old Kiran and when I was forced into a corner in a few tense situations that triggered the roughest of my Ales qualities, my smiles could rapidly turn into a grimace. I felt that my Nut Worth that had been accumulating nicely, was shrinking rapidly. Fearing the thought of being blown back to Cape of Oh No in the next hurricane, I realized I was on the verge of a relapse and needed help. I decided to pause my odyssey and called Dr. Eye Can.

Dr. Eye Can popped up by my side. As he saw my forlorn look, he asked in concern, "Have you just returned from the battles against smiles?"

I replied, "Yes, and I seem to be losing."

After we exchanged a few words about how I thought that some mysterious forces had taken my smile captive and I wasn't making noteworthy progress on my odyssey, he said, "I have a solution to every problem," and brought out his Smileoscope. "Let's measure the level of your smiles."

After laying me on his doctor's couch and attaching the virtual tubes of the Smileoscope to my mind and body, his smile faded as on the Smileoscope dashboard there were a number of lights blinking red. He told me this indicated my smile quotient was precariously low.

"Smile quotient?" I queried, with a worried look.

He replied that the Smile Quotient was a number he got when he divided the number of smiles by the number of grimaces the Smileoscope detected in me. "Kiran, I would like to perform a Smileoscopy to find out why your smile quotient is low. This is strange, as you've put in a lot of effort to learn Cool Moves, so I would like to get to the root cause of why your smile quotient is low and draining all the pillars of your Nut Worth. When my report is ready, we'll know what we need you to do to get you fit so you can restart your odyssey."

With those words, he gave me some literature on how to prepare for a Smileoscopy and asked me to return the next day. As I browsed through the literature, I looked worried, so he said, "Relax; I know your favorite hobbies are cooking, eating, and smiling, the Guts! For the Smileoscopy, I'll use your Guts and the Red Cooking Pot to process all your thoughts, feelings, and actions to understand why you smile and don't smile. There's nothing quite like a steaming curry to cure all the ailments that have stopped making you smile."

This calmed me down, and I left the clinic.

I studied the literature that had an overview of the Smileoscopy. In it, Dr. Eye Can explained what he called 'Finger-Licking Good Curries,' which is one of his specials that he cooks from scratch along with his patients who suffer from the same Ohism problems as I do. The close dialog he has with the patients during the process helps free those emotions that are stuck in their own versions of a hurricane. As they are freed, he maps the emotions into spices that go into making the finger-licking good curry that as you guessed is a curry to be eaten and relished with your fingers. I loved the concept of the finger-licking good curry and was determined to enjoy the Smileoscopy.

The next day when I returned to the clinic, I asked the doctor, "Why among the many options did you choose cooking and eating as the foundation of my Smileoscopy?"

He replied with a smile, "Kiran, in your case, making a finger-licking good curry will not only challenge your Ales and Guts to work as a team, but you and I will need the assistance of all your five senses to help us discover where Oh is being held captive. So, let's get started and start cooking. While you tell me your stories of what you're wondering and worrying about that's hampering your smiles, my Smileoscope will extract the emotions you're generating, map them one to one into spices from my spice collection, and I'll use those to make the masala to prepare one of your favorite finger-licking good curries. Fortunately enough, I've managed to get a handwritten copy of your mom's cookbook. The process you go through as I make the curry and the taste of the curry at the end of your story that you and others in the clinic enjoy determines your Smile Quotient."

Soon, Dr. Eye Can had the Red Cooking Pot bubbling and he asked me to imagine that I had added the Ales and Ex-Factor into the Red Cooking Pot. Soon I was witnessing the doctor in his element, and he enjoyed his version of designer cooking. He was constantly calling out for help to an invisible force that I called Miss ICantFindIt, asking her to find kitchen aids and spices that he wanted to use in his curry. After a while, surrounded by a mess, but happy and content, he had the fire under the Red Cooking Pot glowing nicely.

Returning to his jocular doctor-patient manner when he saw me looking perplexed by this ridiculous Smileoscopy and wondering what I need to do next, he said, "Think of the Red Cooking Pot as a movie screen and you're enjoying the movie with a good ale in your hands. As you narrate your stories that you're wondering or worrying about, I'll make masala to prepare a curry. I'll keep adding spices to the pot and observe what's happening as the new and old spices interact with each other."

I was intrigued, but also ready for my Smileoscopy. I gave Dr. Eye Can a thumbs up to show that I was prepared. He smiled, and under the starlit night sky, strapped up to the Red Cooking Pot, for the next couple of hours I started to narrate stories from my list of thirty story punchlines that made me smile and grimace.

After he had prepared and we enjoyed a few curries, the readings of my Smile Quotient had increased, and the frown on Dr. Eye Can's face had softened. Even though he still had no clue to the root cause of why my smile quotient was low, he seemed confident that after a few more rounds, he would be able to decipher the root cause.

Once the Smileoscopy was over, he freed me and gave me a link to a site called the Eye Tube. When I logged on to it, I found videos of my own Old Cool and Uncool Moves that I've learned since I was a child. He told me, "Here's inspiration for you to start doing these moves more consistently in your life. They're guaranteed to bring a few smiles."

As I flicked through the pages, I saw a list of a few Uncool Moves that were detrimental to my health and inspiration that I needed to start deleting from my life. He said that over the next few months I should try out some of the Old and New Cool Moves in the book to increase my Smile Quotient. He gave me his mobile number and said, "Don't hesitate to call, but I'll also check up on you regularly."

⌇

The value I got from that Smileoscopy is now I have a great toy for when I feel a bad case of SAD coming on. Instead of navel gazing and feeling sorry for myself, I use a Smileoscopy to immerse myself in my hobbies of cooking, eating, and smiling to lower my grimaces for a while. How low I am feeling reflects in how bland my cooking, eating, and smiling is, but with time, a Smileoscopy helps me get over my SAD.

MY DITTY

My ditty is a powerful toy that I use to cheer up when I feel a bout of grimaces are around the corner. I start whistling my ditty to remember that even in my dark moments, I have so many good things in my life. Like a friend once said, "Kiran, chin up. There are a billion people who would exchange your life with you in an instant." Updating the ditty as I progress on the odyssey is also a cool way to measure and monitor that my investment in Cool Moves is bringing me closer to my three goals.

December 2021

One evening, hanging around the fire, chilling with the Guts and the Ales under a starry sky, Dr. Eye Can magically appeared. He went right into preparing my soul food of a fish curry and rice. When he had the pot bubbling nicely, he invited us to join him to gaze into the Red Cooking Pot. When we were taking in the aroma, he handed us a copy of my Oh Ditty and asked us to update it on what we had learned the last few months. This was a fantastic game, and intoxicated by the smell of the simmering curry and our stomachs growling, one by one, we debated each line of the ditty, and when we were in agreement, with a huge smile, I flexed all my emotional muscles that I had been training and read it out to all of us around the fire.

Oh No! Kiran,

you never bother (less) with attention to detail,

you make tons of careless mistakes,

when bored you get (are less) easily distracted,

you do not like to study,

your mind is often elsewhere,

you are always (less) late,

you are (less) messy, forgetful, and lose or misplace things,

you are (less) fidgety, restless, and can never sit still,

you dream too much,

you yap too much, yap too loud, and yap out of turn,

you (still) lack patience and dislike waiting your turn,

you interrupt people (less),

you get (less) easily annoyed and frustrated,

you cannot control your temper, and you fight too much,

you play pranks and tease others a lot,

you (do not) argue for the sake of arguing,

you are defiant to authority and deliberately annoy people (less).

But,

Oh Yes! Kiran,

you are mastering many cool moves and on your way to Cape of Oh.

When dinner was over, Dr. Eye Can asked me to share our experiences of the Cool Moves we have practiced. I brought out notes and read, "There are many Old Cool Moves that already make me smile or have done automatically for years." I told him how I had accepted a few and updated them to include my growing knowledge of the Ales' qualities and how we started mastering them.

The first breakthrough was that I could earn a few smiles by playing a larger role in the family. I call this Family Ties that involve my family in an attempt to help me smile in tough times. I became proactive in shopping and cooking. I also found entertaining ways to transform doing tedious housework like cleaning the house, paying bills, and more into fun. Strangely enough, these tasks also helped me burn my nervous energy and gave me an appetite to start more Old Cool Moves. I found simple ways to smile when doing practical tasks at home, like decluttering the basement and loft, which I never thought I had the patience to do. Doing these practical tasks is very tough at first, but when I look at them as playing a game and break them into small tasks, it's amazing to see how much I've always dreaded doing them.

Dr. Eye Can said, "What other interesting stuff have you done? Something you have never tried before."

I was on a roll now. "The Cool Move to try to paint the house was nothing short of a miracle. I have never tried painting the house before, as I always thought I was clumsy. At the end, the painted house looked okay, and yes, I was messy."

This in the end was a typical Nut Cracker quality as it actually started with me just painting our gate black, but when I saw how good it looked and I could actually paint, slowly, I realized I was getting a kick out of painting. Soon the whole house got a pretty decent coat of paint. I relaxed a lot when I painted, but I also learned to do a decent job at something that doesn't come naturally to me and requires concentration. If I get distracted, the painting gets messy, and I have to redo much of the work. But when I'm in the flow, I get lost in my own world, and like magic, the dull walls become colorful again. The preparation of the surfaces before I paint them is boring and the tough part is cleaning up. "Looking back over the last months and viewing my paint work has left me spellbound," I added.

Dr. Eye Can said, "Cool. A plan, structure, and discipline and a bit of creativity will get you far. Tell me more."

I continued: "The other thing we do as a family now is instead of sitting in front of a TV for a meal, we sit at the dining table and enjoy our meal together. We work hard to avoid distractions like looking at phones or TV when we're together."

Dr. Eye Can beamed, "That sounds so cozy."

I continued, "We also watch hilarious videos together and have formed a family digital group on which we post dinner menus, plans for the day, share memories, photos and congratulate each other for achievements." I described how I had pulled out 20 years of old pictures buried in layers of dust and relived them with the family.

"Some of these Cool Moves have helped the family agree on a few shared roles and responsibilities and improved communication," I added. In the end, these small Moves helped us all appreciate Nut Cracker and get him to help us burn brighter and not burn out. These Cool Moves form a priceless habit that costs nothing and is easy to implement. I clarified that one of the things we also did that cost a bit of money was to get a speed boat license and enjoy sailing together.

Dr. Eye Can's smile was contagious, and he said, "Impressive, Kiran. Well Done! What else have you been up to?"

With a smile that can match Dr. Eye Can's, I replied, "I'm trying to be more aware of the needs of the people in my inner circle."

Dr. Eye asked, "What is your inner circle?"

In a serious voice I said, "My inner circle is about fifty selected family, friends, and foes who have a positive impact on my life. The rest of my family, friends, and foes are placed in my outer circle and I can choose how and when I want to interact with them. In this group are also my leeches and chattering monkeys, and I'm slowly getting rid of them. Interacting with my inner circle has helped me smile, as we can share and spread love and laughter through jokes, funny videos, stand-up comedy, meaningful content like books, podcasts, family outings, and more."

Dr. Eye Can asked, "How did the inner circle react when they heard about your odyssey?"

I pondered and carefully chose my words: "At the start, this was quite difficult, as we are all in different stages of our lives. Sharing my experiences on Cape of Oh No with them, I got them to take part in my odyssey and share my smiles and my struggles. They supported my audacious plan to create a billion smiles wholeheartedly. All was not as rosy as I make it sound, but the wonderful thing was while I shared my struggles with them, many of them shared their own tears and fears and this helped me accept that I wasn't the only one carrying a backpack full of Oh No Emotions on my odyssey." Dr. Eye Can said, "That's great! It's so nice to hear about their support. What else have you done?"

I brightened up and, with a grin, continued: "I watch funny videos and old comedy series from my childhood. I laugh like a crazy kid when we watch episodes of *I Love Lucy, America's Funniest Home Videos, Candid Camera*, and more. I have my favorite comedians whom I follow. Watching and listening to comedy is a really easy and cheap way to get my daily dose of smiles. I also tried to take up dancing to give me great boosts of energy."

Dr. Eye Can asked, "How did that turn out?"

I groaned, "I failed in the New Cool Move I call two left feet."

Dr. Eye Can said encouragingly, "It's okay to fail. What did you learn from dancing?"

"I found some great hip hop and rock music to dance to. I tried to dance to them for a few minutes a day, either with Marianne or by myself. We were terrible together. When I danced by myself, I found catchy tunes that I loved, danced for 10-minute intervals, and my mood definitely perked up. What I learned was that my joints started complaining, and I couldn't make dancing an everyday habit. Even though I was terrible at dancing, it was great fun while it lasted. In the end, I just didn't have a passion for dancing and saved my energy to find another source of smiles."

Another Cool Move, "The Crying Sessions" has also helped me a lot. I told him I had learned that when I'm anxious about something for a long time, I should close myself in a room at a fixed time every day and give myself permission to pour my heart out for 15 minutes. I used to do this at the same time every day till I accepted the impact of what I was anxious or worried about and had a solution for how to live with it."

Dr. Eye Can looks really pleased. "How did Cool Moves help you with your physical wealth?"

"It's going well. I'm in decent physical shape. The 'Walk of Life' Cool Move was an immense help. I go for long walks, treks, and cycling for a few hours at least once a week." I continued by explaining that to motivate me to walk, I bought a good-looking pair of trekking shoes, and this enticed me to walk for a few hours in nature. I also bought a trekking route book, and, often, Marianne and I would drive out to these routes where we would trek for a few hours. I also used to get up early in the morning to walk by myself, and this was a wonderful feeling. "Fresh air and nature are addictive and help me solve a lot of problems."

"The thing to respect is to know my limits. If I pushed too far, I got aches and pains and discovered muscles I've never used before. The worst is when I overdo things and sprain my ankles or get back pain. I also go on a late evening walk. My walking goal when I walk is to wander and wonder for at least an hour a day. For longer walks, I invited friends to wander and wonder with me on any topic under the sun other than the touchy subjects that are in breaking news. These walks are a fantastic way to stay connected," I concluded.

Dr. Eye Can curiously asked, "Walking as a habit is enjoyable but requires discipline. How do you manage?"

I replied that I loved this solution that helped me make walking not only enjoyable but also a learning experience.

Dr. Eye Can's curiosity was aroused. "What did you do, Kiran"?

I blushed as I said, "It was relatively simple and didn't cost an arm and a leg. I bought a good pair of headsets and listened to podcasts and audiobooks. The headsets are priceless. I've learned so much through them in such a short time. Podcasts and audiobooks, especially standup comedy, help me laugh a lot. They've made me appreciate the special skill to take complex subjects, simplify them, and make people laugh."

Impressed, Dr. Eye Can urged me to continue.

"The Cool Move 'learn a new language script' was educational. I practiced learning to write a new language script (I didn't learn to speak the language) and this helped me improve my mind and body coordination. It was a challenge to get the four letters in ADHD to work together. But I enjoyed this challenge, and it encouraged me to spend more time every day on more mind-body coordination exercises. This led me to taking up Tai Chi."

After a sip of water, I continued, "I started learning simple techniques to relax, to manage the stress, aches, and pains I was going through on this path." I elaborated on how I found out that acupuncture was very helpful because, often, I used to get a lot of pain in my neck and shoulders. Relaxing massages were also an effective way to get rid of tension, and, occasionally, I spoiled myself with a massage, adding, "I feel really relaxed after this."

I also told the good doctor how these Cool Moves opened my mind up to admit that some of the main sources of my Oh No Stories stem from being a workaholic and not getting a good night's sleep. These are tough habits to unlearn, but I tried to reduce the impact of these two bad habits. "I'm now focusing more on things that create Oh Yes Stories, and I'm gradually learning to not be a workaholic and to get sufficient sleep every night to smile. This will take a lifetime to unlearn, but I've started."

I then told him how I tried the Cool Move 'Failure to plan is a recipe to plan to fail,' seeking to become a more disciplined planner and be a wee bit less impulsive. I wasn't ready to stop being impulsive as impulsivity has been the fuel of many of my most memorable Oh Yes Stories.

"A straightforward way to start appreciating this Cool Move was to make a grocery list when I went shopping. This was something I tried for the first time in my life. My shopping has always been spontaneous and I never felt I needed shopping lists, as I thought I could remember what I needed." However, in hindsight, I now realized that I always forgot something or the other and came home often with things we didn't need, especially things I fell in love with because the marketing was so enticing. My impulsive shopping habits had been a huge frustration point for the family, so I found a shopping list app, and everybody, including myself, began entering what we needed from the supermarket. "It was a huge saver of time, money, and frustration and a super effective way to shop but also absolutely boring, as it killed all the impulsivity I enjoyed when shopping. However, now, when I go shopping, I don't have to scratch my head for what I need and the amount of hard, annoying, and frustrating time this has reduced is amazing."

I took a break for a while and when I was ready, I continued. "Another very insightful Cool Move was inspired by Stephen B. Karpman's Drama Triangle. This is a model that helped me out in tough situations by identifying who the victim, persecutor, and res-cuer are in every drama I'm involved in." The drama triangle tool is very useful to grasp my roles and responsibility in all my dramas, take them seriously, and try to bring the drama to a happy ending. Using this model, I learned to reduce my Oh No Stories around my leeches and chattering monkeys. For the dramas that I'm involved in, I use it to figure out if I'm the victim, persecutor, or rescuer, and this helps me also create smiles and reduces my grimace.

The Cool Move I love a lot is what I call 'Mind Flyness.' I elab-orated on this, "Very often, when I have a problem that needs a solution, I give my mind the permission to fly to any subject to do reconnaissance and check if there's a source of smiles that I can Mine and Mill for there. I don't try to control these Mind Flyness sessions, and at the end of each of them, I have pages full of ideas that are a great source of inspiration for my next smiles."

After I finished with my last story, Dr. Eye Can was smiling and got me ready for a Smileoscopy. A few minutes later, he grinned and said he was happy with my Smile Quotient readings. "Kiran, the Smileoscopy indicates that you're still not ready for your odyssey. But I think you're not a Smileless Pauper anymore. We have to practice some more Cool Moves to get your Nut Worth in a good balance for the odyssey. I would love to continue to guide you to find inspiration for Cool Moves and be part of the odyssey."

I'm thrilled to have Dr. Eye Can on my team. "It will be an honor," I say with gratitude.

The Ditty is a toy I use actively when I feel that life isn't treating me right. Whistling the ditty does seem to put a temporary stop on my grimaces and helps me to be grateful for what I have.

TOY 4

A Pre-Mortem

After spending quality time with Dr. Eye Can and the Ales, I definitely felt the radiance of my smile return and began to appreciate that a lifestyle where smiles come naturally is contagious. I felt that my enthusiasm to learn more about the Ales and restart my odyssey was coming back. But even though I had great access to my innernet, can rerun my stories at will, and can track and trace my smiles, I still had a nagging feeling that I was, in an unconscious way, inhibiting some of my natural talents from blossoming, those that in future could be a fountain of smiles.

As we continued our Ohism sessions in the Clinic Stop Tuning Yourself, at the age of 55, Dr. Eye Can classified me as a late ADHD bloomer. To help me understand the late ADHD bloomer mindset, he introduced me to a toy called a 'Pre-Mortem.' He said, "It is a process where I imagine I've died and make an 'If Only I Had List' that contains all the things I wish I had done or not done. With this list, in hindsight, I would have a snapshot of what has prevented me from obtaining the fulfillment that I knew I was capable of."

The Red Cooking Pot was once again the diagnostic toy for my Pre-Mortem. This one-size-fits-all aspect of the pot as a diagnostic toy that provides answers to my questions seemed quirky. But, as it involved cooking and eating, I felt that to have the Pre-Mortem toy in my growing odyssey toy kit could be very valuable.

Once again, I enjoyed seeing Dr. Eye Can set up the Red Cooking Pot. He asked me to tell him all the items I had in my 'If Only I Had List' and imagine that the Ales and Ex-Factor were in the Red Cooking Pot. As I rattled them off, he kept adding spices to the pot and after a while, surrounded by a mess, but happy and content, he had the curry, which he says is my mom's Ball Curry recipe, bubbling nicely. I peered curiously into the pot, and I was in heaven as I saw the color and the smell of the curry.

"What do you see happening in the pot, Kiran?" he asked me.

My fertile imagination kicked in. "It is an exotic curry. I see a lot of swirling things that look like pixies, a lot of bubbling, and a lot of steam being blown off. The coolest aspect is that the pot is the playground to a group of pixies who seem individually and collectively intriguing…"

I paused for a while as the doctor added a few more spices. He then closed the lid and, after a while, asked me to open it again. This time I said, "There's a lot of passion on display and happy exclamations can be heard as the spices interact with each other debating who is at fault for not freeing me to achieve what's on my 'If Only I Had List.'"

A few pixies were having fun, a few others were oblivious to what was happening around them. A few seemed lost in their own thoughts, a few were acting like they would rather be elsewhere. The dominating pixies were easy to spot. They had blinking lights on their heads and the loudest voices. A few pixies were tearing out their hair in desperation at the surrounding chaos. I said, "I imagine they all were debating how they can boldly go to places they've never gone before or share their dreams about creating a brighter future for themselves."

"Wow!" said Dr. Eye Can. "What an imagination! You've unconsciously visualized what's going on inside you when you bring your finest qualities to the party."

He closed the pot, and we enjoyed listening to it bubbling nicely and releasing a tantalizing aroma. After a while, he opened the lid to give the curry a stir and throw in a few more spices. He handed me the ladle and said, "Give it a good long stir and tell me what you see."

"Total Chaos! Anarchy rules!" I said as the pot bubbled furiously. "There seems to be a power battle going on between the pixies. Some spice you just added made the peaceful curry become turbulent." With sweat trickling down my brow, I covered the pot, hoping the curry would calm down.

After a while, when the ingredients in the pot appeared to have calmed down, I removed the lid. I give a sigh of relief, as the pixies seemed to have found a solution to their power struggle and were all bubbling together happily again. The curry had returned to normal, with only the occasional contented bubble rising to the surface. Seeing the sense of relief on my face Dr. Eye Can smiled and said, "After the storm comes the calm. What you just witnessed in the pot is how your roughest Ale qualities can stir up trouble in a peaceful gathering as you let them run amok. I love your vivid imagination, but I cannot stomach any more of it today. Let's meet again tomorrow," he concluded.

The next day, Dr. Eye Can said the Pre-Mortem had been a success. He handed me a list of my thirty emotional muscles that had a traffic light indicator for emotion: Use More (Green), Under Used (Yellow), Overused (Red).

He reported, "After studying the results of your Pre-Mortem and the readings on Smiles Quotient Meter, I'm afraid that I agree with you that someone has taken Oh captive. But you now have a list of emotional muscles that you need to train to make you smile more and to stop training to make you grimace less. I'm sure that in a few months, Oh will be smiling again and you will be ready to restart the odyssey."

To help me learn the qualities I needed, Dr. Eye Can said, "I think I have a Cool Move to help you get closer to your Ales. With your love for visualization and storytelling, if you put a face on their names, it will help you to get to know them more personally."

When he saw my face light up, he continued, "Once you understand where, how, what, when, and why the Ales affect your life, and the lives you touch, it would help you make a good plan to strengthen Ex-Factor and Nut Worth."

These wise words from Dr. Eye Can were the answer to my problem that had been nagging me – how to bring Oh back into my life. Seeing the glint in my eyes, Dr. Eye Can said, "Let's start plotting to find the captors. I have a plan that takes root in an activity that you've done unconsciously for years. You've always had the WWoW Factor."

I must have looked like a question mark, so to ease my frustration, he said in his lovely baritone, "Kiran, you have a hobby called

WWoW; that's my acronym for wandering aimlessly, worrying unnecessarily and wondering about the most nerdy things in life."

I smiled when I heard this brilliant observation, and in WWoW mode, I asked myself the WWoW questions or the why, what, how, where, and when questions on the story I'm WWoWing about and how the story will influence my life.

Dr. Eye Can said, "The next toy we have to experiment with is to visualize scenarios on how you could put faces on the names of the Ales. For this, I have the perfect toy called 'Open Kiran Surgery.' Let's meet at the clinic tomorrow. Here's some literature on what the Open Kiran Surgery is about."

⌒

The value I get from my Pre-Mortem confirmed that I'm a typical Alpha male, and I have always been uncomfortable exposing my emotions to the world. It also showed me how important it is for me to be in control of the Ales, as when they're in harmony, I script my most incredible Oh Yes Stories. The opposite is also true, as when I'm not in control, they take charge of me and if they become obsessed with Oh for the wrong reasons, they can lead me down a path that will script many Oh No Stories or superficial Oh Yes Stories. The Pre-Mortem gives me a very tangible list of the Things I Must Do and the Things I Must Stop Doing to help me achieve all my three goals.

TOY 5

OPEN KIRAN SURGERY

As I slowly start enjoying the process of developing my Ex-Factor, my curiosity to learn more about the Ales and decipher the puzzle where Oh is held captive picks up. My skill at operating my innernet and searching for inspiration was becoming addictive and I enjoyed the smiles and the grimaces that spontaneously arose as I browsed through my stories. As I am now at a point where I need professional help to train my emotional muscles, inspired by an Open Heart Surgery, I conjure the Open Kiran Surgery, a toy that makes it fun for me but also gives me a structure when I go deeper on my inner journey to discover more about the Ales than I have ever dared to.

The next morning at dawn, when I arrived at the clinic, Dr. Eye Can introduced me to his new assistant, the Wizard of Oh, whom, at the first glance, resembled a typical wizard adorned in a classic attire. Dr. Eye Can said, "Kiran, as your problems with finding Oh are above my pay grade, I have requested the assistance of the wizard, who is a world-renowned expert in Ohism. He is the best person I can think of to help you find and free Oh. He's a man of few words and will spend most of his time in front of the Red Cooking Pot. We have agreed that today we would like to perform a procedure called an Open Kiran Surgery."

Meet
The Wizard of Oz

I studied the wizard with a frown on my face, debating if I were even ready to trust such a weird looking pixie to advise me on Ohism, let alone perform a complex-sounding surgery on me.

Dr. Eye Can sensed my concern. To calm my growing look of worry, he placed an arm on my shoulder and said, "Relax, even though the wizard will perform the Open Kiran Surgery, I'll be by your side at all times. I suspect Nut Cracker is the captor of your smile, and I would like to look deep inside you and see if this hypothesis is true and, if yes, whether Nut Cracker has any accomplices. To execute this complex procedure, I need help and this is where the wizard comes in."

I had no option but to trust the doctor's instinct.

Dr. Eye Can asked us all to make ourselves comfortable and said, "Let's get the wizard up to speed on your Mission, Purpose, and Goals and the progress and obstacles you've encountered so far."

I rattled off the thoughts bubbling in my head, while the wizard kept nodding his head gently. When I finally stopped, he asked, "The concept of Ex-Factor can be confusing. Can you visualize your Ex-Factor as a pixie?"

I thought for a while and told him that I could visualize Ex-Factor as a detective who is a constant presence in my life, helping me find ways to identify all the emotional muscles I need to train to create more Oh Yes Stories and less Oh No Stories. With a poof of his wand, a pixie called Ex-Factor was soon flying around the clinic. When he settled in my hand, I noticed his features in fascination. This was a perfect visual of what my Ex-Factor looked like.

Meet
Ex Factor

When he saw I was thrilled with his magic, the wizard said, "Before we start the Open Kiran Surgery, as the concept of Cool Moves can be confusing, can you visualize your Cool Moves as a pixie?"

I thought for a while and then smiled the largest of smiles in a long time: "Someone who looks cool and content without a fear in this world." With a poof of his wand and a few words, I was holding the coolest pixie in my hands. I was delighted at the wizard's creation of Ex-Factor and Cool Moves.

Meet
Cool Moves

Lying on the couch, still nervous over what was about to unfold, I spoke aloud to no one in particular, "What is the plan now and how do Ex-Factor and Cool Moves fit into it?"

The wizard, as calm and collected as ever, laid out the details for the Open Kiran Surgery. Seeing the perplexed look on my face, he said, "An Open Kiran Surgery is a noninvasive surgery during which I'll guide you on what to do as I prod and poke the well camouflaged nooks and corners of your mind and body to smoke out the captors. Ex-Factor and Cool Moves have critical roles to play to help you find and free Oh."

I wasn't sure if this answer calmed my nerves, but, once again, I trusted the process I had agreed on with Dr. Eye Can.

The wizard took out a few strange looking instruments and said that now he was going to do a complete mind and body check. After 20 minutes, all through which I'm a bundle of nerves, I'm relieved when he finally says in a monotonous tone, "Let's meet again in a few days."

The next few days were spent worrying about the outcome of this exotic-sounding surgery. So, when I checked into Dr. Eye Can's operating theater, I was still nervous over what to expect. It was only when I caught sight of the Red Cooking Pot humming with a comforting sound and surrounded by the intoxicating smell of food, that I relaxed a bit and began to feel at home.

To get me ready for surgery, the wizard said, "For the duration of the Open Kiran Surgery, I'll place the two pixies, Ex-Factor and Cool Moves, inside you and then give you a few Cool and Uncool Moves to practice. These include actions that will give you smiles as well as grimaces. Then we'll observe what is happening within you based on monitoring the reactions of Ex-Factor and Cool Moves. Are you with me?"

When I nodded my head, still confused as to what this surgery is about, he attached virtual tubes to my mind and body that were connected to the Red Cooking Pot. He said that these tubes would capture the Oh Yes and Oh No Emotions that I would generate while practicing the Cool and Uncool Moves and, similar to the Smileoscopy, he would capture them and map them into spices that went into making the masala of the finger-licking good curry. The only difference between a Smileoscopy and the Open Kiran Surgery is that the surgery can last for many hours over many days and will require that I focus to the best of my ability throughout.

I looked at Dr. Eye Can and said, "The wizard knows that I have ADHD, right? What he is asking me to do is nearly impossible."

The doctor said, "Kiran, trust the process. Believe me; it works."

When the surgery was underway, I started randomly practicing the Cool and Uncool Moves on the instructions of the wizard. I didn't quite enjoy a few of them, but followed the process, as it was part of the surgery. Naturally, when I executed the ones I enjoyed, I smiled. And, when I practiced the ones I didn't, I grimaced, cursed, and swore.

All the while the wizard prodded and poked inside me, he asked Ex-Factor and Cool Moves uncomfortable questions, all aimed at identifying who the captors of my smile could be. At the same time, in silence, Dr. Eye Can was jotting his observations down.

When I asked Dr. Eye Can what he was doing, he said he was recording all my nitty gritty thoughts, feelings, actions, and the words I was uttering and mapping them to the various unknown spices with exotic names the wizard had in his bag. He then handed the spice to the wizard, who now was making a chicken vindaloo from his well-worn cookbook while Dr. Eye Can was analyzing the reactions of spices with each other and jotting them down.

When I looked at him dumbfounded, he explained, in nonmedical jargon, that if I were enjoying myself practicing a Cool Move, he added a dash of spice like chili (it had a more exotic name in the wizard's spice bag) to the vindaloo, which, generally, is a spicy dish. If he spotted a grimace coming on, he would add another bland spice to the vindaloo. Whenever we took a break from the wizard's prodding and poking, he invited me to gaze into the pot to see if I could recognize any of the captors among all the exotic swirling pixies in the pot.

While the wizard cooked, my mind and body as well as Ex-Factor and Cool Moves were exhausted as he prodded and poked through five decades of emotions hidden in me. After a few days of non-stop prodding and poking, the Open Kiran Surgery was getting to be an uncomfortable experience. Thankfully, one day, when I woke up in a sweat in what seemed like the middle of the night, Dr. Eye Can was clutching an agitated pixie whom he introduced as Nut Cracker. Dr.

Eye Can said, "Meet the liveliest spice in one of the spiciest vindaloos the wizard has ever made."

Nut Cracker was almost all that I had imagined he would be. He had a tomato-red face with dark black eyes. He had springs for a spine, and I couldn't spot any feet. His hands seemed to resemble a Nut Cracker and he just doesn't appear to be able to be still. He had all the four letters of ADHD in different combinations that encapsulated my brand of ADHD brilliantly.

Meet
The Nutcracker

Handing Nut Cracker to me, the doctor said "While you were asleep, Nut Cracker had confided in me that he was one of the mysterious forces and a key root cause of your hurricanes. He had been one of the captors of Oh, who was scared of the hurricanes. Unfortunately, under captivity Oh was overwhelmed by his rough qualities and those of his fellow captors, and unable to take any more of them, escaped from their clutches. They had followed after him but before they could catch up with him, I was diagnosed with ADHD. Subsequently, I had become obsessed with my ADHD and had started taking Mr. Spectacles to learn to survive a life with ADHD. In the process I had learned a few ways to get to know him better and how to control the disruption he brought into my life. As a result, he had calmed down a bit and had to give up trying to recapture Oh. When I asked him who his accomplices were, he would not name them."

I took the time to reflect on what Dr. Eye Can had just said. When I was ready I gave Dr. Eye Can a thumbs up, and the wizard restarted the Open Kiran Surgery. As Nut Cracker joined us in gazing into the pot, he too couldn't pinpoint who his accomplices were. The wizard continued to go deeper and deeper with the Open Kiran Surgery and he found a lot of other interesting pixies hovering inside me. From my gut he extracted three who from their hearty demeanor I knew at once we're Cooking and Eating, and Smiles, but there was still no sign of my Oh.

Meet
Cooking

Meet
Eating

Meet
Smiles

After a few more hours of the wizard prodding and poking inside, I was tired and ready to abandon the Open Kiran Surgery that was wearing me out. Just then, Dr. Eye Can appeared with a big smile, clutching two pixies. "Kiran," he said, handing two extremely dirty pixies to me, "Meet P Leader and Spark Plug, your Leadership and Entrepreneurship pixies."

When P Leader and Spark Plug were safely in my hands, he said that in a final effort to smoke out Nut Cracker's accomplices, the wizard set about making the spiciest vindaloo ever. As he blended the spices, he spotted Spark Plug, the ringleader of a motley crew of subordinate pixies causing a lot of commotion as the vindaloo became spicier, while P Leader was trying his best to calm down the motley crew. Seeing these two beauties in action, the wizard knew at once he had found Nut Cracker's accomplices.

Dr. Eye Can took the two pixies from me and gave them a wash. When he handed them back to me, I studied the two pixies with interest. Spark Plug was casually dressed in yellow. With a funky hairdo, I saw a resemblance to a spark plug. He beautifully captured my entrepreneurial spirit, looking vibrant and always ready for some energy to ignite. P Leader is dressed in an elegant suit, tie and with well-greased hair and polished shoes, he's the epitome of a corporate leader.

Meet
P Leader

Meet
Spark Plug

The jovial doctor continued explaining that once he had the three pixies firmly in his powerful surgeon's hands, he had to do a lot of arm twisting before all three of them admitted they were the root cause of my most contagious smiles and the hurricanes that have made me grimace.

The wizard continued on the Open Kiran Surgery in a last attempt to find Oh. I hear him mutter to Dr. Eye Can, "I can hear a faint sound of Oh humming but as I get closer to the point from where it seems to originate, it suddenly disappears. Let me try for a while more."

After some more prodding in the deepest parts of me, Oh was still nowhere to be found. The wizard indicated that he was done with trying to find my Oh and Dr. Eye Can concluded the Open Kiran Surgery.

Dr. Eye Can lets the Ales and the Guts free and as they hovered around the clinic, I curiously asked the Ales why they chose me as their home and why they make me spend precious energy to survive the hurricanes in my life. In unison they said, "When you create Oh Yes Stories that we are part of and we enjoy, we're best friends, and help you with our finest qualities to create the story that gives you your contagious smile. When you create Oh No Stories that none of us like, you irritate us, so we tap into our roughest qualities, we fight bitterly with each other, and this makes you grimace. If you continue to script endless Oh No Stories for your own reason, we get so fed up with you that we whip up hurricanes that make you grimace. After a long period when you seemed chronically grumpy, to protect our sanity and to protect Oh from being tainted by your grumpiness, we decided to take him captive for his own protection."

I loved their explanation. It was now clear to me that when I was in Cape of Oh No, to get my attention that they were unhappy with me, led by my Nut Cracker, they had taken Oh captive and forced him to stop making me smile. Somehow, they knew when Oh is gone, I would stop smiling. Without my smile, my life became unbearable, and I would do whatever it takes to find, free, and bring Oh back into my life.

When the wizard was ready to finish the surgery, I said "Please wait. Before you finish the surgery I would like to hold a ceremony to baptize Nut Cracker, P Leader and Spark Plug. I would also like to find all of them a safe home within me."

The wizard looked and said "Ok."

In my most official voice I said, "I baptize you my Entrepreneurship pixie as Spark Plug. You are the primary source of the audacious ideas I often have. They misfire more often than not, but when they catch fire, the energy they add to my life makes me smile. I'm sure that from now on, as I get to know you better, and my entrepreneurial qualities bloom, I will remember to give you credit for my most audacious ideas."

Watching Spark Plug react to my words increases my heartbeat, and I'm full of smiles.'

I continue, "I suggest that Spark Plug make himself at home in my heart."

With a whoosh of his wand, the wizard replies, "Your wish is granted."

With a huge smile, I continue, "I baptize my Leadership pixie, P Leader. This is to acknowledge that for most of my life, he is often in pleading mode, trying hard to lead me down the sensible path. I'm sure he'll be in pleading mode on the odyssey as he tries to lead me, Nut Cracker, and Spark Plug down the sensible path to attain my three goals. As leadership has always been in my blood, I suggested that he make himself at home in my bloodstream."

Once again with a whoosh of his wand, the wizard replies, "Your wishes are granted."

On a roll I say, "Nut Cracker, you are the newest pixie in my life, I don't know you as well as Spark Plug and P Leader. But from the time I've spent with you, you have dazzled me with your flashes of intelligence and intuition. As I have a penchant for making critical decisions on impulse, usually followed with a pounding heartbeat and rising blood pressure, I feel it is time to involve my brain in the decision-making process. I know I will need a lot of brain power on the odyssey and baptize you as Nut Cracker. I suggest that you make yourself at home in my brain."

Once again with a whoosh of his wand, the wizard replies "Your wishes are granted."

The Ales loved their names and their new homes. Watching the Ales together, I began to recognize the source of my attitude and my fiery, intuitive, and intelligent personality. But on encountering the Ales, I faced the mouthwatering question: Was I a late bloomer not only in ADHD but in Entrepreneurship and Leadership as well?

With the Ales and the Guts by my side, Dr. Eye Can said, "Make yourself at home in the Clinic of Stop Tuning Yourself and continue finding Cool Moves to strengthen Ex-Factor."

〜

The value I find in my Open Kiran Surgery is tremendous. The art of visualizing my family, friends, foes, heroes, villains, advisors, and more as pixies helps me have meaningful conversations with them on a wide variety of subjects in my life, especially as I am WWoWing about something particular and how it impacts my life. If I think I am missing an emotion in Ex-Factor or need inspiration to a Cool Move, I can perform an Open Kiran Surgery to learn more about what this emotion could be. I could do the same if I ever needed to replace any of the Guts with another hobby most suited to the problem in my life that I'm trying to solve.

TOY 6

A LOT OF SMILES

After many weeks of playing with my growing list of toys, I slowly began to appreciate that each of them was helping me smile more and grimace less. I was also learning that to become a good leader takes time and that life as an Entrepreneur is a constant struggle. But I had also set myself three complex goals that required me to become an Entrepreneur with ADHD who can lead with a smile. Not one to shy away from the challenge, I designed the 'Lot of Smiles' toy to help me balance my natural inclination to keep trying anything that seemed new and exciting and sharpen my ability to focus on what exciting new things (i.e. Cool Moves) serve me best to meet my three goals.

When I visited the Clinic Stop Tuning Yourself, to get the latest results on all the consultations and surgeries I had undergone, I was met by Dr. Eye Can who ushered me into his office where Ex-Factor, Cool Moves, and The Wizard of Oh were seated with serious looks. Seeing their overall demeanor, I got a bit nervous, but Dr. Eye Can once again reassured me as he offered me a hot cup of coffee. He said that they had analyzed all their data and it seemed that, although I was progressing well, I would still need a lot of Cool Moves integrated into my life to attain my three goals.

"Kiran," he said, "I know I had jokingly said that I was a doctor and could only help you bring back Oh into your life and help you burn brighter and not burn out. And I had qualified it by adding that as I am neither an artist, management consultant, nor finance guru, I would be unable to help you with your two goals: to Pioneer the Art of Extrapreneurship and become an Extrapreneur; and Become a Smiling Billionaire. But, given that you need a lot of help in achieving these goals too, Ex-Factor, Cool Moves, The Wizard of Oh and I are, together, going to mentor you to achieve these two as well."

I was relieved to hear this, especially as I was dreading the demanding work and the trial and error experience I would have to endure to achieve these latter aims. With a smile, I replied, "That will be amazing. What do I do now?"

Dr. Eye Can put on his best serious smile and said, "We suggest that to become an Extrapreneur you must not treat the training you need as a hobby or an activity to kill time. It must be viewed as a business and run like a business. To reach your three goals, we have designed a structured process that you must follow. But to be true to this process, you will require to develop a greater mindset, discipline, and determination than you ever tried before."

I puffed my chest out like a proud peacock and said, "Hard work has never frightened me."

Dr. Eye Can then walked me through the A Lot of Smiles toy that he explained is made up of three interconnected parts and is built to help me get the most bang for my investment of resources (time, money, energy, sacrifices, and more) to find Oh. I browsed through the literature he gave me on the A Lot of Smiles and said I was ready to start.

After a few more days in the company of my mentors, the Smile Quotient Meter was buzzing and registering a lot more smiles. I could feel the tiniest power of Oh in me again. But I still had no clue where he was being held captive. Smiling had once again become addictive.

When Dr. Eye Can felt I was eager to learn more, he explained some of the ways to discover how the finest qualities of the Ales could help me become an Extrapreneur. He said, "We have just been able to clone a bit of the Ex-Factor and Cool Moves from the lives of the leaders and entrepreneurs we have analyzed. Now, Kiran, as the first step in the A Lot of Smiles toy, you'll have to understand more deeply your own leadership and entrepreneurship qualities. Fortunately, I've been able to extract these from the data I've been gathering in the Open Kiran Surgery. From this list we now have to find what qualities of yours the Ales dreaded and what qualities of the Ales you dreaded. We need to find a way in which you could coexist with all of them and work together to move yourself up the Extrapreneur Ladder."

I took his words in slowly and replied, "I have some ideas on how to do this but have no clue over how to get them started."

Soon, he had grasped my challenge and said, "Kiran, you already have all the answers you're seeking inside you. We just need to ask the right questions. Why don't you spend some quality time with the Red Cooking Pot and see if you can shortlist the questions you should be asking yourself."

Over the next few days, as I cooked, ate, and shared the pieces of the puzzle in my mind with the Ales and the Guts, the questions I should be asking myself came like whispers from deep within the pot:

- Who am I?
- Who am I, now that I know the Ales?
- What impact do the Ales have on my life?
- How can the Ales help me become an Extrapreneur?
- What am I good at?
- What do I feel now that I have ADHD?
- What do I love to do?
- What do I actually see, hear, feel, smell, and taste?
- How, When, and Where do I enjoy doing what I'm good at?
- How, When and Where can I help the world with what I'm good at?

These were tough questions and as I tried to answer each of them, I could see that my answers to them were superfluous. Watching my grimace growing, Dr. Eye Can suggested we should take a break from cooking. Closing the lid of the pot, he led the way out into the fresh air of Oh Landia and walked me through the A Lot of Smiles toy and how I can best use it.

"The first part," he said, "Is called 'A Lot Filter'." He then walked me through each stage of this part and it all seemed quite straightforward.

For each inspiration I had for a Cool Move, I would be bombarded with millions of data points that I would have to filter through. I would then have to zoom in only on those Cool Moves that would have the most impact on me developing Ex-Factor.

Dr. Eye Can emphasized that once I have shortlisted these Cool Moves, I would then have:

- To Learn A Lot
- To Plan A Lot
- To Practice A Lot
- To Integrate A Lot

When I had grasped the rudiments of each step of the filter, he continued, "To achieve the impact I want the Cool Moves to have, the filter is also designed to help you increase or decrease the complexity of the data points to meet your three goals."

This led to the next part, which he called the 'SMILE' toy that interfaces with the A Lot Filter. As he walked me through each step of the SMILE toy, he said, "All Cool Moves must be Simple, Meaningful, Intelligent, Lucrative and Educational for you. They must also be Scalable, Marketable, Inspirational and help you develop your Leadership and Entrepreneurial qualities."

- Simple and Scalable
- Meaningful and Marketable
- Intelligent and Inspirational
- Lucrative and Leadership
- Educational and Entrepreneurial

When I had grasped the rudiments of the SMILE, he continued, "While the terms Simple, Meaningful, Intelligent, Lucrative, Educational will help you attain new qualities in your Ex-Factor for personal and professional fulfillment, the Scalable, Marketable, Inspirational, Leadership and Entrepreneurial will help you attain new qualities in your Ex-Factor for you to develop Extrapreneurship and share it with your loved ones to create a billion smiles every day!"

The power of the A Lot Filter and SMILE was daunting. I was exhausted and done with learning any additional new things today.

Agreeing that we would not explore any more new territory today, Dr. Eye Can handed me a fresh link to Eye Tube and said he had updated me to a Premium User and told me to enjoy it. We logged on and he showed me the videos on the A Lot Filter and the Smile concepts. As we studied them, I was relieved that they both helped me solve what I had been struggling to do: select the high-impact Cool Moves that will have the most impact on my attaining all three goals.

As I closed the link, Dr. Eye Can said, "Be careful when you work with the A Lot of Smiles toy not to focus only on the most exotic Cool Moves that Nut Cracker and Spark Plug will be naturally drawn to."

That brought us to the third part of the A Lot of Smiles, which is called the Three Dumb Bells. It's key to building a solid and lasting foundation to help you achieve my three goals, the doctor told me. He explained that the Three Dumb Bells would help me focus on training a set of emotional muscles linked to a category of a Cool Move. And you can guess from the name the Three Dumb Bells, the categories are flyweight, middleweight, and heavyweight Cool Moves.

I looked perturbed by a few more buzzwords coming our way, but Dr. Eye Can, unfazed, continued, "The value of the Three Dumb Bells is that it gives you a process to understand the risk factor and the complexity of the Cool Moves you're integrating into your life.

Inspired by the world of boxing, which I only enjoy as a spectator, I chose these three categories of Cool Moves:

Flyweight – Oh Yes or Oh No Cool Moves that will take less than three months to integrate or get rid of from my daily life,

Middleweight – Ooh Yes or Ooh No Cool Moves that will take between three to six months to integrate into my daily life, and

Heavyweight – Oooh Yes and Oooh No Cool Moves that will take more than a year to integrate into my daily life."

When I understood the concept behind the three weight classes, Dr. Eye Can continued, "The Three Dumb Bells will help you identify lots of flyweight Cool Moves, a balanced amount of Middleweight Cool Moves and an occasional, but highly effective, Heavyweight Cool Move. Until now, you've mastered dozens of Flyweight and Middleweight Cool Moves. They're helpful, but glittery and lack the knockout punch. They will help you to find and free Oh and keep him in your life, but to share Oh and your smile with the world, you need to learn the hardest of all punches, and this is to master Heavyweight Cool Moves that are so powerful that they will help you bring and keep Oh in your life.

I was really happy with today's discussion on Cool Moves, and I summarized them.

Cool moves are:

Daily short-duration, simple, fun, repetitive activities, and actions (e.g., exercise, spend time with family, write a few pages, read a few pages)

Weekly short-duration, simple, fun, activities, and actions (e.g., swim, dance, play Sudoku, clean the house, mind-body coordination games, help a few deserving people, play a sport)

> Life-changing activities that will shake the foundation of any of the four Nut Worth Pillars like authoring a book or consciously changing my career if it's detrimental to my health.

We should always try to break down a Cool Move into a series of short-duration fun activities and actions, as this will help us grimace less.

The value the A Lot of Smiles toys brought into my life was to help me firm up my fluid odyssey plan. They were the toys I needed to plug the holes in Daddy's hose pipe. They would help me stop going around in circles and learn to navigate my way toward the Cape of Oh. They would also give me valuable feedback on my progress toward achieving my three goals. When I'm struggling in DontDoNation with problems, I can use this feedback to find solutions with the help of my Miners and Millers who share with me their time and genius, two commodities money cannot buy. Their mentoring helps me to achieve my three goals. Working with the A Lot of Smiles toys helped me answer tough questions, and they also led me to defining my Life's Principles

- I deserve to be happy, healthy, and wealthy.
- I will enjoy unwrapping my Ale gifts.
- I can run a business by myself.
- I must remember to give more than I take.
- I will spend time helping deserving people.
- I will inspire others in all things I do.
- I will be a proud Extrapreneur.

When I was playing with the A Lot of Smiles toy, I realized that every year in the future there will be a lot of people around the world who will receive the ADHD label and will search for help to answer tough questions like I did and that is why the A Lot of Smiles toy became important to me if I want to create a billion smile everyday.

TOY 7

SWEET AND SOUR SPOTS

The more I invest in Cool Moves, the more clearly I realize that not all of them make me smile. In fact, it is only after I have endured my fair share of grimaces in training them that they give me a few smiles. As I analyze the changes of my Ex-Factor during the process from which a Cool Move shifts from a source of grimaces to a trickle of smiles, inspired by a favorite dish of mine a "Sweet and Sour curry," I tumble upon the "The Sweet and Sour Spot," a cool toy that helps me refine the ideal combination of my Ex-Factor that I will need to achieve my three goals.

Dr. Eye Can's Eye Tube came to my rescue when I browsed the videos on Sweet and Sour Spots and thought, "Maybe this could help me learn more about my perfect and imperfect qualities of the Ales and also perhaps about the sweet and sour things in my life."

At the Clinic Stop Tuning Yourself, as we continued to train Ex-Factor, I thought that over the last few weeks, I had enjoyed the company of the Ales. I had felt a growing sense of excitement when I was in their company. I loved the way they were bonding together. I closed my eyes and enjoyed reliving the recent Oh Yes Emotions that washed over me when I smiled. Soon, I began to wonder why the emotional muscles behind these enjoyable Oh Yes Emotions when the Ales are in harmony were at complete odds with the dreadful Oh No Emotions when the Ales ravaged my life.

In no time, I was restless once again. Unable to truly relish these Oh Yes Emotions any longer, I needed to find a solution to help me make them last longer. I was ready to try out Dr. Eye Can's Sweet and Sour Spot toy.

So, the next time I sat down with Dr. Eye Can, I told him I would like to try out his Sweet and Sour Toy. He was delighted, quickly performed a Smileoscopy and after analyzing the results said that the Smile Quotient was healthy, and I would soon be on my way to seeing a five-digit number in my Smile Quotient.

Let's get started, he said, and after he explained how we were going to use the Sweet and Sour Spot toy, he asked me to get a fire going. Under Dr. Eye Can's watchful eye, I fire up the Red Cooking Pot and following the instructions in the Sweet and Sour toy "How to" recipe, I start preparing an Indian version of a Chinese Sweet and Sour Curry. When I was ready, I called on the Ales to come out and, as they did so reluctantly, invited them to join me in a cozy team building session to make the Sweet and Sour Curry that we could enjoy with Guts. I assigned each of them a role in preparing the ingredients to make the curry. As the chopping and stirring began and the kitchen was buzzing with laughter and complaints, I asked them which of their individual qualities that make me smile and grimace would describe them best.

Spark Plug, always the first off the block, said his favorite quality, one that gave him a stream of Oh Yes Emotions, was generating ideas, and his ideas were usually the best. If he got his way and could try these out, the impact on me was a bucket full of smiles. But if I shot them down, he would play the spoilt child and display all his rough qualities; something that would make me grimace for days.

Before he could say more, Nut Cracker cut him off abruptly. Bobbing up and down, he said that his best quality was to get me to do things his way, which was the best way. Like Spark Plug, when he got his way, he could make me feel magical. If he didn't get his way, he too could make me grimace for a prolonged period. Hearing Spark Plug and Nut Cracker drone about their fine qualities, I knew I was looking at the sources of many of my smiles and the vitality and inspiration they brought into my life.

Finally, as Spark Plug and Nut Cracker had no more to boast about, it was P Leader's turn. In a calm voice, he informed me that his finest quality was to make plans to bring order into my life. In his humble opinion, when I followed his plan, I was successful in finding a good balance between the four letters in my disorder and establishing some order in my largely disorderly life. When I didn't follow his plan, he could be as rebellious as Spark Plug and Nut Cracker and could make me grimace for quite some time.

I loved these descriptions that made me realize how easily they could get me to smile or grimace. Now that I knew in broad strokes how the Ales functioned, I thought it best to draw them into a conversation over why they spent so much of my energy creating all the hurricanes in my life. Unfortunately, the question rubbed them the wrong way; suddenly, my cozy team builder turned into a nightmare.

Soon, I had the curry boiling and was watching the passion pouring out as each answered the question in their own way. Dr. Eye Can helped me observe all their emotions and mapped them to the spices from the recipe, carefully adding them to the pot that was now hissing furiously.

When the Ales had exhausted themselves trying to answer my questions, we tasted the curry. With a loud "yuck!" we all realized that the combination of spices I had added while observing their rough qualities pouring out hadn't worked. What was meant to be a Sweet and Sour Curry, had turned bitter; it was a curry with just a dash of Sweet and lots of Sour tastes.

Each of us contributed our two cents of wisdom on what spices we should add to save the curry. The result actually made the taste worse, and we finally had to throw it away. Dr. Eye Can, sensing our growing irritation, retired to the sofa for a nap and left us to sort our problems out.

As we sat around the empty pot, hungry, P Leader suggested we hold a retrospective to see why we had messed up what seemed like a perfectly simple recipe for making a Sweet and Sour curry. For 15 teary minutes, under P Leader's guidance we poured our hearts out about why we all appeared to be in discord with one another. When we were all done, P Leader summarized our observations. We all agreed that in my late forties, as my life became bland, lifeless, and boring, very similar to that of an OhDear, the Ales began to hate it. Frustrated at failing to get my attention, they pooled their roughest qualities and enticed me to do things that go against my nature, constantly making me grimace and start to burn out. Their tactic worked miracles; soon, as my Ex-Factor faded, Oh lost all his power to make me smile. I became a Smileless Pauper struggling to survive in the Cape of Oh No.

Once in Cape of Oh No, with all of us hating every moment, and me physically and mentally exhausted, it was easy for them to kidnap Oh and with this I lost my ability to smile. This was how they wanted me to realize how much I needed Oh in my life.

Grateful to the Ales for sharing their frustrations and respecting their quirky destructive methods, I learned a lot more about both their perfect and imperfect qualities. I realized that if they could effectively work together to burn me out, they could work as effectively to help me burn brighter. P Leader concluded our retrospective by saying, "It's clear that all of us want to get as far away as possible from Cape of Oh No, and we agree on working together to burn brighter."

We now had to figure out a model to work together! I started making the sweet and sour curry all over again, once again beginning from scratch. This time, I asked the Ales to recall our most poignant memories over the last five decades. Soon I had the curry boiling in the pot and watched the passion pour out as we shared each other's versions of my stories. As each answered my questions in their own way, I carefully observed all their emotions and mapped them to some new alternative spices from the recipe. Adding them in carefully, I noticed that the pot soon settled into a soothing bubbling.

Happy with our attempt to follow the recipe, I called Dr. Eye Can to help us analyze what was happening.

Looking into the pot, he said, "Kiran, ever since you could crawl, you have the skill to complicate the simplest actions that others perform effortlessly. But, you can also make highly complex actions appear ridiculously easy to others.

"When the Ales are in the sweet spot of their fine qualities, they're on fire and help you burn brighter. In their sweet spot, they effortlessly connect, coordinate, and communicate when you ask them to respond to a call to action or perform a task that needs their individual or collective qualities. Their magic happens and you execute the action perfectly and burn brighter.

"But," he continued, "when you call upon the Ales to respond to a call to action that's outside their sweet spot, they effortlessly misconnect, miscoordinate, and miscommunicate, and so you execute the action so disastrously that it has grave repercussions and enhances the risk of you burning out."

I understood what the doctor was saying, but to make sure, I asked him, "What exactly is our Sweet Spot?"

Dr. Eye Can replied, "The Ales' Sweet Spot is the optimum combination of their individual perfect and imperfect qualities. You can learn how to execute Calls to Action from the Sweet Spot that will help you achieve all your three goals. The opposite is also true and that is their Sour Spot."

As I pondered on his answer, gazing deeply into the curry, Dr. Eye Can asked us to keep quiet. He picked up a spoon and started furiously stirring the curry. Soon he was sweating profusely, even as he seemed to be in a tug of war with something inside the pot. He cried, "Kiran, play some Cool Moves that make you smile. The bigger the smile the better."

I scratched my head and started cracking one corny dad joke after another that had all the Ales rolling on the floor laughing. Suddenly, with a roar and a relief spreading all over his face, Dr. Eye Can dug something out of the pot. He showed it to me, and I saw an almost lifeless pixie in his strong surgeon's hands.

He covered the pixie in a cloth and disappeared for a while. When he returned, he handed the pixie over to me and said in a sad voice, "Kiran, meet Oh. I've done a Smileoscopy on him and his reading is on the lowest level on the grimace scale."

I held Oh in my hands and looked at him in dismay. I was horrified to see what my years on the Cape of Oh No had done to him. I asked Dr. Eye Can, "Where did you find him?"

"Kiran, he was being held captive by a few of your Oh No Emotions in the darkest corner of your Oh No Story archives. Ex-Factor had to fight an army of your Oh No Emotions that refused to let him go. It was only when you all started laughing and you could feel it in your gut, Ex-Factor suddenly found the power to free Oh from their clutches."

I looked at the Ales with gratitude and thanked them for the role they played in freeing Oh.

Dr. Eye Can continued, "I have spoken to Oh briefly and though we agree he is free from his captors, he feels he is still mesmerized by the power a few of your Oh No Emotions. When I asked him what this mesmerizing power felt like, he explained that it was difficult to put it into words . But, he said that when you were in your miserable state he was so afraid that these emotions seemed to provide him with a relative sense of security, even comfort. It made him feel safer than when he had to face the full force of your misery. I understand his point of view, though he now agrees with me that what he experienced was only a false and transient sense of security. These few Oh No Emotions, let's call them Oh's former captors, I imagine from previous cases like yours, have a vested interest in keeping you miserable. This is because when you are miserable they thrive the most and play out the role they are designed for in your life."

I looked surprised and commented "Do you know which these few emotions are, so we can prevent them from capturing Oh again in the future."

Dr. Eye Can frowned "I tried to ask Oh the same question, but he unfortunately cannot put a name on them. My hypothesis is that the Oh No Emotions he is most mesmerized by depends on situation you are in. Sorry I cannot be of more help."

"That's fine. Thank you for the feedback, doctor," I said with a huge grimace on my face. "At least we know in broad strokes who his former captors are and we can work out deciphering them in the future. What else did he mention about his captivity?"

"I told him all about your odyssey, your mission, purpose and goals and the team you are gathering that have helped you find him. I told him all about Mr. Spectacles, SAD's, Fonges, your Ex-Factor and Cool Moves and how hard you want to work to keep him in your life. He was impressed by how much he means to you and all the effort you have invested to free him. But, he is skeptical if you can continue to work this hard to keep him in your life forever."

I put my hand up and asked "Why?" I was disappointed. "I have done all this to bring him back into my life."

"Sure you have, and I re-emphasized your three goals to him. But he says what happens if you stop taking Mr. Spectacles, what happens if you get bored of Cool Moves, what if, there are too many - what if scenarios he rattled off for me to remember even though he is weak. He is still very insecure about accepting what I told him in good faith. He just does not want to come back into your life and then land up in Cape of Oh No again. My guess is that he will still be wary of you for a while until he gets to know you again. I fear that Oh will always try to return to the false safety and mesmerizing power of his former captors whenever he is insecure in your company. But let me quickly add that the negative mesmerizing power only provides false safety. The positive mesmerizing power of your Oh No Emotions is very useful to help you find ways to avoid the Oh No Emotion again."

"Wow!" I exclaimed. "I love the distinction of the positive and negative mesmerizing power of the Oh No Emotions. The same is true for the Oh Yes Emotion. They too have both positive and negative mesmerizing powers."

"You got the idea Kiran, but let's focus on the Oh No Emotions for now," said Dr. Eye Can. I nod in agreement and the doctor continues, "What is even worse is that his former captors have a vested interest in keeping you miserable. They know the power they have over you when they have Oh in captivity and they will always try to use this power over both of you to capture Oh again. To keep Oh as far away from these few Oh No Emotions for as long as possible will require you to strengthen Ex-Factor even more. The only way to ensure you smile more than you grimace is to have a healthy relationship between Oh and your Oh Yes and Oh No Emotions. Remember Oh is an integral part of Oh Yes and Oh No, so like it or not we all need Oh No Emotions in our life. We just have to learn to deal with them in the best possible way we can. All the events of the last few months have exhausted Oh and what he needs now is a lot of tender loving care to help him recover his strength so he can make you smile again."

I was amazed at this novel way to rescue Oh and looked at the Ales and the Guts and said, "Now that Dr. Eye Can has helped us find Oh, it is our duty to help free him from the false safety and negative mesmerizing power of his former captors. To do this we need to up our effort to train more Middleweight and Heavyweight Moves so we have the skills in our Ex-Factor to support Oh to free himself from the fake security and mesmerizing power of his captors."

All this while the curry was bubbling nicely. I tasted it and it was perfect. As we enjoyed the Sweet and Sour curry, Dr. Eye Can brought the Smile Quotient Meter out; it was buzzing merrily, and he was thrilled at the readings.

⌒

The Sweet and Sour Spot is a toy that showed me how important it is for "me to be me" and not someone else. When I succeed, I smile, but, when I compare myself to someone else, I fall short, get anxious, depressed, or envious, and this makes me grimace all the more. I knew that now that I've found Oh and have him by my side, I would find out which emotions lay in the Ales' Sweet and Sour Spots, so I could train them myself to smile more and grimace less. I'll never be able to live in my sweet spot always, but if I know where I am relative to it and have contact with Oh in whatever state he may be, I'll be okay. The sour spot is also a reminder as a leader and entrepreneur with ADHD, I am also vulnerable to a case of SAD, if I operate mostly from my Sour Spot.

TOY 8

SMILE AND GRIMACE P&L

As I was well on my way to discarding my Smileless pauper status, I needed a rock-solid toy to measure and monitor my smiles and grimaces. I knew this was the toy that would be my north star as I navigated my way to become a Smiling Billionaire. I knew that successful businesses invested resources and the best talent in financial management. This inspired me to build my own Smile and Grimace P&L that along with my Smileoscope, could help me measure and monitor all my investments in Cool Moves to ensure they were taking me closer to becoming a Smiling Billionaire.

While Oh recuperated, I spent six more months in Oh Landia. I was thrilled and exhausted. We, as a quirky team, had come a long way from Cape of Oh No, and I would go to bed each night smarter and wiser. We were also learning a lot of Cool Moves that helped strengthen Oh and relax the grip my Oh No Emotions had on him: one fewer grimace and one extra smile at a time.

Sure, I was overloaded with information and struggled now and then to get to know the Ales and their likes and dislikes. But, overall, I was happy to be where I was. Oh was back in my life. I now had to measure and monitor my smiles.

To share our progress and our victories, and get objective feedback, I called Dr. Eye Can and asked if he could visit us. He was delighted and, in a puff, was back in my life. After exchanging pleasantries, he went straight to business and told me he would like to do a Smileoscopy again. As he connected me up to his Smileoscope, he said he would like me to share our experiences with the Cool Moves we had practiced. When he was ready, he asked me to begin. I brought out our notes and began to read out the main points:

"The Cool Moves train all my thirty Emotional Muscles in some way or the other. Not all of the thirty Emotional Muscles are trained equally. I still have to find a process for how to do this. These are some of the Cool Moves that have worked well:

Cool Move – the Wok of Life. I always thought that speed cooking was for busy people who were forever on the move. But the wok opened a new dimension in my cooking skills. Cooking in a wok looks easy but requires a lot of skill to orchestrate the many ingredients that are put into it at a high temperature. It has really helped me control my attention deficit because when working with the wok, I must have unwavering focus, as I continuously toss in ingredients, move them around, remove them, and then repeat the whole process again with the next set. A delicious meal is ready in minutes, and a wok is a source of many of my smiles.

Cool Move – 'Physical Alarm.' A lot of aspects of my physical health are in my control and mine to enjoy or neglect. Many physical health issues are loaded in my genes. I cannot control when or how they will play havoc in my life. The best thing I can do for myself is to use an automated physical alarm system, set thresholds that help me keep an eye out for them and before the alarm goes off, make sure I go for my regular planned maintenance checkups.

Cool Move – The 'Good Life.' This combined my love for food and fun. I've learned to enjoy and put a high value on simple actions like feeling the sun and wind on my face. My favorite activity is to enjoy a cup of freshly brewed coffee in the morning while I do a mind-stimulating activity like a word game. In the evening, to appreciate a good day, I pour myself an excellent whiskey or rum. I love the few moments when I indulge in unhealthy living. These moments are best enjoyed on chocolates and homemade ice cream, an overdose of potato chips and peanuts with a cold beer. To counter the unhealthy aspects of the Cool Move, I spend time outdoors and enjoy simple pleasures like flying a kite, running obstacle courses, swimming, and more..."

Here I paused, but, when I saw everyone nodding in agreement, I quickly continued. "When my physical wealth was robust and reaping smiles, I looked into how I could enjoy increasing my mental wealth.

Cool Move – inspired by 'The Running Around Like a Headless Chicken' cartoon. This one helped me to get started increasing my mental wealth. I began by noting simple things that frustrated me, things that could be fixed with a little more focus. Soon, thousands of grimaces that plagued my life and had made me run around the house like a headless chicken – trying to find a mobile phone, keys, purse, computer, and more – were solved quite simply. I found fixed spots to keep them safe when I didn't need them. I also forced myself again and again to place them in these spots each time I finished using them.

Cool Move – the 'Power of Winding Down.' Another change that I mentioned was how I had become a firm believer of the need to develop a good sleeping routine so that I could get sufficient sleep. To improve my sleep habits, I learned the 'power of winding down' at night. I was inspired by a procedure used in my sailing days to start and stop the engine of a ship. Step by step, I followed those five stages – Full Astern, Half Astern, Slow Astern, Dead Slow Astern, Stop – as my 'power of winding down' routine. It starts with a 30-minute walk listening to a podcast to slow down, followed by writing my Extrapreneur Herald, my personal newspaper about my daily life as an Extrapreneur. I write my breaking news headlines and about Cool Moves that helped me learn more about sports, art, cooking, health, wealth, as I document the highlights of my day. After this, I try to learn at least one new thing or fact before going to bed. This could be as simple as tying my shoelace in a new way. After this is bathroom hygiene, a few breathing exercises, watching a really boring TV drama series. The sleep comes slowly, and I'm ready for dreamworld.

Cool Move – 'Thirty-minute boring work.' This was another of those uncomplicated moves that assisted me in getting through the mind-numbing administrative tasks that I had to do to run a family and business. These tasks would make me grimace and I kept procrastinating over taking them up. By adopting the Thirty-minute boring work cool move, I put together a solution that works for me. In the morning, preferably before 10 am, I assign 30-minute slots to pay bills, read business mail and reports, and do other admin tasks.

These 30-minute slots help me get the most tedious tasks out of the way as early in the day as possible and have a clear conscience to WWoW the rest of the day on stuff I enjoy.

Cool Move – 'The Brain Tax.' I mastered this to use for work that requires me to tax my brain. With it, my routine involves working for 30 minutes and then taking a five-minute break. I continuously repeat the cycle until I don't have to tax my brain anymore. To help me implement this 30-minutes rule, I put an alarm for 30 minutes in another room. When the alarm goes off, it has a high-pitched sound that can wake up the dead. This jarring noise forces me to stop work and turn it off.

Cool Move – the 'Cycle Man.' I use this whenever I want to WWoW deeply about something complex that had a significant impact on me. "I jump on my bicycle, and when I reach a beautiful spot, I stop. Here, I give myself permission to get lost in my own thoughts and practice Mind Flyness. I visualize as many scenarios as possible using the WWoW formula, and this helps me gain a bit more clarity. I jump back on my bicycle with a smile, as I now have an idea on how to proceed with these complex issues.

Cool Move – 'Unstretchable Time.' This was really amazing. Most of my life, I have tended to be late for leisure activities. This has always driven my family crazy. I realized that with a bit of better planning and discipline, I could remove a few grimaces this usually caused quite easily. So now I try extremely hard not to be late. I also use Unstretchable Time to be more consistent in doing household chores. To do these chores effectively, I use the time boxing technique and allocate a fixed time to a planned activity and do my best to complete it in the time box. For example, I clean the house on the same day every week in a 2-hour time window between 3 and 5 pm."

Cool Move – 'Yes, But.' This was another that I found to be quite fantastic. When asked to do something that I don't have the resources to do, to not disappoint the requester, I say, "Yes, I can do it, but you must do this for me." Using this Cool Move, I'm learning to say "No" to things that have little meaning for me on my path to being an Extrapreneur. An example is to save a few grimaces caused by doing jobs for the 'chattering monkeys' and 'leeches.' I would say, "Yes, but you have to do this for me." That irritated them, and they slowly stopped loading their work onto me.

Cool Move – 'Spend-less.' With a spend-less mindset, I forced myself to remove a lot of material clutter from my life. I cleared out my cupboard and basement and, as I did this, I decluttered my mind. A simple action like not buying new clothes for a year and reducing my wardrobe to the bare minimum helped me develop a lean and mean mindset. It also made the choice of clothes I have to wear ridiculously simple. The cherry on the Cool Move was that it helped me contribute to saving the world's resources in my own way. Using the Spend-less analogy, I always try to get rid of an Uncool Move to make space for the new Cool Move. If I cannot get rid of an Uncool Move, then I know I'm overloading my poor mind and body with new stuff that I'll never appreciate.

Cool Move – the 'Dark and Quiet Room.' I found this effective in that It helped me use a structured technique to sort out my never-ending stream of maverick business ideas. The method I used was that every Monday morning for 45 minutes in a closed room, I would think over the pros and cons of my ideas. If at the end of 45 minutes, I was still on fire about a maverick idea, I invested time and energy looking deeper into what it would take to bring it to life.

Cool Move – 'Nerd.' This was a great way to keep Spark Plug invigorated. I enjoy courses on creativity and the digital economy to understand the role of advanced technology in my life. I also invest in the digital currency markets. Trading digital coins is a great learning experience to observe my Oh Yes and Oh No Emotions that swing like an uncontrollable pendulum between ecstasy and despair.

Cool Move – 'To Give Back and Learn.' This was one of the most rewarding. I spent more time now mentoring deserving people, especially young entrepreneurs. While I shared my experiences with them, I also learned from them. I also got more involved in the local community and helped charitable organizations. Working with the homeless was among the greatest lessons I'll ever learn in living a selfless life.

Cool Move – 'Social Media Diets.' This was a great Cool Move, as it helped me limit my time on social media to 15 minutes a day. It was an incredible way to break free from chattering monkeys and leeches and avoid getting sucked into their perfect make-believe world."

Cool Moves – 'Mindlessness,' the art of minding my own business, 'Restmoreness,' the art of resting more when I feel restless, and GiGo - 'Get Involved or Get Out.' The first two are also really powerful Cool Moves that interlock with the GiGo, the art of telling myself that if I'm not part of an activity playing out in my life, I must enjoy the activity only as a spectator, without getting involved.

Cool Move – 'Frequent Flier Rewards.' From the time I spent on social media, I learned how both positive and, even worse, negative stories spread like wildfire. I adopted this approach on my own Oh Yes Stories and I shared the joy with my inner circle with simple gestures like thank you posts. These leave a lasting impression, and many people started reciprocating in the same way to me. When I experienced an Oh No Emotion, I also started flagging my vulnerability to my inner circle so they would give me some leeway till the emotion passes.

(Coolest) Cool Move, – 'Dating.' I discovered that there are many things that allow one to spend cozy moments, but don't have to cost a fortune to enjoy or are limited to one's imagination. I took a few hours every week for a date with Marianne where we would try something unusual that we didn't have time to do in our busy everyday lives. I also went on solo dates with myself to discover, learn, and do new things such as sketching, antique shopping, bargain hunting, sailing, visiting new places, dinner by the beach, painting the house, and making collages.

Cool Move – 'Money Matters.' This one helped me prepare myself for the difficult conversation about the importance of money with myself first and then my family. When I didn't have money, I would always think that when I did get enough money, I would change the way I lived for the better. Now that I do have a decent amount of money, I know that the pursuit of money can change me into a person I don't want to become. When I was comfortable discussing the importance of money in my life, I involved Marianne, Kristin, and Kia in my future fiscal management decisions. I then created a relationship with dependable advisors who have the specialized knowledge I lacked and whom I felt comfortable and safe with discussing sensitive important financial matters. I also built a network of 'life coaches,' who aren't Miners and Millers but professional accountants and financial advisors to help me with personal and financial decisions."

After I finished with my last story, I handed Dr. Eye Can my Cool Moves Log and Vulnerability Log that I hadn't shared. He looked at it with interest and asked me to read it out aloud. Slowly and clearly with a smile I started reading line by line from the logs and Dr. Eye Can was watching me and my pixies in earnest.

My Cool Move Log:	
COOL MOVES THAT HELP ME EARN	SMILES
Physical Wealth Matters - Good physical wealth makes managing the other three variables in the Nut Worth equation easier to build and maintain.	
Do not be afraid of a doctor and get regular health checkups. Enjoy my mischievousness. Spread my smile and charm.	Oh Yes
Push my existing physical and mental boundaries (I started Tai Chi).	Ooh Yes
Laugh so hard till it hurts. Finding a bargain in a flea market also brings smiles.	Ooh Yes
I learned a new sport called Pétanque that I played with senior citizens in my local community. This was a very hard decision to make, as before I joined I thought this was a game for old people. But, it was a source of much joy, and I looked forward to our games with anticipation.	Ooh Yes
Mental Wealth Matters - Good mental wealth makes managing the other three variables in the Nut Worth equation easier to build and maintain.	
I started enjoying doing Tai Chi and have found diverse ways to use hot and freezing water to boost my energy.	Oooh Yes
Discovered the hidden opportunities that ADHD has given me.	Oooh Yes
The benefits of breathing The benefits of meditating	Ooh Yes
The secret to smile is also attained by the mindset Communicate, communicate, communicate. Learn to reduce my natural inclination to multitask.	Oh Yes
Identify people in my Inner Ring and put them first.	Ooh Yes

Start documenting my successes and failures doing Cool Moves as stories to share with the world by learning to be a storyteller.	Ooh Yes
I did a few courses to learn new things and I attended courses on Creativity and the New digital economy.	Oh Yes
Use more fixed rules in my life to replace useless rules that make me grimace. Plan-Do-Check-Act method is very helpful when I start new projects. How to identify and prioritize actions that matter by using the Moocow method (Must have, Should have, Could have, and Will not have) to have the best return of investment of my resources measured by my smiles. 20% rule - Keeping 20% of my working hours to learn new things keeps me smiling. 90% rule - 90% of what I worry about never happens. 80/20 rule - 80% of all joy or pain in my life is caused by 20% of my actions.	Oh Yes
Develop rhinoceros' skin to manage all the well-meaning feedback I get in my life.	Ooh Yes
For each of the many processes I adhere to, achieve something that creates an Oh yes story to remember. If it's not broken don't fix it. Improve it but remember the baseline so I can always come back to it if the improvements don't work. Never change more than one parameter in my Nut Worth at a time, because if it improves or fails, then you won't know which parameter made the difference. If you think something is breaking or broken, ask for professional help to fix it. This can be as simple as a broken household appliance, or my physical and mental wealth.	Oh Yes
The power of grinding down means that even when life is hard work, if I approach it through the lens of fun, at some point, I'll reap its rewards.	Oh Yes

Communication diets In all written and verbal communications, the method called RACI works well for me. RACI is the acronym for Responsible, Accountable, Consulted, Informed, and it has helped me work effectively when I communicate with people. When I correspond through written social media, I must write with the same tone as I would use in verbal communication to a person standing in front of me and we are looking into each other's eyes.	Oh Yes

Financial Wealth Matters helped me pressure-test my money holes. Money allows me to live in a comfortable home, drive a car, take vacations, and provide well for the family. But now I know that there is more to life than the pursuit of more.

I baselined all my financial assets.	Oh Yes
I revisited my insurance, pension, and investments.	Oh Yes
I got professional financial advisors to manage my assets.	Oh Yes
I started learning about digital currency and traded a bit to see how my mental wealth was impacted by the high price volatility in this asset class.	Oh Yes
For my business, I need to think about how I'll operate it in my absence.	Oh Yes
I wrote my last will and testament.	Oh Yes

Social Wealth Matters

Do more mentoring of deserving people, especially young entrepreneurs. Get more involved in the local community.	Ooh Yes
Volunteer for organizations I believe in.	Oooh Yes
Never be the sheep that's sacrificed on the altar of someone else's success. I'm always responsible for what I do. If people misuse my abilities, then I'm responsible for giving them the mandate to create disturbances in my life.	Oh Yes

Understand the concept of a Gift as I share my entrepreneurial wealth. A gift has a giver and receiver, or it can be snatched by a taker. I'll always be aware of takers, who are people who take more from me than they give. Giving is an art that I must master, as giving does not come naturally to me. Receiving things or words of appreciation or criticism is an art I must practice.	Oooh Yes

I took a break and then also gave Dr. Eye Can a list of areas in my life in which I'm still vulnerable. As he browsed the list, he said "Please continue to read this out aloud."

Slowly and clearly, with my face wracked with emotions, I started reading line by line from the logs and Dr. Eye Can was watching me and my pixies in earnest.

My Vulnerability Log:	
AREAS IN WHICH I'M STILL VULNERABLE	GRIMACES
I still feel tired and have mood swings	Oh No
Still worried about a visit from Mr. Fonges and the SAD that could send me back to Cape of Oh No	Oh No
I'm struggling to be a giver and a taker. To give more of myself than I take from others is a difficult balance, as I'm still not sure if I've gotten rid of my leeches and chattering monkeys.	Oooh No
I know I run a business by myself. I know it will take time to get a business running, and I'm still struggling to find out what exactly will make me happy in the long run.	Oh No
I try to help deserving people, but I'm still struggling to find my definition of a deserving person.	Ooh No

Just for the fun of it, I try to not spend any money for one weekend but have not yet succeeded.	Oh No
I tried to forgive a few people who have hurt me deeply but have not yet succeeded. I think doing this will take a lot of courage and a lot more awareness to learn and accept that they can hurt me once again.	Oooh No
I'm trying to learn what spirituality means to me, but this is a tough question to find answers to.	Oh No
I'm trying to go on "Information Rations." I need to do this to free up a small part of my brain from information that I'm bombarded with. Every day, I struggle to learn how to be diligent about what information I let into my brain, how it can influence my judgment, and how I can get it out of my brain again. This is really hard.	Oooh No

When I was done, I was sweating and exhausted but proud that I had been able to share some of my vulnerabilities with Dr. Eye Can. I told him that for future reference, I will maintain an updated log on our website www.kiranvas.com

He loved the idea of keeping a log of my Cool Moves online and he stopped the Smileoscopy. When Dr. Eye Can had disconnected me from the Smileoscope, he said, "Kiran, thank you for your honesty. Let me first check Oh to see how he's doing. I'd like to visit him alone."

⌐

My Smile and Grimace P&L is one of my favorite toys to help me with fun but serious ways to measure, monitor and change the impact of my Cool Moves in helping me attain my three goals When I was done with designing the Smile and Grimace P&L toy, I realized how very grateful I am for the support I get from my Miners and

Millers. I think I have a better understanding of why my Miners and Millers still support me today in my good times. It's because when I was struggling in Cape of Oh No, I didn't shy away from telling them I was physically and mentally exhausted. They appreciated my honesty and because they recognized my determination to move away from the Cape of Oh No, they gave me support to get me smiling again from sources I didn't even imagine."

BASECAMP AND BOOTCAMP

Today even as my Nut Worth is flourishing, I'm still very vulnerable across all its four pillars. The hurricanes still blow my way. The frequency and severity are less and with the help of Mr. Spectacles and Cool Moves, I'm becoming more robust at riding them out. I've developed my own hurricane early warning system. When this system senses a hurricane coming my way, I can retreat to a more robust hurricane shelter with the Ales. From here, we can either minimize the ravages the hurricane may create or find ways to divert it from blowing my way. But to get ready for the rigors of the odyssey ahead, I designed my Basecamp and Bootcamp toy.

Dr. Eye Can went to check on Oh. After 30 minutes, he came back smiling along with Oh. The doctor remarked that he had done a Smileoscopy on Oh, and his smile quotient was much stronger, though it was still on the lowest level of the smile scale. He also was more robust than when he had first been fished out from me six months ago. He also said that Oh had confided in him that he was blossoming day by day and had made peace with the Ales, forgiving them for kidnapping him.

As Oh gurgled like a baby, Dr. Eye Can started the Smileoscopy on me and after a while he said, "I'm happy with your Smile Quotient readings. You seem to have hit the 6-figure mark."

He then said he would like to try something new and perform a Smileoscopy of each one of the Ales and Guts. Over the next hour, one by one, he performed a Smileoscopy on each of them. The rest of us could hear the Smile Quotient Meter ring up a lot of smiles.

When he was done, Dr Eye Can looked pleased and said with a cheerful voice, "Kiran, well done. All of you are blossoming. In general, you have a healthier Smile Quotient. The feedback you gave me and the Smile and Vulnerability Log indicates that your Net Worth is stable enough to start training for the odyssey to free Oh from the last and powerful Oooh emotions. I am impressed with the extra strength in your thirty pack emotional muscles. It is just a question of time before you can free Oh and bring him back into your life."

Dr Eye Can however, warned me, "Though your Nut Worth is stable, if we started the odyssey again now, the largest risk we face is that you could still be susceptible to a mild case of SADS. If we got bogged down in a severe hurricane during the odyssey, the energy you would use to survive would steadily deplete your Nut Worth, and you would land back in Cape of Oh No."

We all looked downcast, as we had thought we were ready to restart our odyssey. To comfort us, Dr. Eye Can said, "Let's have fun now. No more boring stuff. Kiran, if you thought you had reached the apex of your personal and professional life, the Wizard and I think otherwise. We think that all the effort put in till now has brought you to the basecamp of what you are capable of achieving in life. With the right training and guidance, you can learn to tackle the tougher obstacles ahead on the odyssey. The next step to free Oh from the negative mesmerizing power of your Oh No Emotions is to go on a bootcamp."

"Basecamp and bootcamp, why?" I asked.

Dr. Eye Can replied, "Well your ICE packs in reality are virtual games. With the word games in mind, remember all professional athletes and also anyone serious about transforming their lives use versions of basecamps and bootcamps to prepare for all major events in their life."

"I buy that, but what do you mean by a basecamp and bootcamp," I say impatiently.

"Ok, but first let me start by saying that I know a perfect location for the basecamp and the bootcamp. A basecamp is a good analogy for a secure place or a place you can call 'A home away from home.' It's in the heart of Oh Landia in a place called Nutty Woods. Here you'll have all the infrastructure and support you need to prepare for the odyssey and will be close to your mentors. In Nutty Wood there is an abundance of experiences that will make you smile. Here you and the Ales will receive instruction on how to train all the four pillars of your Nut Worth. The bootcamp is also a perfect analogy for you to learn to train like a professional. Only if you train with the mindset of a professional can we develop the Extrapreneur Mindset that's required to bring back Oh in your life. The bootcamp will also take place in Nutty Woods and sets the stage to prepare you for the hard work ahead. Here, you will learn to simulate training your Ex-Factor, and simulate scenarios to rescue, focus on team-building, etc., under the guidance of your mentors."

Seeing that we were a bit confused with the basecamp and bootcamp analogies, he smiled, "Let's imagine you are a boxer and want to train your Ex-Factor so blow by blow you can help Oh free himself from the negative mesmerizing power of his former captors. But everybody who has the ambition of becoming a professional in every field usually has a world-class team of mentors to train them. This world-class team is the difference between those of us who say, "I want to" and "I did it." I would love to be part of the bootcamp, be one of your mentors, and help you plan and execute the bootcamp."

I was relieved to hear that Dr. Eye Can wanted to remain part of my odyssey, thanked him for his motivational words, and said, "As always, it will be an honor. Cape of Oh No is a pleasant nightmare that I'm thankful for, as it opened up a new world of hidden opportunities. I have no intention of going back to Cape of Oh No and I'm dreaming of a life in Cape Oh. The reality I know is that I'll end up transitioning in and out of sweet spots between the Cape of Oh Yes, Cape of Oh No, and Cape Oh for the rest of my life, but as long as I have a healthy Smile P&L and Nut Worth, I'll be thankful and do my best to keep Oh in my life."

Dr. Eye Can hands me a map, points to where Nutty Woods is located, pinpointing a building called the "Bungalow" and as he closes the door to Clinic Stop Tuning Yourself says, "Take some time off; I'll see you in the Bungalow whenever you feel ready to come. I'll tell them to expect you in The Bungalow at some point in the near future. Don't get lost in Oh Landia. We have a job on our hands."

STRATEGIC TIME OUT 3

Though I had gotten to know my Ales a bit more and we had found Oh, the hard work of a bootcamp still lay ahead. But I was ready for it. I was still nervous, so to pep myself up before moving to Nutty Woods, as I have a bragging gene, I told anyone who was willing to listen about my odyssey. People actually listened. I onboarded a few more Miners and Millers, people whom I respected and trusted. Others committed to hopping on and hopping off my odyssey when I restarted it. And, of course, the leeches and chattering monkeys were back, waiting for juicy solutions that they could claim to be their own.

As I write this, I work hard on training my emotional muscles and can feel my Ex-Factor being strengthened. I am thankful for my ADHD label, as it definitely helped me open my eyes but also my mind and heart to appreciate that I need to have a new type of physical, mental, financial, and social strength if I were serious about restarting my odyssey. Yes, every day is still hard; a part of me wants to escape to the good old days and continue to be a sidekick in somebody else's story. But most of me wants to stay and discover ways to reach all my three goals, the ones that focus on helping me burn brighter and not burn out: Find ways to bring Oh back into my life;

Pioneer the Art of Extrapreneurship and develop as an Extrapreneur; and Become a Smiling Billionaire.

Before we move on to my next adventures, where I start experimenting on how to thrive even more with ADHD, I was ready to cross over to the invisible world of Nutty Woods. Standing in front of the Clinic Stop Tuning Yourself, I took a selfie of my emotional muscle as it looked one year after I was diagnosed with ADHD.

Punch lines of my new stories

I'm more:

Alert, Confident, Courageous, Competitive, Diligent, Enthusiastic, Energetic, Focused, Friendly, Funny, Grateful, Humble, Heroic, Playful, Thoughtful

I'm less :

Aggressive, Argumentative, Chaotic, Egoistic, Envious, Greedy, Materialistic, Helpless, Impatient, Irritated, Forgetful, Frustrated, Guilty, Lethargic, Restless

My Incredible Emotions

The emotions I enjoy:

Admiration, Amusement, Appreciation, Awe, Calmness, Excitement, Interest, Joy, Nostalgia, Relief, Romance, Satisfaction, Surprise, and Sympathy

The emotions I am better at managing:

Anger, Anxiety, Awkwardness, Boredom, Confusion, Craving, Disgust, Disappointment, Embarrassment, Fear, Sadness

With a few more of my emotional muscles in the best shape of their lives, I was ready for the next adventure in Nutty Woods. I was energized, I had a team that was growing every day, and I could measure and monitor my smiles. BUT I still found it very hard to deal with some of the more complex Oooh Emotions like disgust, horror, fear, and pain.

PART 4

Powerful Execution

My fertile imagination and clumsy creativity gave me my stories, concepts and toys. But it was only when I learned the craft of coupling my five decades of powerful execution skills to my imagination and creativity, that my first collection of ICE packs could further enhance my ability to process the new information and experiences, especially those that I was now more conscious of in my changing world. I have organized the ICE packs into hierarchies with each ICE Pack playing a pivotal role in helping me smile more and grimace less.

CHAPTER 8

THE OH SAFARI

Spark Plug in me wanted to create a billion smiles.
P Leader in me wanted to lead the way to a billion smiles.
Nut Cracker was thinking, why stop at a billion smiles?

It's crunch time for me, now. I have to start training my emotional muscles like a professional athlete to bring Oh back into my life. To model my behavior like these professionals getting ready for an important event in their careers, I opt to use the metaphor of a base-camp and bootcamp to prepare myself for my odyssey that I hoped to restart soon.

To visualize my basecamp and bootcamp toy, I settled for the scenes from a safari to Tanzania in 2014 when I lived for a few weeks in the Simanjiro with the Maasai. Building on my visual of the crater formed by my meteor, I was inspired by our visit to the Ngorongoro Crater, a large volcanic caldera that is home to a diverse range of animals, flora, and fauna to visualize Nutty Woods as my ethereal basecamp, a natural wonder and home to the most exotic nuts. The visual of a safari also serves as a reminder of a place where wild animals wander free in nature and I, enclosed in a jeep, am awestruck as I admire the elegance they display while roaming in their natural habitat. This is exactly what I needed to do in Nutty Woods. Go on an Oh Safari, where Oh is free and I can learn from the way he reacts to my Oh Yes and Oh No Emotions as a bystander.

I call my ethereal bootcamp SafarE with a capital E, to remind me that my odyssey is also about getting more comfortable dealing with my emotions and to bring Oh back into my life. The SafarE will have a number of programs designed to strengthen my Ex-Factor. The first of them is The Induction Program.

As I was getting ready for the bootcamp, I encountered a new complication. While in DontDoNation, I had my Miners and Millers who could mold, guide, and direct me to bring Oh back into my life, I realized that I could not take them with me to Oh Landia. So I needed to find an ethereal team that could replace them.

TEAM INDUCTION PROGRAM

Over the last few months, I had learned that before I jump into anything, I should have some sort of a plan ready. This time, before I jumped right into my basecamp and bootcamp, I decided that I would break it into a series of smaller programs, and, in each program, I would visualize situations and study the impact they could have on my Oh Yes and Oh No Emotions.

The first program was the Induction, inspired from similar programs in a few companies who strategically invested in structured training programs to onboard new employees. I decided that I would design my Induction Program using visualizations and role play so that I could simulate many of the experiences on the odyssey ahead. By doing that, I would be able to identify a few things that may remain beyond my control and understand how to deal with them. This would help me find my feet in the basecamp and bootcamp and also build strong relationships with my mentors and future teammates.

After waving Dr. Eye Can goodbye at Clinic Stop Tuning Yourself, with Nut Cracker in the lead, we went on a long trek through the stunning landscape of Oh Landia and finally arrived at The Bungalow. A rustic structure on the top of a hill, it was elegantly designed and added beauty to the luscious flora and fauna of Nutty Woods. From the impressive terrace we had a magnificent view of the hills, rivers, lakes, forests and the tiny town of Nutty Woods. At the end of the horizon was a beautiful white beach that danced with the blue ocean.

Dr. Eye Can invited us into The Bungalow, and, as we settled in, he didn't mince words. "I'm not surprised that you all came directly to The Bungalow. You can't wait to get started." We all nodded in agreement.

Then he put on his serious voice and said, "The reason you landed in Cape of Oh No was that you hadn't yet learned to use the most complex features that ADHD brings into your life. Even though over the last few months, you had learned more about your ADHD through Ales and Oh, now, the skills to develop Ex-Factor professionally will start with guidance from world-class teachers, who could mold, guide, and direct you in Ohism. They will help you steer clear from the Cape of Oh No that you would otherwise have been drawn to for the rest of your life."

After I grasped the enormity of what Dr. Eye Can had just said, he laid out a high-level plan for the bootcamp. As he walked us through it, he concluded, "The goal of the bootcamp is for you and the Ales to learn to work as a united team through thick and thin. I will meet you here tomorrow morning at 9 am on the dot."

TEAM INSPIRATION

As inspiration is a key to kick start my fertile imagination and find Cool Moves that suit my brand of Ales, I dream up the concept of Team Inspiration, an ethereal version of my Miners and Millers based in Oh Landia, who will inspire me with Cool Moves to bring Oh back into my life.

The next morning on the dot of 9 am, Dr. Eye Can ushered us all around the dining table. He got straight down to planning the bootcamp in more detail. When we reached the question of who will mentor us on the bootcamp, he said, "Fortunately, I know some ethereal world-class Miners and Millers in Oh Landia who can mold, guide, and direct you to strengthen Ex-Factor before you depart for the next stage of the odyssey. I have shared your story with them as well as all the artifacts we have compiled in our consultations. I have nicknamed them Team Inspiration and they possess all the skills you need to train Ex-Factor in the bootcamp." With a shrill whistle, eight pixies magically appear.

As we curiously watch these delicate pixies, he announces proudly, "Meet Team Inspiration, your source of inspiration to bring Oh back into your life. Let's start introducing the four pixies who are the Nut Miners or, in your terminology in DontDoNation, you will call them Entrepreneurs. They'll guide you on how to develop your entrepreneurship spirit, focusing on your thirty Oh Yes and Oh No Emotions and in the discovery of the role they play in your life."

We're excited to meet the Nut Miners, and Dr. Eye Can calls Acrobat to introduce herself.

Acrobat, a dainty pixie, steps forward with a swivel and, in an exquisite voice, says, "I'm an athlete, and, like you, Kiran, I too can chase a ball the entire day if given the option. My role is to guide you to develop a mindset to view actions in your life, however serious or joyous the situation may be, as a game. I spend a lot of time on obstacle courses, trying to find ways to navigate the course. I look forward to spending many hours with you learning to tackle the obstacles that appear in your life."

Meet
Acrobat

With a bow, she exits, and the doctor calls on Spam Fighter, whom he introduces as a warrior geek. Spam Fighter is tall, muscular, lean, and mean.

Meet
Spam Fighter

Without fuss, he says, "My role in the odyssey is to direct you to find simple yet incredibly hard ways to improve Ex-Factor. I have some high-tech devices to keep harmful data and information, the type that tends to make you grimace, as far away from you as possible. Together, we'll figure out the use-less qualities you need to unlearn from your life and find the use-more qualities you need to add to your life." With these few words, he went into the background.

Spam Fighter is impressive and a tough act to follow, but as Dr. Eye Can calls on the next pixie, Dragon Slayer, a fearsome knight, clasping a beautiful sword, steps forward. "Dragon Slayer," he says, "is a fearsome warrior who is a specialist in mentoring his students to fight off the imaginary dragons that symbolize evil forces that try to enter their lives and the lives of their families." We're spellbound!

Meet
Dragon Slayer

Dragon Slayer opens his visor and, in a lively voice, says, "With my dragon-slaying sword in your hands, I'll mentor you to grasp what attracts the inner dragons that disturb your peace of mind. Together, in the bootcamp, I'll teach you to foresee the appearance of these dragons and how we can turn off their fire power."

Nut Cracker is captivated by the sword, so to amuse him, Dragon Slayer gives us a demonstration of his dragon-slaying abilities, then flutters away and gives a firm push to Mr. If On-Lee.

Even before Mr. If On-Lee says a word, he brings a smile to my lips and a cheer to my heart. He's completely relaxed and as he slouches down in a chair, he mumbles, "I'm an entrepreneur in the making. I have tons of innovative ideas, start many businesses, but cannot get any of them to succeed. My therapist says that I give up too easily and am plagued by an 'if only I did this or that attitude.' I have authored my own book *7 Keys to Failure*. Just hanging around with me will teach you what you must not do if you want to convert any of your wonderful ideas into a source of a billion smiles."

Meet
Mr. If Only - Lee

The four Nut Miners had given us much to think about, especially how they would help us free Oh. Spark Plug and Nut Cracker were in a daze, and I had to prod them out of their stupor as Dr. Eye Can started to introduce the Nut Millers.

He said, "The Nut Millers have complementary qualities to a Nut Miner. In DontDoNation, you will call them leaders. They'll guide you on how to develop your leadership spirit, focusing on your thirty Incredible Emotions and in discovering the role they play in your lives."

We are excited to meet the Nut Millers and Dr. Eye Can introduces Mrs. Bolt, whom we recognize from the Story Archives. "Mrs. Bolt," he says, "is a multidimensional leader, librarian, teacher, and project manager, as the matriarch of Nutty Woods. Mrs. Bolt will teach you to bolt all your nuts together."

Meet
Mrs. Bolt

As we snicker at the doctor's humor, Mrs. Bolt kills any opportunity for a wisecrack and says, "In the libraries of Oh Landia, I'll introduce you to a myriad of new ways to accumulate your Nut Worth. Through the simple art of reading and listening to the words of the most brilliant minds, you can learn more about any topic you desire and learn to find and free Oh. From literature, philosophy, fiction, arts, history, science, cooking, comedy, and more, we will find simple ways to help you accumulate your Nut Worth. You have all the knowledge you ever need to become an Extrapreneur inside you. You just need to find ways to access it."

We're all in a somber mood after Mrs. Bolt's speech, but lighten up as Miss Chef, a happy lady with a lovely infectious smile, steps up with a ladle in her hand. "In my kitchens, using the art and science of cooking, I'll teach you to relish the assorted flavors of life that each of your thirty Oh Yes and Oh No Emotions brings. As we cook, clean, eat, smile, and more, I'll guide you to look for opportunities in every mistake, crisis, or problem you face and see if we can turn them into smiles. I look forward to learning your famous designer cooking skills and tasting your finger-licking good curries that Dr. Eye Can keeps raving about."

Meet
Miss Chef

As Miss Chef sits down, Colonel Cocktail, a retired army colonel, comes forward with his chest sticking out. The doctor introduces him as the Miller who is going to help us work with discipline. "Without discipline, you will go around in circles in your odyssey and struggle to bring Oh back into your life," he stresses.

Meet
Colonel Cocktail

In a booming voice, as if addressing his platoon, Colonel proclaims, "I'll direct you on the qualities you need to learn to become warriors. I'll teach you to unravel the mystery of leadership and teamwork. If you put in the hard miles, I will, as a reward, give you a copy of my cocktail book on how you can mix all the wonderful nuts in your life into mouthwatering cocktails." With a sarcastic smile, he says, "There's nothing more refreshing than a bowl of nuts to go with an ale or, in my case, a cocktail full of Dr. Eye Can's ICE, that I look forward to enjoying with you after a hard day's work on the bootcamp."

Before the Colonel's bravado got us into warrior mode, Nutty Nanna, a gorgeous lady, steps up and taps the belligerent Colonel on his shoulder, saying, "Step back, Colonel." In a comforting voice, she announces, "While you may think, by my looks, that I'm a powerhouse of wisdom, what I enjoy most is a good laugh.

Meet
Nutty Nanna

I'm also a self-proclaimed fabulous storyteller and love to spin a good yarn. I'll guide you on how the art of storytelling can spread this Extrapreneurship and Smiling Billionaire stuff you keep talking about. Over the next few weeks, in my company, you'll appreciate how the art of enjoying eating loads of sweets, great food, comedy, the pun, and storytelling will help brighten your life, however serious the situation you're in may seem."

We're all blown away by Team Inspiration and are eager to get to know them better. But before we can start bonding, I ask the doctor, "What about Team Perspiration?"

The doctor says, "In a minute, but let's take a break and a deep breath," and calls upon Colonel Cocktail to explain further.

"If your Team Inspiration is amazing, Team Perspiration is going to blow all your senses away," the Colonel begins. "On the odyssey, inspiration can only get you started on a path, the rest of the time spent on it is pure hard work and perspiration. Before I introduce you to Team Perspiration, a few last words on Team Inspiration to make sure you understand their roles. Always remember, a Nut Miner is an entrepreneur whose passion is to mine the flora and fauna of Nutty Woods for nuts that have a significant impact on lives. Like you, they love to explore the unknown. Finding solutions to complex problems is what makes them smile…" He pauses and looks around as if he's inspecting his battalion.

When he sees he has our attention, he continues, "Back to the analogy of the nuts. The Nut Miners will mentor you on how to be inquisitive and find new sources of Cool Moves that may never have been done before. Learning these types of Cool Moves from them will have a significant impact on how fast you crawl up the Extrapreneur Ladder and attain your three goals. A word of caution: the Nut Miners will only inspire you to find these Cool Moves, but you yourselves have to put in the hard work to integrate them in your life. So, in their company, be prepared to fall down from the Extrapreneur Ladder many times, as many of their Cool Moves may not work and cause you plenty of grimaces before they start working and make you smile. On the other hand, Nut Millers are leaders, excellent in communication, coordination, and connecting people. They're experts in the leadership process and enjoy, as opposed to the

Nut Miners, planning and risk management, strategy, tactics, and operations. In their company, you'll learn to find inspiration on how to savor the thirty Incredible Emotions."

As he takes a sip of a liquid in his glass, we look around a bit concerned, wondering whether we are capable of meeting the colonel's expectations. He puts his glass down and continues, "Back to the analogy of the nuts, the Nut Millers will mentor you on how to make both Old and New Cool Moves a part of your daily lives. Learning from them may not be as exciting as being in the company of the Nut Miners, but the time spent with them will help you develop leadership skills that will have a significant impact on how fast you can crawl up the ladder, and how long you stay on the highest rung. Let's take a break before I present Team Perspiration."

⌐

The value I gained in finding the characters in Team Inspiration, was I spent hours thinking about my role model leaders and entrepreneurs, both those I knew and those whose lives I've read about and studied to understand what qualities of theirs will help me build my Ex-Factor. I appreciate that ADHD, Leadership, and Entrepreneur all are sources of smiles and grimaces, and it's up to me, with their guidance, to find my sweet spot between my ADHD, Leadership, and Entrepreneur that will make me smile more and grimace less.

TEAM PERSPIRATION

Having a mission, purpose, and goals is good for my ego. But at the end of the day, without results, they just look good on paper. As perspiration is a key to convert my Cool Moves into results, I dream up the concept of Team Perspiration, who will perspire alongside me as I integrate Cool Moves into my life.

Dr. Eye Can whistles and five new pixies magically appear.

I vaguely recognize these pixies as the doctor says, "Here's Team Perspiration. Can you think of better partners to help you do the hard work to train your emotional muscles? I could not, and settled for your five sensory organs: Touch, Smell, Taste, Hearing, and Sight. Like Team Inspiration, each of them have unique and complementary abilities. They function seamlessly as a team. They know you intimately. They've stood by you in Cape of Oh Yes and Cape of Oh No. On the odyssey, they've promised me to help me put all the theory on Cool Moves into action. Young as they look, they bring 55 years of transformation experience, as their individual qualities have matured along with you Kiran."

I digest what the doctor had said about Team Perspiration and buy into it. I think to myself that if I cannot bear a life without Oh, I'm sure it will be hard for me to live without any one of Team Perspiration. I mutter, "I get your point doctor, and I am dependent on Team Perspiration to bring Oh back into my life."

Dr. Eye Can is thrilled that I accept his maverick suggestion for my teammates on the odyssey. "Kiran, remember each member of Team Perspiration is a leader and entrepreneur. You can learn a lot from them. They all have enormous potential and you can look forward to learning to enjoy them. The odyssey is the perfect environment for you to explore how to use your senses more. Another important function that Team Perspiration will play on the odyssey is that of quality assurance. They're a living version of your Crappy Alarm Button that you love so much. In this, they're the best team to ensure that all the Cool Moves you practice in Oh Landia are relevant in DontDoNation and can help you achieve your three goals."

I am touched when I see Team Perspiration, and the doctor calls Worried Eyes to present himself.

Meet
Worried Eyes

Sporting a classic worried look that can in a split second change to a smile when I'm up to mischief, Worried Eyes says, "Yeah, my awful name is pretty awful. But when Kiran enjoyed life in the Cape of Oh Yes, I was shining brown, twinkling, and helped Kiran to look out for opportunities to be mischievous. The last few years after he lost his smile, I got dark circles, as I was his constant lookout for things to worry about. But worried or not, I'm still razor sharp and my role on the odyssey is to help to spot the most beautiful opportunities in life and keep an eye out for trouble of the sort that Kiran is always interested in being part of."

I get goosebumps as I hear Worried Eyes speak and thank him for his support through thick and thin.

The next pixie, Hard Nose, sporting a classic bump and a wrinkle flies in.

Meet
Hard Nose

"I'm Kiran's comrade-in-arms when he wants to explore new things. When Kiran is impulsive, it gets us into a lot of trouble and causes Kiran to fall on me often, so I'm a wee bit crooked. On the odyssey, I'll help sniff what's going on around us and will lead Kiran toward the delightful smells in life and away from the things that smell rotten. I'm always ready to take a few blows for the team when needed, and I'm sure there will be quite a few on this odyssey." I couldn't argue with anything that Hard Nose said and I gave him a thumbs up.

Then with a loud cheer from the other senses, Tough Skin takes center stage, and I know I'm about to blush.

Meet
Tough Skin

Imitating Dragon Slayer, he says, "Once upon a time, I was spotlessly clean and free of scars. But this period lasted the first two years of Kiran's life. Ever since I can remember, I've had to put my skin on the line in Kiran's hair-brained adventures and I've taken a few hard knocks for him. Hopefully, as Kiran learns to be an Extrapreneur, I won't have to take any more hard knocks on his account. But then I fear my life may become boring. My role in the odyssey is the bodyguard, who will complement Dragon Slayer to protect the team from dangers lurking around them."

I'm loving these emotional speeches made by my body parts and enjoying seeing them in real life. The next is Ear Wax, who mimics Colonel Cocktail's demeanor.

Meet
Ear Wax

"For most of my life, I helped Kiran hear only what he wanted to hear. I call this skill selective hearing. I also helped him to stay balanced as he walked, but as he wobbles so much, I'm not performing this role well. When Kiran was young, I got my ears ruffled a lot when he was mischievous. Nowadays, I have a lot of hairs in me, which irritates Marianne, and she tries to pull them out, and boy, that hurts. On the odyssey, I'll assist Spam Fighter to help the team shut off the constant stream of noise pollution that surrounds us."

The last but not least pixie I spend time together with day in and day out, Taste Buds, flies in.

Meet
Taste Buds

Dressed like a band majorette, accompanied by blaring music that has all of us dancing to her tune, she spins her baton in her hand and says, "I'm Kiran's best friend. In my company, I help him orchestrate all the other senses and he experiences the magic of the five tastes: sweet, sour, salty, bitter, and savory. I help Kiran when he's engrossed in designer cooking and I'm often called upon to determine if the dish tastes right or to help save it from disaster when he, in his enthusiasm, adds too much salt or chili. The role I'll play in the odyssey is to help Kiran taste the thirty nuts to see the role they play in strengthening Ex-Factor. I'm sure that, as Kiran is determined to train like an athlete, I'll be tasting a lot of mud every time he hits the dirt."

If I thought I was impressed by Team Inspiration, the chivalry of my five senses was an eye opener to how well they've protected me in life. I appreciated Dr. Eye Can's mastery in identifying Team Inspiration and Team Perspiration and the roles they'll have on the odyssey.

Once we had all made each other's acquaintance, the doctor does a quick Smileoscopy and the Smile Quotient Meter is soon buzzing merrily. He's extremely happy with the quality, quantity, and frequency of my smiles. And, with a solemn look, he says that because our smile quotient reading is healthy, we're accumulating smiles, and we now have a baseline that we can refer to at the end of the bootcamp to ensure that we are definitely ready to proceed on our odyssey. The doctor sees that we are all pumped up and calls The Ales, Guts, Team Inspiration, Team Perspiration, the Wizard of Oh, Cool Moves and Ex-Factor to gather around him. As he clicks a selfie, he says, "I hereby call all of us Team Smiling Billionaire. Together we will help Kiran explore all his thirty Oh Yes and Oh No Emotions and strengthen his Ex-factor. Let's close our first day of the induction program. Let's get cracking and find ways to help Kiran smile more, grimace less, burn brighter, not burn out, and inspire him to create a billion new smiles every day! Could he not have been less ambitious and content to start with a few hundred smiles every day? Tomorrow morning, Mrs. Bolt will pick you up and we'll meet in a place that will tickle your senses."

⌒

To find the characters in Team Perspiration, I spent hours thinking about all the hard work I've put in over five decades. Though I've lived in harmony with my five senses, there's so little I know about their true potential. Each Cool Move involves not only strengthening my Ex-Factor but also developing one or more of my senses, and I look forward to seeing how I can develop them to help me bring back Oh to my life.

ICE PACK 4

The Dining Room

I have so many moving parts in stories, concepts, toys, pixies, and more to help me achieve my goals. But I now need a way to mix and match all of them together and work like a well-oiled business to reach them. I dream up the concept of a buffet, one that inspires me as it has so many amazing things to offer. With so many choices, at the end of the day, it's up to me to ensure that I enjoy mixing and matching the offerings to suit my brand of ADHD and make sure that my teammates, especially my five senses, are activated and engaged to bring Oh back into my life.

Our second morning of the Team Induction program is a reminder that we're not on a holiday. I'm lying on a comfortable king-size bed, in the middle of a dream relaxing on the beaches of Cape of Oh, sipping coconut water laced with rum. As I take a sip, I'm awakened by a knock on the bedroom door. "Enter," I say, annoyed.

Meet
Mrs. Bolt

Mrs. Bolt enters with steaming cups of coffee. She orders us out of bed and hands us our coffee. After our morning ablutions, we're on our way to Nut Quarters. As we enter Nut Quarters, we are engulfed by the intoxicating aroma of spices, and I say, "We have reached spice heaven."

Mrs. Bolt ushers us into a plush boardroom. I was all smiles when I saw it was aptly called "Bored Room" and we are thrilled to see Team Inspiration, but I can't spot Miss Chef.

When we have our bearings and sit down, Mrs. Bolt welcomes us and says that over the next few days, we will explore Nutty Woods with Team Inspiration. This will help us feel more comfortable in Nutty Woods, get familiar with our roles and responsibilities on the odyssey, and work more on the Purpose, Hobbies and Passion, Cool

Moves, Toys, and other things that will be needed to bring Oh back into our lives.

Then Mrs. Bolt leads us to the Dining Room and on the way tells us that The Dining Room is Miss Chef's Mill where she created the most amazing food using the spices of Nutty Wood. We enter The Dining Room and are thrilled to see a buffet has been laid out for us. The color and fragrance of the buffet was really out of this world. But it also looked intimidating. Introducing us to the buffet, Mrs. Bolt says, "This Dining Room is Miss Chef's domain and she uses a combination of the spices made in Nutty Woods to prepare the most delicious meals. She has specially made the buffet today to give a taste of all the exotic spices of Nutty Wood as well as to get to know the basic spices used in most of the dishes." She steps aside, and Miss Chef, dressed in spotless white overalls with the cutest dots and a ladle in her hand, magically appears.

"Welcome to my Dining Room. Like Kiran, my best friends are Cooking, Eating, and Smiles," and looking around, she asks, "Where are you?"

Cooking, Eating and Smiles on hearing their names appear and flutter around the buffet.

Miss Chef looks pleased and continues, "The buffet is prepared with all the thirty Incredible Emotions that Kiran has identified as the core of his smiles and grimaces. Each dish of the buffet will make all your five senses tingle, but each spice used in a dish has a clear role in creating the dish. We enjoy blending the spices to create our favorite dishes, but what differentiates our buffet is that just before the cooking is done, we add a pinch of one of our Nutty Woods' Pixie Dust Spices or just Pixie Dust to our dish that act like magic to enhance the flavor of the dish and only then are we ready to serve our masterpiece to the world."

Nut Cracker is intrigued with the Nutty Woods' Pixie Dust Spice and asks, "Is the Nutty Woods' Pixie Dust Spice similar to the final touch of a dash of this and that, which Kiran adds to the dish before he thinks it's ready to eat?"

Miss Chef recognizes that trait in herself and says, "Exactly, we love the subtle difference the Nutty Woods' Pixie Dust Spice imparts to our creations. It's like an artist signing off a piece of art when they're done. We have eight Nutty Woods' Pixie Dust Spices in our collection. Each one of us in Team Inspiration has their own Pixie Dust Spice that they've invested years to perfect. They all have unique names that reflect our philosophy of life in a few words. They've carefully selected the combination of nuts that represents their passion for life that they want to share with others. My Pixie Dust is called Mischief and I create it intuitively every time I make one of my signature dishes. Mischief has no recipe but is made on the fly by me by adding the right mix of the others in Pixie Dust to my signature dish. But while we can only prepare the dish to the best of our taste buds, it's up to each of you to enjoy the dishes in your own way. Let's dig into the buffet. A tip is to start with the dishes on the left. They're made with a few of the basic spices, and when you can taste and savor the basics of those dishes, get adventurous."

Miss Chef gave me a shining steel plate that was divided into 10 smaller sections, asked me to follow her, and started helping herself, filling each section one at a time. When our plate was full, I sat down, but was still confused where to start on this eating orgy. Mrs. Bolt told me to follow her cue. "Fingers were made before forks and spoons," she said as she showed us how to taste each dish separately. When she saw that we got a taste of what flavor each dish had to offer, she started to mix two dishes with her fingers, and, as we followed suit, we enjoyed savoring their combined flavors. Soon, two became three, and we started enjoying the symphony of flavors that were possible with all the dishes in the buffet.

Flavor by flavor, we smiled when we enjoyed a flavor or grimaced when we tasted something that we didn't like. After a few more helpings, we had tasted all the dishes, and we enjoyed identifying the flavors. When our stomachs were full, we thanked Miss Chef for this unforgettable experience. Mrs. Bolt said, "Well, now that the eating part is over, let's get to work."

She led us back into the conference room where there was a digital Map of Oh Landia and gave each of us a pair of Virtual Reality glasses to put on. When we were ready she took us on a virtual tour through the streets and gardens, forests, and fields in which the nuts are cultivated. We enjoy tours of the beach and then on to visit a few Mines and Mills where we see how the Nuts are mined and milled into spices. The grand finale is a tour of the Vault where all the spices are stored.

Blown away by the fascinating introduction, we sit back in our chairs and let the beauty of what we just experienced sink in. Finally, as Mrs. Bolt sees us getting restless, she smiles and says, "Let's continue with our induction program tomorrow. Same time, same place. It's going to be about mindset by one of my favorite millers."

⌒

The value I got from this adventure on the Buffet concept was it made me realize that I had infinite ways of becoming a Smiling Billionaire to choose from. But the most potent way that suited my brand of ADHD was my inclination to learn new ways to activate my senses. I knew that as they developed, they would guide me to strengthen my Ex-Factor. If this happened, then bringing Oh back into my life was just a question of time.

CHAPTER 9

THE EXTRAPRENEUR MINDSET

I had been doing well and my Smile Quotient Meter was ticking along nicely. But as in many situations in life, when things were going well, my ability to worry kicked in and I thought "Is this too good to last?" To ease this worry, I once again leaned on my experiences in the corporate world. A decree, "Failure is not an option," that's used to motivate a team to go above and beyond the call of duty to reach a farfetched goal came to mind. This is a fantastic team-building motto, but now, I asked myself, perched on my Extrapreneur Ladder, enjoying the 360 degree panoramic view of Nutty Woods, "When is failure a valid option?"

As we settled down in the Bored Room, the experienced Mrs. Bolt was quick to spot that I had fallen in love with the concept of bootcamp to get us ready to continue on the odyssey. My positive body language was radiating smiles, but I was given a reality check when Mrs. Bolt commented, "Looks like reaching the Cape of Oh has become a 'failure is not an option' project for you. The best way to succeed in such an audacious odyssey ahead is to focus your energies and build a formidable team. So, let's start getting to know each other and, more importantly, our weak points and focus on building a strong mindset."

I agreed with her, and Mrs. Bolt continued, "Over the next few weeks, you all will spend time with Team Inspiration discovering Nutty Woods. Every day, we will introduce you to our Nut Mining and Milling process to understand how it can support you in training your emotional muscles. As a bonus, they'll also introduce you to the secret of their Pixie Dust Spice. But first, I've asked Colonel Cocktail, my favorite Miller, to share a few words about how we can develop a strong mindset."

Colonel Cocktail stood up, stretched, cleared his throat, and in a deep baritone that commanded our attention, said, "As we will spend months together on this SafarE—by the way, I dislike you mucking around with the English language—let's focus on establishing a strong mindset that will be our foundation to bring Oh back into your lives. Don't let the word 'mindset' make you nervous. During the SafarE, you'll be exposed to many new situations that will trigger strong emotions. Many of these emotions will definitely make you nervous at the start, but one member of Team Inspiration will always be there to inspire you to see a positive, even in the most desperate situations."

I had little time to savor the sense of reassurance provided, as the Colonel continued, "During the initial programs in the SafarE, we will only observe your emotions; we will not start training. That will happen in the subsequent stages. Throughout the SafarE, we'll gather data and analyze this data together to ensure we're developing a good mindset. I have a suggestion on the mindset I would like Team Billionaire to develop to bring Oh back into your lives. Let's refine it during the SafarE so when you're ready for the odyssey, you have your own mindset that you will all live up to."

He added some further words of advice: "A word I want you to ponder on is 'try.' This word will be useful to you when an hour, day, or program on the SafarE is hard, and you want to give up. Irrespective of the outcome of a Cool Move, try your best to contribute to the team performing the Cool Move, as in this way, all of you and the team will learn to support each other, have fun, and build lasting relationships. If we fail in the bootcamp to get ready to free Oh, we have at least made new friends, enjoyed the process of getting to know each other, and learned lessons in life."

He handed us out a piece of paper with the words

The Extrapreneur's Mindset
Enjoy Truth Trust Guts Love Relationships ☺

After we've studied these words, Colonel Cocktail said, "We'll know we're well on the way to bringing Oh back into your lives when we're comfortable with this chain of words and believe in them. This is my interpretation of them, and I hope over the next many months you will refine them and make them your own:

"**Enjoy:** Everything I do as an Extrapreneur must start with a mindset that says, 'Even though I'm on the most difficult path ever in my life, I must TRY to enjoy every moment of it. Enjoyment is the starting point to build relationships.'

"**Truth:** In good times and in bad, I need to be truthful to myself and accept that I'm vulnerable to many unknown things that will unfold on the way to bringing Oh back into my life.

"**Trust:** As I get to know my perfect and imperfect Ale qualities, start integrating them into my daily life through Cool Moves, I'll get positive and negative feedback, but I need to trust myself and stick to doing what's best for me to bring Oh back into my life.

"**Guts:** Always remember, it takes Guts for you to achieve your mission, purpose, and goals in life.

"**Love:** Day by day, as we walk the Path to Cape Oh, searching for Oh, remember to love yourself and loved ones, as without you and them smiling, it will be impossible to bring Oh back into your life.

"**Relationships:** Never forget to acknowledge the people who were there for you when you were in Cape of Oh No, those who will be there every time you land back in Cape of Oh No, and whom you should be there for when they need you."

These were heavy words on mindset. We couldn't digest more. With my grimaces growing larger by the second, Miss Chef says, "It's snack time" and leads us to the dining room, which is filled with the aroma of samosa and lassi. We enjoy Miss Chef's creations, and when all of us, especially the Guts, are happy, we head back to the Bored Room.

Mrs. Bolt is in charge again. "I know this may sound strange, but for the next few days please be open to your five senses – Worried Eyes, Ear Wax, Taste Buds, Tough Skin, and Hard Nose or, in plain English, see, hear, taste, touch, and smell. The best treat you can give yourself in the induction program is to do what you're famous for, that is, to daydream and imagine. Also remember to WWoW as much as you want and remember that Team Inspiration is always there for you. Are you ready to push on to the next activity in the Induction program?"

I replied with bravado, "Yes, we are. We've been training for this SafarE unconsciously for five decades."

Mrs. Bolt is amused as she sees how eager we are to start. When we've all settled down, she turns on a large digital screen and zooms in on what she calls The Energy Grid.

⌁

The value I got from this adventure on Extrapreneur Mindset is the importance of building a strong team around me who will help me develop a robust mindset that suits my brand of ADHD as this will serve me well on the days I find myself back in Cape of Oh No. In time, I also came to appreciate that many members of my team, both physical and ethereal, will hop on and hop off my odyssey as their situations demand.

CHAPTER 10

THE ENERGY GRID

I realize more and more everyday how important it is for me to have a steady supply of Cool Moves that create energy to make me smile more and grimace less. As I reflected on my multiple energy sources and how to manage them effectively, the analogy of an energy grid fascinated me. I had learned how the infrastructure of an energy grid generates, distributes, and stores energy that lights up people's lives. As I experimented with my own Energy Grid, I realized how important it was to focus on having easy and quick access to sources of positive energy within me and around me. I should learn how to tap energy sources that make me smile and to learn how to dissipate the negative energy that makes me grimace. Most importantly, I should learn the importance of saving my surplus of positive energy for Cape of Oh No days.

Mrs. Bolt dims the lights in the room. and starts a presentation on the screen. Pointing to a map of Nutty Woods, she says, "The Energy Grid is the heart beat of Nutty Woods, and we look after it with great care. Just like Oh is the algorithm of your Smile Making Machine, the Energy Grid has a number of Mines and Mills that are clearly marked on the map. I have chosen a few Mines and Mills to be the centerpiece of the bootcamp. Each of these mines and mills will help the team build up the holistic skills you need to gradually free Oh from the fake security and mesmerizing power of his former captors."

She flips to the next slide, and we see a room full of gadgets and people trying them out. She continues, despite a few hands going up to ask questions, "Each Mine and Mill has an emotion simulation room or ES room. And, Kiran, ES room is not an abbreviation for escape room. Here, visitors can virtually interact with a number of concepts and toys to get an experience of how the nuts of Nutty Woods can help train their emotional muscles."

When she comes to a picture of a Mine, we see a lot of people with enormous teeth, all busy smelling and biting nuts. "These workers in the Mine are called Biters," she says. "Their main role is to mine Nutty Woods for nuts. Their names come from an important quality-control action they do. That is, they bite a few of the nuts they're mining and the amount they smile or grimace determines how much effort will be used to harvest these nuts so they can be sent to the Mills to be made into spices."

She flips to the next slide that has a picture of a stately-looking building with a lot of people having strong jaw lines. "This is a typical Mill and the workers in the Mills are called The Chewers. As you can guess by their jaws, their main role is that they spend a lot of time chewing on the nuts during the process of being milled into spices."

I loved these funny looking Biters and Chewers and knew we were in for a fantastic experience. I ask excitedly, "The Energy Grid? What does it do?"

Mrs. Bolt replies, "The best analogy I can think of is, if your Ales or, as you call them, your extras, are your powers, then you need a grid to manage the power." We love her humor.

Mrs. Bolt continues, "The Energy Grid is like an energy grid on DontDoNation that generates energy that lights up people's homes. During the SafarE, you'll be spending most of your time on The Energy Grid. To learn to generate, use, and store your energy and find a good balance between your smiles and grimaces, we have chosen four Mines and four Mills for you to visit during the Induction Program. At each Mine and Mill, under the tutelage of a Nut Miner or Nut Miller, you'll experience different emotions. You've already experienced Chef's Mill, the Dining Room and as an extra treat for Team Perspiration, you will spend a lot of your time during the SafarE with the Chef there."

"I'm thrilled and also a bit confused about what to expect on the Energy Grid, Mrs. Bolt," I say. "Please elaborate before you lose me even before I start traveling on it."

"Imagine your body and mind as an energy grid that was built more than five decades ago," she says.

I smile and say, "Life was simple when I was young."

Mrs. Bolt nods. "Exactly. In your younger days, your energy needs were simple. An example is you just needed a bit of energy to light up a smile. As you grew older, your energy needs change and now you require energy to make yourself, family, friends, foes, OhDears, chattering monkeys, and leeches smile. So, you need to produce more energy not only to light up your life but also the lives you touch."

"Okay, I'm with you, but still not sure where this is leading to."

Mrs. Bolt continues, "Imagine you don't have enough energy to light up your life and the lives you touch."

"Ouch! It's a day in the life of Kiran in Cape of Oh No," I respond.

Mrs. Bolt nods. "So, as your energy levels decrease, your light bulbs don't get energy and a few burn out. Now imagine there's a community of people like you on The Energy Grid. If Kiran is having a good day, you're producing a lot of energy through your Oh Yes Stories."

Nut Cracker chips in, "That would be a nightmare for me. He would be so irritating. But for certain, there's never a boring day for me when Kiran is around."

Mrs. Bolt is not amused by Nut Cracker's snide remark. "If Kiran is producing more energy than he can consume himself, instead of wasting the energy by irritating you, he can feed some of it back to The Energy Grid so others in his community who need it can plug into it."

"Okay," I say, "So The Energy Grid is like a battery that stores the excess of my energy for later use and then sells it to others. It's like a hoarder or, even better, black marketeer. I love this Energy Grid."

Mrs. Bolt's feathers are ruffled, and she grunts, "Focus, and don't let your imagination run wild. Imagine you're having a difficult day full of Oh No Stories. You're consuming more energy than you're producing. But, as you're plugged into The Energy Grid, you can tap into someone's excess energy, and this will help brighten your day."

"I like this Energy Grid more and more. It's like stealing energy from The Energy Grid. Boy, this Energy Grid sounds mischievous," I comment with a smile.

"Not everybody is a crook, Kiran. Think of it as sharing not stealing. In this way, The Energy Grid facilitates a partnership in the community of people like you, Kiran. This is a WIN WIN situation for the whole community," she points out.

"How does everyone win?" I ask, and Mrs. Bolt replies, "If someone's energy level is down, hopefully, there's an excess of energy on The Energy Grid that they plug into that will brighten their day."

"A beautiful, corny concept, but now I get it," I nod.

Mrs. Bolt looks relieved when she sees I have no more irritating questions. "Fantastic! Now back to The Energy Grid. Each one of us in Team Inspiration has their own Pixie Dust Spice that they've invested years to perfect. They've carefully selected the combination of nuts that represents their passion for life that they want to share with others. As you explore The Energy Grid, you'll get a chance to observe and experiment with some of the nuts and spices of Nutty Woods, and this is a good way to prepare yourself for the next programs in the SafarE where we'll focus on how to use all of them through Cool Moves to make you smile more and grimace less."

I say in a worried tone, "The Energy Grid, Mines, Mills, and ES room sound complicated."

Mrs. Bolt laughs when she sees the frown of confusion and the sweat dripping down my face. "Let's take a break, freshen up and get ready for our next session. Your day will liven up from now."

After we've enjoyed a chai and are all refreshed, we head to the conference room where Team Inspiration is waiting for us.

Mrs. Bolt once again turns on the screen. "Let's take you on a tour of The Energy Grid and visit a few Mines and Mills that I've chosen that are best suited for you to learn more about your perfect and imperfect qualities and how you can evolve these qualities to develop Ex-Factor. We'll spend a few hours only at each Mine and Mill but after the Induction Program when the next program of the SafarE starts, we'll spend as much time as necessary at the Mines and

Mills and you'll have a chance to train through what we call the 4 by 4 Training Plan, or four Oh Yes and four Oh No Emotional muscles. Let's hit the Energy Grid."

The value of The Energy Grid is that it helps to appreciate that I need to constantly monitor my energy levels and remember to store some energy for my Cape of Oh No days and to help loved ones and other deserving people who are having a difficult day boost their energy levels.

THE VAULT

The Vault is Colonel Cocktail's Nut Mill where he mills his Pixie Dust Spice called Wealth.

Meet
Colonel Cocktail

As I reflected on my Nut Worth, which was accumulating gradually with the help of Cool Moves, I realized that I need a place to safeguard my Physical, Mental, Financial, and Social Wealth from being squandered or from being misused by people like my leeches and chattering monkeys. This led to the concept of the bank that's used to safeguard financial wealth. It made me realize that I should also have a bank or a vault to safeguard my physical, mental, and social wealth, as these, together, will probably have a larger impact on making me a Smiling Billionaire than just my financial wealth.

To get us on the move, Mrs. Bolt says we'll start at the heart of the Energy Grid called the Vault, the fortress of Colonel Cocktail. The colonel beams a smile that I wish I could replicate, takes charge of us, and leads us out of the Nut Quarters. We follow, chattering away and after 15 minutes, reach the Vault. Colonel Cocktail takes out a huge key and opens the heavy door that leads into it. As we enter, the Colonel says, "Savor the fragrance."

We close our eyes and feel we are in a nut and spice paradise. The colonel explains to us that the Vault is the Nut and Spice hub of Nutty Woods. All the nuts gathered in the Mines every day are brought here and stored till they're sent to the Mills where they are milled into spices. The finished spices are stored in the Vault before they're shipped out to the spice merchants.

The inside of the vault reminds me of a prison housing a lot of cells with iron bars. Each cell is filled with bags of spices carefully stored in neat piles. We catch sight of someone who looks like an accountant standing near a huge mountain of nuts admiring them with great affection. The mountain of nuts is well protected by a glass dome with blinking red and green alarms and other fancy gadgets. Anticipating our next questions, the Colonel tells us that the lights and alarms are to keep unwanted spice treasure hunters away as well as store them in the correct conditions so their flavor is retained as long as possible.

Curiosity gets the better of me and I ask, "What's behind the glass dome?"

"That's where all the nuts we gather in Nutty Woods that will soon be ready to be milled into spices are stored," the Colonel says as he presses a button on the glass dome and asks Pole Vault, the accountant to join us.

Pole Vault writes something in a book and, irritated at being disturbed, comes out with a frown. After introductions, the Colonel asks Pole Vault to give us a tour of the Vault. Pole Vault leads the way and mutters, "Each cell is specially designed according to the nuts and spices stored in it." He gives us a few samples of nuts and spices to touch, smell, feel, and taste and, in amusement, watches our expressions change as we savor the flavors of the nuts and spices.

Pole Vault takes us to the room where the Chewers are putting the finishing touches to Colonel Cocktail's Pixie Dust Spice, 'Wealth.'

"What's the secret behind Wealth?" I ask.

Pole Vault replies, "Wealth is a reminder to people that money matters but good Physical, Financial, Mental, and Social wealth are important to enjoy life."

At the end of our tour, Pole Vault leads us to the ES room of the Vault, and the Colonel joins us. He serves us a bowl of steaming rice with a sprinkling of Wealth. As we eat, he says, "On the SafarE, we'll spend many days in the Vault and learn many Cool Moves to strengthen Ex-Factor. My plan is that when you spend time in the Vault, we can focus on training these emotional muscles."

He hands Ex-Factor a 4 by 4 Training Plan that has a diagram of Pole Vault demonstrating how to do Cool Moves to train the emotional muscles to be more Alert, Confident, Diligent, and Focused and to be less Egoistic, Envious, Greedy, and Materialistic.

We skim through the 4 by 4 Training Plan and when we're done with our rice, the Colonel tells us to play around with the gadgets in the ES room and Pole Vault will guide us to train for a few of the Cool Moves. An hour later, we've learned a lot from Pole Vault, and Ex-Factor feels that these Cool Moves will make us stronger. The Colonel tells us that he needs Pole Vault back to work on increasing his Wealth.

Pole Vault is happy to get rid of us. As he waves us goodbye, we see that in his hand he has a book called *Colonel Cocktail's Smile and Grimace P&L*. We wave goodbye to Pole Vault, and the Colonel leads us to the next Mill called the Library.

⌒

To find the smile punch line of the Vault I spent hours thinking about all the hard work I've put in over five decades to curate my stories and accumulate my Nut Worth and how important it was for me to protect them so that I use the power in them judiciously. *Perfectly Imperfect* was the answer to script my stories and store them in a safe place so I can read them in good times and in bad and save them for my progeny to learn from my success and mistakes I've made. The Vault is also a constant reminder to me to remember to safeguard what's mine and share it with deserving people. I learned this lesson the hard way, as I've often squandered my energy by interacting with the leeches and chattering monkeys in my life.

ICE PACK 6

THE LIBRARY

The Library is Mrs. Bolt's Nut Mill where she mills her Pixie Dust Spice called Book Worm.

Meet
Mrs. Bolt

As I reflected on how to educate myself on diverse topics that could inspire me with Cool Moves, I spent a lot of time in various physical and digital libraries and the concept of the Library took shape. Wandering around libraries I was amazed by the enormous number of books of knowledge that sit on prime real estate in the libraries authored by really smart people. Unfortunately, I was not accessing this freely available knowledge strategically. The time I spent in libraries after I realized this really enlightened me to the fact that the more I learn from these authors, the clearer it becomes that most of my problems had solutions. I just had to unlearn a lot of

Uncool Moves from my life to make way for this new knowledge to have meaningful impact in my life.

⌒

The Library is in Mrs. Bolt's Mill and kingdom. She is engrossed in reading the *Oh Landia Herald*. In classic librarian style, precise and to the point, she welcomes us, and, as we start with a tour, she says, "Today, I'll introduce you to a world filled with wise words of wise people whom I call the Gold Minds."

The library is very silent, and I blurt out that it reminds me of a graveyard. "Why do you call them Gold Minds? Shouldn't you call them Scary Ghosts?" I ask, and the silence that follows is eerie. An irritated Mrs. Bolt says, "Quiet!" and whispers, "Funny. Yes, it's a graveyard of millions of beautiful words that you can enjoy. Within this library lies the secret to becoming a Smiling Billionaire."

"Who are these Gold Minds?" I ask Mrs. Bolt.

"A Gold Mind is a brilliant mind in any field who shares their knowledge with us through words. Through studying their words, you can learn philosophy, history, science, cooking, comedy, and more. Many of them have also figured out the equivalent of your Nut Worth and made this knowledge available to you in their words. But to get to these words, you have to have the patience and endurance to read their books or in your terminology, crack open their gold nuts, though I think gold nuggets is more appropriate, as that will help you bring Oh back into your life."

Mrs. Bolt saw that I was not sure I understood what she meant by gold nuggets, so she continued, "You will get what I mean by Gold Minds and Nuggets. Let's walk around and I'll show you where I mill my Pixie Dust Spice 'Book Worm.'"

Nut Cracker makes a face and blurts out, "Book Worm, Yuck!"

As we walk around the bookshelves, looking at the amazing collection of books, I lament, "I've forgotten all about my own passion for reading books."

We follow Mrs. Bolt and are in awe as she introduces us to her world of books. As we end the tour of the Library, Mrs. Bolt leads us to the ES room of the Library that's hidden in the basement where she introduces us to Night Suit, a scientist who works with Mrs. Bolt on the Book Worm.

Night Suit is as opposite as one can ever be to Mrs. Bolt. Crunching potato chips, he's lovingly talking to his computer that Mrs. Bolt says is called Daisy. As he spies us, he gives us a thumbs up and returns to talking to Daisy.

"What's he doing?" I ask curiously.

Mrs. Bolt frowns as she says, "Ever since Mr. If On-Lee heard about how you use the Red Cooking Pot as your search engine to your innernet, he has asked Night Suit to build him his own search engine to Daisy that they've called Lazy Daisy, so he can sit on the couch the whole day with Daisy and Lazy Daisy and asks her questions that he's too lazy to find answers to himself. Right now, Night Suit is loading all the knowledge contained in my books into Daisy so he can use Lazy Daisy to find answers. If he succeeds, there will be very few book worms left in DontDoNation."

"That will be sad," I replied, adding, "I can also see how using Lazy Daisy a lot will make your mind lazy. I love the name of the search engine."

Mrs. Bolt tells us to wander around the ES room and enjoy the aroma of the nuts that go into curating the Book Worm, she tells us to play around with the gadgets in the ES room but not to disturb

Night Suit as he is also programming Daisy with data to find the perfect combination of nuts for a new version of Book Worm.

When I ask her why a new version, she replies, "In Nutty Woods, we're constantly experimenting with our Nut Collection. The experimentation never stops. Once in a while, we get a new nut or make an existing nut more potent and all the Miners and Millers will try to use this new nut to improve the power of their Pixie Dust Spice."

After we've tried out most of the gadgets in the ES room, we head for the Cafe and settle down in the comfortable armchairs, helping ourselves to a cold juice flavored with the Book Worm. We study the paintings of famous Millers and Miners who look so serious as they gaze down disapprovingly at us. Another wall is the Wall of Frames, which is covered with pictures and stories of travelers like us who have also been successful in solving their Nut Worth Equation. "One day, our picture and story will hang here," I say.

When we've filled our bellies with juice, we go back to Mrs. Bolt's office and keep bugging her to tell us what the Book Worm is made of and the effect it will have on us.

Unperturbed by our nagging, she whispers, "That's something we'll find out during our SafarE. Before we discuss the secret nut that goes into Book Worm, I would like to present you with a gift." She hands me an old leather-bound book that's titled, *Dummies Guide on How to Solve Nut Worth Equations.*

After we have skimmed through the book, I look up and say, "Thanks a lot, Mrs. Bolt. I never imagined you would have a book for dummies. Are you the editor of the *Oh Landia Herald*?"

"Yes, I am," she replies. "We write the most brilliant articles on our equivalent of the Nut Worth. I will send a copy to the Bungalow every morning."

Mrs. Bolt gives me a thumbs up and continues, "On the SafarE, we'll spend many days in the Library mingling with the Chewers and learn many Cool Moves to strengthen Ex-Factor. My plan is that when you spend time in the Library, we can focus on training these emotional muscles."

She hands Ex-Factor a 4 by 4 Training Plan that has a diagram of Night Suit and a few somber looking Chewers demonstrating how they do Cool Moves to train the emotional muscles to be more Grateful, Humble, Heroic, and Playful and to be less Argumentative, Impatient, Irritated, and Restless.

An hour later when we have tried out a few of these Cool Moves in the ES room, Ex-Factor feels that these Cool Moves will make him stronger. He has two more questions, but Mrs. Bolt says, "Stop, no more questions today, but try out a few of these Cool Moves for the next 30-minutes. After that, please head to Dragon Slayer's mine called The Forest. He's waiting for you at the North entrance of the Forest." She points to her map. "Keep a lookout for the Dragon Slayer there," she says and closes the ES room door behind her in relief.

⌒

The Library is a constant reminder to me that "I have knowledge at my fingertips" and must remember how much I can learn from all the knowledge contained in books, videos, and pictures made by Gold Minds, etc. I have such easy access to these, yet unfortunately, I use them so sparingly. I also learned how authors of children's books have this ability to simplify complex messages and make them easy to grasp using words and pictures. The Library concept changed all this and taught me the importance of freeing up time every day to enjoy consuming valuable knowledge. Today, I focus on finding a select handful of Gold Minds whose wisdom inspires me to become a Smiling Billionaire.

ICE PACK 7

THE FOREST

The Forest is Dragon Slayer's Nut Mine where he mines for nuts that are milled into his Pixie Dust Spice called Pacifier.

Meet
Dragon Slayer

When I was in the Cape of Oh No, for the first time in my life, I experienced severe anxiety. Since then, I haven't suffered anxiety, but as these moments are scary, I needed Cool Moves to train me to counter any future anxiety attacks. After a lot of contemplation, using many of the techniques I had learned to deal with my anxiety, the concept of The Forest led me to create The Dragon Slayer, a fearless warrior who could teach me skills to keep my inner dragon, leeches, and chattering monkeys, the ones that disturb my peace of mind, as far away from me as possible.

~

Dragon Slayer is waiting for us at the entrance of the Forest with his dragon slayer sword. He looks menacing. As he spies us, he lowers his visor, draws us around him, hands us a bag filled with clothes, and says, "As we'll be out in the Forest the rest of the day and as you can never predict the weather here, you may be exposed to heat, damp, rain, scorching sun, cold, strong winds, leeches, monkeys, mosquitoes, dragons, and more, all in one day. These clothes will help protect you from any extreme weather."

I shiver and say, "You mean dragonflies not dragons, right?"

Dragon Slayer, with a stony look, replies, "No, real dragons." He presents me with an ebony stick. "This is a prop to use instead of a Dragon Slayer Sword that will help you slay all the invisible dragons in this forest and later in your life. One day, you may earn the right to inherit my Dragon Slayer Sword."

The Dragon Slayer takes out a map of the forest and traces the route we'll take. "For the next few hours, as we trek through my Nut Mines, we'll learn how to fight dragons and keep blood-sucking leeches and chattering monkeys at bay. The Cool Moves you'll learn from me in the SafarE are about how to build healthy relationships with different personalities. So today, as an appetizer for what is to come, I'll introduce you to unconventional ways to learn to spot the unwanted dragons, leeches, and monkeys by keeping your eyes, nose, and ears open, and your mouth shut."

Nut Cracker shudders. "Book Worms first, now leeches and dragons. Yuck!"

Dragon Slayer shrugs his shoulders at Nut Cracker and leads us into the forest. At the entrance, there is a garden filled with flowers, trees, flowing streams, fountains, and beautifully groomed lawns. As we walk through the garden, we admire the beauty and, unable to stop myself, I splash around in the stream. Time stands still.

When we're ready to move on, The Dragon Slayer points to the horizon above the forest and says that we'll head in that direction. After half an hour, we finally reach the real forest and, before we enter, Dragon Slayer shows us some basic skills in the art of hunting and slaying dragons. As he instructs us on how to hold the Dragon Slayer Sword, he says, "These dragons, even though they blow great balls of fire at people, are sneaky and appear out of nowhere like magic especially when you're lost in thought. So be alert."

Under his direction, we carefully maneuver our way through the dense undergrowth and learn a few tricks about observing signs of a dragon's presence, how to prod the undergrowth and flush them out. When a few imaginary dragons of all shapes and sizes and various fire power appear, he teaches us a few simple sword tricks to fend them off or, when needed, to slay them. .

After this quick introduction to dragon slaying, we walk on toward the top of a hill and slay a handful of them. An hour later, tired but excited at our growing dragon-slaying capabilities, we reach the hilltop and the entrance of the Forest Mill. From here, looking around, we have the most beautiful view of the Forest. The Dragon Slayer opens a gate to the Forest Mill, and as we enter the building, we hear a lot of laughter. We're surprised to see Mrs. Bolt, with her poker face gone for a change, surrounded by a group of jolly workers relaxing after an enjoyable day mining for nuts in the forest.

We're welcomed, ushered in, and handed mugs filled with hot soup. The Dragon Slayer explains that the soup is flavored with his Pixie Dust Spice called Pacifier, made of the most delicate of all nuts gathered in the Forest.

I look at him quizzically. "Delicate nuts? If they're delicate, will they not be consumed or destroyed by the dragons wandering in the Forest?"

Dragon Slayer has answered this question many times. "True, but the dragons cannot consume or destroy the nuts. These nuts are hard on the outside and soft on the inside. The dragons cannot use their firepower to toast them or the weight to crush them, so they cannot enjoy the secret power contained in the heart of the nut. But it's different when the same nuts are brought to one of the Nut Mills. Here, the millers have a method that dissolves the hard shells, and they can extract the delicate flavors that are used to make the Pacifier."

"Wow! This soup has a mouthwatering sensation that's so hard to describe. Why is it called the Pacifier?" I ask curiously.

"Whenever the dragons appear and you feel vulnerable, think of a baby and how much it loves its pacifier. When you suffer from anxiety, your own version of a pacifier may help you to calm down till the anxiety disappears. The pacifier can be like the Dragon Slayer Sword, a smooth stone, or just a piece of cloth that smells nice. Our mantra in the Dragon Mill is 'Beware of both your good and bad thoughts.' The good or bad dragons are symbolic of our good and bad thoughts. Having a few good dragons is great fun and they'll make you smile. They can also help you fend off a few bad dragons. However, despite this, when the bad dragons appear closer in your life, bring out the

Dragon Slayer Sword and practice your dragon fending and slaying skills to reduce the amount of anxiety they bring to your life."

After the soup, we wander around the mill and mingle with the other miners and millers. We find the ES room and it's filled with amazing Dragon Slayer gadgets. We try out many of these gadgets and mimic slaying dragons. We could stay in the Dragon Mill for many more hours, but we have a long way back to the Bungalow and many more dragons to slay before we reach home.

As a parting remark, I ask Dragon Slayer why we didn't see any leeches today.

Dragon Slayer says, "Lift up the legs of your pants." As I do this, to my amazement, I see a number of leeches on my legs happily sucking my blood away.

Dragon Slayer says, "That's the power of the leech. In life, you'll meet people who will suck your blood without you knowing it. You need to learn how to identify them and find ways to get rid of them without them hurting you. Let's leave them on you for now."

We are a bit fidgety when we hear this but Dragon Slayer grins and says, "A leech cannot harm you. Next time, I'll bring a few chattering monkeys on our walks in the forest to irritate you. On the SafarE, we'll spend many days in the Forest and we'll learn many Cool Moves to strengthen Ex-Factor. My plan is that when you spend time in the Forest we can focus on training these emotional muscles."

He hands Ex-Factor a 4 by 4 Training Plan that has a diagram of Dragon Slayer and a bunch of merry Biters in the Forest demonstrating how to do Cool Moves to train the emotional muscles to be more Alert, Confident, Courageous, and Competitive and be less Egoistic, Envious, Greedy, and Guilty. "Till we meet again, under Ex-Factor's guidance try out a few of these Cool Moves, without getting hurt."

Late in the evening, exhausted but happy, we return to our bungalow and are greeted by Mrs. Bolt. "Rest your weary legs. Here's a manual on how to remove the leeches in your life. Sleep in tomorrow but be ready at noon to meet the Nutty Nana at her Mill called Pickle Street."

⌢

To find the smile punch line of the Forest, I spent hours thinking about all the times I suffered from anxiety. The value I got from The Forest is to remember the 90% rule - 90% of what I worry about never happens and helped me appreciate the need for a virtual Dragon Slayer and a Pacifier in my life.

PICKLE STREET

Pickle Street is Nutty Nana's Nut Mill where she mills her nuts that are used to make her Pixie Dust Spice called Raja.

Meet
Nutty Nanna

When I was in the Cape of Oh No, determined to get out of there, my love for cooking played a major role in energizing me, and I realized how a powerful hobby like cooking food from scratch can help me process my thoughts to find solutions to my problems. To make the art of cooking food from scratch a dependable source of smiles in the future, I laid the foundation for Pickle Street that helps me enjoy the variety of flavors that life has to offer me.

"Home is where the curry is, so wherever I may roam, I always want to come back home." Humming these lines, I knock gently on Nutty Nana's door. She welcomes us with a fake frown that changes into a hearty laugh when Nut Cracker blurts out like a love-struck teenager, "How do you stay so glamorous?"

She answers in song, "By being as nutty as I can; that's why they call me Nutty Nana."

She takes us to her cozy garden, and as we sit down, she says, "Today, we'll enjoy discovering my Mill the charming Pickle Street, and you can spend time getting to know your nuts."

"Why is it called Pickle Street?" I ask.

"I'm sure you'll know the answer by the time we come back here. Follow me and get ready to discover the treasures of my mill that I call Pickle Street."

We can smell Pickle Street a mile away. As we get near, we know that we are in for a colorful, aromatic, and sensory experience. When we enter Pickle Street, we're met with rows of stalls with baskets full of spices. It was similar to a farmers' market with a cacophony of sounds, smells, games for the children, shops selling drinks and snacks, and people sitting in the shade, gossiping, snoozing, and playing board games. Shopkeepers and customers sit sipping tea and bargaining over prices. It was a happy atmosphere.

We wander around Pickle Street, and are fascinated by the nuts and spices, pickles, and condiments sold in the stalls. The air is saturated with the intoxicating smells of chili, pepper, oil, vinegar and turmeric and other roasted spices. The roasting spices tickle our noses and make our eyes water. All of us have sneezing and laughing fits, and some of us are worse off than others.

Hard Nose says, "Boy, my nose tickles," with a giggle. "I'll take some spices back to the prim and proper Mrs. Bolt to see if I can get her nose to tickle too. What fun it would be if she has a sneezing fit in her Library. I wonder who will have the guts to say 'Shhhh' to her. This street should have been called 'Tickle Street'," he adds as he starts sneezing uncontrollably.

We poke our noses into as many stalls as we can to chat with the merchants, who are great fans of Nutty Nana and offer us fragrant teas made with the spices that their stalls are famous for. They introduce us to the nuts, share their history, usage, where they're found, how they're mined and milled, and, of course, they try to sell us their wares.

We taste quite a few of the nuts, pickles, and chutneys as well and my mouth is drooling. After many hours wandering around Pickle Street, we have a great introduction to many of the nuts and are beginning to understand the roles many of them could play in shaping our Ex- Factor.

Stuffed, we go back to Nutty Nana's house, and she greets us with a smile. She leads us to her ES room that I consider is the best ES room till now, as it has an outdoor wood fire place. She says that, as a treat, she'll fire up her outdoor wood fire and prepare for us one of my favorite dishes, a 'Mutton Mulligatawny' curry with a dash of her Pixie Dust Spice that she calls Raja.

Watching Nutty Nanna cook was calming. She said that for the next few hours we would just have to hangout and enjoy the aroma as the flavors of ingredients she uses melted into one another. The wait for the curry to get ready was close to torture. Passing Miners, Millers, Biters, and Chewers got a whiff of the aroma, and they came to chat with us about our experiences on the Energy Grid. After a few hours, Nutty Nana tells me to remove the simmering pot from the fire. I do this with care and when the pot has cooled down a bit, we enjoy the most delicious tender mutton and, of course, eat too much. When the meal is done and we've cleared Nutty Nana's kitchen, relaxing on the sofa feeling drowsy, I ask Nutty Nana what her Raja means.

Nutty Nana replies, "Raja is the equivalent of King in Hindi. I call it Raja to remind people that they should treat themselves once in a while like kings and queens."

I nod to agree with her, and she says, "One way to treat ourselves like kings and queens is to give ourselves all the time in the world to enjoy a tasty curry cooked from scratch as often as possible."

With our stomachs full, as we gaze into the fire, Nutty Nana starts telling us about her other passion of being a sit-down comic.

"What is a sit-down comic?" I ask.

Nutty Nana smiles, "I'm too old to stand-up and be a comic, but will never be too old to sit-down for hours and be a comic."

She brings out her computer and shows us her streaming channel called "The Voice of Oh Landia" where, as she teaches young Biters and Chewers and other citizens of Oh Landia the art of living life like a Raja, she reels off one funny joke after another.

After we binge watch a few episodes that are shot in her kitchen and garden, I can see we are in the presence of not only a Gold Mind but also a natural comedian who can take complex words of wisdom and wrap them into a powerful comedy vitamin pill for all age groups. "This is an art worth learning from Nutty Nana!" I say out loud.

As we near the end of our visit, Nutty Nanna says, "On the SafarE, we'll spend many days in Pickle Street and we'll learn many Cool Moves to strengthen Ex-Factor. My plan is that while you spend time in Pickle Street, we can focus on training these emotional muscles."

She hands Ex-Factor a 4 by 4 Training Plan that has the merchants of Pickle Street demonstrating how they do Cool Moves to train their emotional muscles to be more Competitive, Enthusiastic, Friendly, and Funny and be less Chaotic, Forgetful, Frustrated, and Lethargic. As she douses the wood fire with water, she signs off, "Till we meet again, try out a few of these Cool Moves without burning your kitchen down."

When the sun has set, after cooking and eating to our heart's content, we have to take a long roundabout walk on our way home to digest the Mutton Mulligatawny curry. When we reach the bungalow, Mrs. Bolt has pinned a note on our door that says we must be at Acrobat's Mine, the Obstacle Course, at 10 o'clock tomorrow morning.

$$\backsim$$

To find the smile punch line of Pickle Street, I spent hours thinking about how I can engage all my senses to help me discover how to appreciate the beauty of the world that I've been blind to for so many years. The simple solution was to cook more exotic foods that use exotic spices that taste, smell, and feel differently from what I'm used to.

ICE PACK 9

THE OBSTACLE COURSE

The Obstacle Course is Acrobat's Nut Mine where she mines for nuts that are milled to Pixie Dust Spice called Enjoy.

Meet
Acrobat

When I was crawling my way out of Cape of Oh No, I learned that I needed to improve my mind and body coordination, as this would help me amplify or calm my fine and rough qualities, particularly those that are inherent to my brand of ADHD. Instead of spending sums of money on gadgets, I chose the motto of "the best things in life are often free" and the concept of The Obstacle Course took root here. It inspired me to find simple and affordable ways to improve my mind and body coordination. As I felt I was crawling like a baby out of Cape of Oh No, I mimicked the movements of a baby learning to crawl, walk and run and found many stimulating mind and body coordination exercises in the recreational areas in my neighborhood.

～

Being sporty, I look forward to the Obstacle Course. We spot the Acrobat and a number of Biters doing stretching exercises. She waves and runs toward us, and as she approaches, does a somersault, then swirls on her toes and, with a perfect bow and radiant smile, says, "Hi! Let's hit the dirt, follow my cue." To help warm up my aching joints and activate Team Perspiration, we follow her doing stretching exercises.

When we're warmed up, the Acrobat presents me with a black blindfold with the words, "Know your obstacles, Focus on things that excite you, Dissolve the things that frustrate you."

I try on the blindfold and ask, "What does dissolve the things that frustrate you mean?"

"Well, that's what we'll find out today; let's start to get to know your obstacles."

We follow the Acrobat to the Obstacle Course, and she tells us, "Today on, I'll teach you a few basic moves to coordinate your mind and body movements."

Looking each of us in the eye, she continues, "Be prepared for a few aches and pains and don't be afraid to shout with joy, smile, and grimace as you fall down and get dirty. Remember the word 'Try' as Colonel Cocktail mentioned when he spoke about Mindset. Irrespective of your individual ability to maneuver an obstacle, try your best to contribute to the team getting past this obstacle. No matter how much you may be suffering, try your best and join the others in the team as they run, jump, and crawl over the obstacles."

I'm delighted when I hear this. "Wow, this sounds like fun."

When we reach the course, we're thrilled when we see the variety of obstacles we'll have to climb over, crawl under, balance, hang from, jump into pools of muddy water, walk across ropes and nets, and a lot of other fun stuff.

When we've walked around the course a bit to acquaint ourselves, Acrobat says, "The Cool Moves I've planned for today are to give you a preview of what you'll experience on the SafarE. The end in mind for today is to get a feel for how much we must learn to trust each other and get to know each other's skills, capabilities, strengths, and weaknesses. The Course has 10 obstacles. Today, we'll only practice enough to get familiar with the obstacles. Please don't try to break any records or bones. To start, Kiran and Worried Eyes will navigate the course alone, and identify any obstacle that he cannot overcome by himself. After he's confident, he can navigate the course, to make things a bit more difficult, we'll blindfold him and Worried Eyes. Then the rest of you will guide Kiran to navigate the obstacle course without breaking any bones."

We loved the plan. Worried Eyes and I make my first attempt to cross the obstacle course, while the others get their bearings, familiarize themselves with the layout of the obstacle course, agree on roles, responsibilities, and commands and stop signals so they can give me instructions about what I need to follow to complete the course.

When we're ready, Acrobat says, "By the end of today, Kiran will have found new muscles he never knew existed, but you all will also learn how, as a team, you can train your emotional muscles on the Obstacle Course."

Impatient to get started, I shout, "I'm ready. Please let me survive the Obstacle Course without landing up in the Emergency Room."

Nut Cracker seems to have been appointed as my guide and nervously says, "We've got your back; don't fret. We'll guide you across the course."

Nut Cracker then briefs me on the commands he'll use to help guide me across the course. He says the most important command is when he shouts STOP! I should stop at once. This is because I'm about to get into a tricky situation trying to overcome the obstacle. When I have stopped, we will regroup, take a status update, and agree on what needs to be done to continue on the course.

With that, the Acrobat blindfolds me, gives me a spin and when I stand still, Nut Cracker hops on my shoulder and starts screeching instructions, trying to guide me to navigate the Obstacle Course. Not yet trusting Nut Cracker's instructions completely, I stick out my hands and feet and use them as sensors to detect if I'm about to walk into flower beds, or bang into benches, garbage bins, and bushes. Nut Cracker's instructions often hardly make sense and after what seems to be a few minutes, I try to ignore them. I'm soon walking into several obstacles, and Nut Cracker falls off my shoulders quite often. With each bang and bump, I say, "Ouch!"

Soon, I've fallen a few times; I'm dirty and scream a few expletives at Nut Cracker for not guiding me properly.

Later, we all get mad at each other. After a few minutes, we're all bickering. With no instructions, I wander off on my own, get confused and dizzy and feel like I'm walking around in circles. Nut Cracker senses my panic and admits to himself that he's not the best person to guide me across the obstacle course. In all humility he shouts, "Stop!"

I'm relieved to hear this command, stop at once, and pull off my blindfolds. As I take in the scene around me, I can see I have hardly walked a few meters from where I started though it felt like miles.

When we all have our breath back, Nut Cracker says, "P Leader please take over and give Kiran instructions he should follow to complete the course."

P Leader accepts the role and says, "Let's gather together team." P Leader gives us a clear goal and assigns clear roles and responsibilities to each of the team. He then starts issuing instructions for me to follow.

With P Leader issuing instructions in a calm voice, a few bumps and bruises later, I get better at avoiding the obstacles, and I start to trust his instructions. Soon, I'm in the flow, as P Leader guides me to climb over, crawl under, balance on wooden beams, hang and move across bars, jump into and across pools of muddy water, walk on tightropes, and cross nets.

Finally, I hear him say, "Stop!" Reluctantly I stop and pull my blindfolds off. These last few minutes have been an exhilarating experience. We're excited by the challenge and enjoy learning how to get my mind and body to work together.

My confidence in P Leader's ability to work with his team to guide me across the obstacle course was now boosted. So, I readily agree with the team, when they say that, to make things tougher, I should start traversing the obstacle course backwards. We now have quite a sizable audience of Biters staring at us in amazement and cheering us on. The Acrobat knows we're not following her instructions only to practice so as to get familiar with the obstacles without breaking any records or bones. But, as she sees we're having fun and not doing anything dangerous, she chooses not to say anything. Instead, she gives P Leader the thumbs up to continue.

Soon, I'm blindfolded and even though navigating the obstacle course walking backwards is scary, I trust P Leader's instructions. We're now working well as a team and navigate the obstacle course with ease. P Leader says, "Stop!" I do so at once, pulling off the blindfold to see that the whole team and the audience of Biters is full of smiles. The Acrobat asks us to gather around her. Tired and with my body sore from all the bangs, but exhilarated with the fresh air and exercise, the Acrobat leads us into the Obstacle Mill and, in the ES room, which is a virtual version of some of the most complex obstacles we know in DontDoNation, she serves us ice-cold lime juice.

When we're refreshed, she tells us, "Enjoy the ES room and try to simulate a few of the obstacles you'll face in DontDoNation. All the bumps, bruises, aches, pains, running, walking, sweating, cheering, ups, and downs you faced today are part of life. At my Mine, I have both a mantra and a Pixie Dust Spice. Our mantra is Figure It Out, and my Pixie Dust Spice that I've added in the lime soda that adds an extra fizz to it is called Enjoy. The Figure It Out helps you to remember that as a Miner you'll fall flat on your back many times, even as you learn to mine a world full of opportunities and discover new solutions to problems. As your abilities to mine improve, you'll gain confidence to succeed in mining and, gradually, you'll keep wanting to push the boundaries of your limitations. The best analogy I have for this is the desire you find to progress from excelling in Flyweight to Middleweight and finally Heavyweight Cool Moves."

Nut Cracker, the curious one, asks, "Why have you called the Pixie Dust Spice - Enjoy?"

"Well, did you not all enjoy yourself today? Enjoy is a really worthwhile investment that gives you a great return by making you aware that there are three sources of smiles and grimaces."

My curiosity perks up when I hear these words: "Three sources, what are they?"

Acrobat takes us to the window and, pointing at the obstacle course, says, "As you smiled and grimaced today, you experienced the three sources of smiles and grimaces. The first source that comes from within you is one that you can control by your thoughts and actions. The second is the smiles and grimaces you enjoy with your team or others whose lives you touch, for example the audience today. You may be able, through your thoughts and actions, to convert a few of these grimaces into smiles. What you get from these sources will depend on how you react to others' thoughts and actions. The third is the smiles and grimaces from the surroundings in which you live, like nature, that you have no control over. In this particular case it was the obstacle course, where you were all enjoying the pleasures and challenges of a carefree outdoor life. How are you feeling, Kiran?"

I reply with a big smile, "Wow the three sources of smiles and grimaces make sense. I can now recognize all of them. I'm feeling great, and I did have fun. I smiled a lot and grimaced a lot even though I'm hurting badly. Thankfully, I have no broken bones or bad bruises that will leave a scar for life. I think it was great for us to learn how we could pool all our talents together to guide me across the course. It's been a good introduction to prepare us to train for the obstacles ahead."

Acrobat agrees. "Even though you were angry with each other, you learned to listen and to trust each other's instincts. You learned simple problem solving and conflict resolution skills that got you through the Obstacle Course. I think you now know what I meant by: Focus on things that excite you; Dissolve the things that frustrate you. Remember, as a team, to be like Velcro. Stick together at all times."

"That's so true," I say. "A fun fact is that the Obstacle Course today was a master class in - The best things in life are free."

Acrobat says, "I cannot agree with you more. The Obstacle Course experiences of today are going to pioneer several more Cool Moves that will make us play and smile till our guts hurt."

I thank Acrobat and say, "Today, I felt I was the most authentic version of myself. I also learned that if I have a training coach who understands my strengths and limitations while guiding me, I can push myself outside my comfort zone to try Cool Moves to crawl up my mythical Extrapreneur Ladder, which seems to be becoming more and more of an Obstacle Course."

Acrobat was happy with our performance at the course. "On the SafarE, we'll spend many days on the Obstacle Course, and we'll learn many Cool Moves to strengthen Ex-Factor. My plan is that when you spend time on the Obstacle Course, we can focus on training these emotional muscles."

She hands Ex-Factor a 4 by 4 Training Plan that has a diagram of her and a bunch of Biters profusely sweating while demonstrating how they do Cool Moves to train their emotional muscles to be more Confident, Courageous, Competitive, and Enthusiastic and be less Aggressive, Helpless, Impatient, and Frustrated. We try out a few Cool Moves, and though they're hard, Ex-Factor feels that these will make him stronger.

With that Acrobat says, "Do try a few Cool Moves and please don't break any bones or sprain any muscles. Please be ready at 10 o'clock tomorrow morning when Mr. If On-Lee will be taking you to meet an old friend of yours at his mine, The Experiment."

"And old friend? Who is this?" I ask.

Acrobat smiles and says, "You'll be surprised."

To find the smile punch line of the Obstacle Course, I spent hours practicing how to navigate the most severe obstacles I faced in my life when I was going through periods of anxiety and depression in Cape of Oh No. Even today, I still simulate practice navigating on my obstacle course whenever I feel a bad case of SAD and FONGES coming my way.

ICE PACK 10

THE EXPERIMENT

The Experiment is Mr. If On-Lee's Nut Mine where he mines for nuts that are milled into his Pixie Dust Spice called No Expectations.

Meet
Mr. If Only - Lee

The concept of The Experiment is another way for me to use a daily activity as a source of smiles. A simple way to do this was to find an activity that I had to do every day and use it as an experiment to work in a structured manner to study my Oh No Emotions and convert them into Oh Yes Emotions. I decided to do this by using the time spent with our family cocker spaniel Charlie, who I had to walk with every day whether I liked it or not in all weather conditions, morning, afternoon, and night.

When Mr. If On-Lee rings the doorbell, I'm delighted to see our dog Charlie, my 14-year-old golden cocker spaniel. Charlie sports a vest with the phrase, "Can you control this bundle of energy?"

Charlie is happy when he sees me. Many licks and barks later, Mr. If On-Lee hands me Charlie's chain. "Kiran, walking a dog is an interactive way to deal with all your emotions in real time. The energy you get walking Charlie is as good as any of the nuts you can find in Nutty Woods. Tell me a bit about your relationship with Charlie?"

"Well, I have a love-hate relationship with Charlie. Charlie is my best friend and I've walked ahead of Charlie for more than 15,000 kilometers."

"Walked ahead? How?"

"Yes, when we go on our walks together, I walk ahead, and Charlie follows reluctantly. For most of these 15,000 kilometers, I've been trying to make Charlie walk at my rhythm, which reflects the mood I'm in. But it seems like Charlie has his own agenda, as he stops and sniffs and marks his territory as often as he can and does what we call "reading the neighborhood newspaper." The slower Charlie walks, the more frustrated and impatient I get to return home and I pull and pull and swear at Charlie to "give back to nature what he has consumed" so we can get this walk over and done with. Over time, the walks became more of a duty for me than an enjoyment for both of us."

Mr. If On-Lee understands my dilemma. "I can see why Mrs. Bolt asked me to help you out. Walking Charlie seems to have given you both a classic case of "If only you do this and not that, we can enjoy our walks together." Let's see how we can bring back the fun of going for a walk with Charlie. Learning how to guide somebody who loves you unconditionally is a very rewarding experience. It's also an effective way to learn to have fun together as you draw on each other's positive energy. Let's walk Charlie together and start with observing a few ways to improve your verbal and nonverbal communication skills that can be useful to bring back Oh into your life."

We set off for a walk and are soon walking through the colorful streets of Nutty Woods. Mr. If On-Lee tells us, "The first thing we should do as we experiment with your emotions walking Charlie, is to have no expectations about what to expect during the walk. A way to do this is to start the walk with this mindset: 'This is Charlie's time. Let him enjoy it'."

We agree on this mindset, let Charlie lead the way, and follow. Easier said than done. Charlie chases after whatever attracts him, and, much to my discomfort, I take a back seat and follow him. He pulls on the chain so strongly that he almost wrenches my shoulders out of their sockets. But after his initial enthusiasm burns out, he calms down and settles into a gentle walking and sniffing rhythm.

Mr. If On-Lee tells us to observe how Charlie uses his five senses. This was great advice and I enjoy observing what catches his eye, what smells excite him, what noises catch his ears, what he chews on, or how he licks a friendly neighbor's hand. I also enjoy watching how he reacts to dogs he likes or dislikes. I realize that I too, am like Charlie. If he needs a variety of sights, sounds, smells, and tastes to keep his Cocker Spaniel instincts sharp, I too need similar things to keep my natural instincts sharp.

Mr. If On-Lee says, "Let's head for The Experiment to observe how Charlie reacts in various scenarios, we'll walk a couple of routes in the mine so he can familiarize himself with smells on these routes."

After an hour's walk, during which we try three different routes, we reach Mr. If On-Lee's plush headquarters and put our legs up for a bit. I'm irritated with Charlie for all his pulling that has almost wrenched my arm out of its socket, and Charlie is panting from all the walking and barking. Mr. If On-Lee tells me to relax and, after we and Charlie are refreshed, he says, "Let's go walking again. The compound is full of Biters going about their daily chores. This is a perfect place to let Charlie exercise his cocker spaniel instincts. Let's take him for a walk around the headquarters' gardens."

We set off to walk, and I observe Charlie taking in all the new smells. His tail is like a windmill every time a Biter comes and pets him. Charlie thinks they smell wonderful and licks them with great enthusiasm.

We complete a round and when we come back to the place we started from, we venture on a new walk. We let Charlie lead, and after doing a few rounds, he always seems to head in the direction from where he sees and hears the most action or the loveliest smell. "This is so much like me," I comment with a sheepish smile.

At the end of an hour, I can take no more of walking after Charlie. Mr. If-On-Lee too seems exhausted. As we head back to the head-quarters, he asks me to share my experiences. I admit, "The time at the Experiment walking Charlie has been educational. The concept of a frequent Charlie Time Walk is powerful. If I learn to set off on these walks with no expectations, I can take a backseat. If I can do this, I'll learn to be more patient with him and can convert most of my grimaces into a few smiles. I have to just let him lead the way."

The rest of the team agrees with my observations, and we head back to the Mill for lunch.

After a nice lunch and cup of herbal tea, Mr. If On-Lee leads us to the ES room that's filled with all sorts of crazy gadgets.

"What are these gadgets?" Spark Plug asks and with a sheepish smile.

Mr. If On-Lee replies, "One of them can change the world, but I'm too lazy to take any of these experiments and convert them into a tool that can help make a difference to the world. Anyway, today is not about me, but you. The reason I chose a dog for our induction today was - the life of a dog is pretty straightforward. Eat, play, sleep, fight a bit, and sniff a lot. They're faithful friends and show us how to make new friends and find ways to protect us from danger. They're a great example for us, they inspire us to focus on what's entertaining them here and now. When you have a grimace that you cannot bear, or a problem you cannot solve, just spend a few hours enjoying Charlie Time; let yourself be curious and sniff out new opportunities, as there may be a mine of smiles just waiting to be discovered around the corner."

These were very wise words from Mr. If On-Lee.

I realize after today's experience, that to learn to take a back seat is hard as it goes against my natural instinct to be in control. I start worrying whether I have the ability to take a backseat in many activities in life that engage me.

To cover up my worry, I say, "I get what you're trying to say. What's your Pixie Dust Spice?"

Mr. If On-Lee replies, "It has a strange name, but I call it "No Expectations." In many trivial situations in life, having No Expectations is a really good starting point to learn how to manage your own expectations and those of others too. No Expectations helps you create, own, and be in control of your own stories. If you have lofty expectations and cannot live up to them, you'll be disappointed, burdened by what you call the SAD. If you have No Expectations but always do your best, you'll always overachieve. No Expectations is a major source of smiles."

"Wow, that's a unique way to think about the path to achievements. I definitely learned a lot more about mindset and leadership today. I love Charlie Time and think, in the future, I can also have Nut Cracker Time, Spark Plug Time, and P Leader Time, so I can learn to enjoy their company too."

Mr. If On-Lee appreciated my insights into the experience he arranged for us today. To round off the day, he continues, "On the SafarE, we'll spend many days at the Experiment and we'll learn many Cool Moves to strengthen Ex-Factor. My plan is that when you spend time at the Experiment, we can focus on training these emotional muscles."

He hands Ex-Factor a 4 by 4 Training Plan that has a caricature of Charlie demonstrating how he does Cool Moves to train his emotional muscles to be more Enthusiastic, Energetic, Friendly, Heroic and be less Aggressive, Argumentative, Chaotic, and Helpless.

To bring our stay at the Experiment to a close, we are overjoyed when Mr. If On-Lee says, "Hang around for a while and try out my gadgets. Try to invent some cool gadgets yourself. I'm going to close my eyes for a few minutes."

We walk around Mr. If On-Lee's lab and all of us try out his half-completed experiments. In a while, the ES room is filled with commotion that switches between laughs, screams, flashing lights, and more. Ex-Factor bears the brunt of all this commotion but feels that these Cool Moves will make him stronger.

We are enjoying ourselves so much that our faces fall when Mr. If On-Lee says, "Let's conclude; we all had a cool day today, including Charlie who seems to be the most exhausted of all of us. Tomorrow, you'll visit Spam Fighter at his amazing Mine called the Space Center. Get ready to learn about flying objects tomorrow."

To find the smile punch line of The Experiment, I reflected on the hours I've spent walking Charlie and trying to control him. This was an almost impossible task. Nowadays, as he gets older, and his five senses lose their sharpness almost every week, I really have to be patient with him, respect his aging faculties, and walk at his pace so that we both spend quality time when we're together.

ICE PACK 11

SPACE CENTER

The Space Center is Spam Fighter's Nut Mine where he builds Spam Filters, his equivalent of a Pixie Dust that when you use wisely in an online world, makes your life more secure.

Meet
Spam Fighter

One of the areas that I knew was key to stirring up my Oh No Emotions, was the amount of time I spent online consuming information from social media, digital newspapers, watching the news on television, and more. I knew that most of this information was spam that I had to learn to manage to bring Oh back into my life. Once again, the 'best things in life are free' motto came to my rescue and I saw the concept of the Space Center as an analogy for my own custom designed personal spam filter. It should let in only the most relevant information that would help me keep abreast of world events and ensure that the focus on bringing Oh back into my life was rekindled.

⤳

As I walk into the Space Center, I can see a space warrior with a remote control looking up and controlling what seems to be an Unidentified Flying Object (UFO).

He spies us, walks toward us, and, without a warning, hands over the controls of the UFO to me, and, with a thumbs up, opens a soft drink and sits down to watch the fun.

With a fancy-looking remote control winking at me clasped in my butter fingers and with the Ales all excited by the gadget trying to be my guides, I try to get the UFO under control.

With no idea how to use the remote control, and with each one of the Ales shouting brilliant ideas on what to do, chaos reigns supreme. The UFO develops a life of its own and, with a loud bang, crashes into a tree nearby.

Horrified at what we've just done, we immediately play a blame game among ourselves. The space warrior walks toward us, lowers his face mask, and, to our embarrassment, we see it's Spam Fighter. He tells us that we just destroyed his gift to us, and, with it, goes all he has planned for us today, which was just hanging out and enjoying the experience of flying the UFO.

Our disappointment is obvious. Spam Fighter pats us on the back, and hands us his program for what we'll experience in the Space Center. We read the program and are astounded by the activities he has planned for us. We have lots of why and what questions on how to perform these activities. A patient Spam Fighter listens to them, doesn't answer them, and when we see we won't get answers from him, assures us that when we leave the Space Center today, we'll have answers to our questions. Putting on his glasses, Spam Fighter lets us start with the first activity of the day and introduces us to the Oh Landia Space Program that builds space objects, a few of which we'll try to fly today.

He says, "When you're involved in flying drones, UFOs, planes, spaceships, and more, you easily remember the three sources of smiles and grimaces that Acrobat told you about: those that that come from within you and which you can control, those that come from sources external to you from your team or the lives you touch, and those from the surrounding in which you live like nature or, in this case, the airspace above us."

"In the Space Center," he continues, "we use the terms for the three sources a bit differently. We describe the elements you're in contact with as you fly one of our space objects as natural, unnatural, and supernatural elements. Many of these elements are in your control, but some are not in your hands. To master how these elements impact your flying abilities, let's go to the ES room . I've chosen a Cool Move to show you how flying a space object, like dealing with your emotions, is a complicated process with many moving parts. Today, building on your introduction from the other Mines and Mills, I'll use futuristic technology to challenge your smiles and grimaces and your team-building skills."

I'm thrilled that, finally, we'll get our hands on some futuristic technology and look forward to flying a UFO.

Spam Fighter brings out a bag that's full of odds and ends and says, "Let's get back to basics and build and learn to fly a kite before we move on to flying the UFO."

Everybody's face drops when they see they'll be building a plastic kite and not a UFO. After a while, when I realize that he's testing us, to pep up my team, I tell Spam Fighter, "I'm excited at the prospect of flying a kite, it was one of the most exhilarating experiences I had as a child."

Spam Fighter appreciates my effort to get the team spirit up and asks, "What did you do, Kiran?"

I light up as I describe how my best friends and I built many kites using odds and ends together. When we flew the kite, we all had our roles and responsibilities on what to do to get the kite airborne, keep it airborne, and as we did not have much money to buy another kite, we focused on bringing it back safely so it could live to fly another day. We participated in kite flying competitions and each of us knew our role and responsibility as we tried to win each fight. Because I could run fast and wasn't afraid of getting into a fight, my role was to hold the kite as the flier got it into the air, and then to standby to run after a kite when the thread was cut by another kite, and as it drifted away to freedom, to fight with others chasing the kite to claim the kite for my team."

Spam Fighter loved my story, gave us the *How to Build a Kite* manual, and asked us to build the kite together.

At first glance, it seemed easy, but in a matter of minutes, we were all frustrated, as nobody was following the instructions, and instead were clowning around with some even holding the instruction manual upside down just to see how a kite would look if it flew upside down.

Spam Fighter watched in amusement as we swore and fought with each other to build the kite. When we finally made it, it looked all wrong.

My rough quality of never being able to follow instructions was being exposed while trying to assemble this simple kite. After a lot of arguments, we dismantled the kite and reassembled it. Even though we used all the pieces it looked nothing like the picture of the kite on the box. I joked, "Looks like we've built a designer kite."

We were demotivated and ready to throw in the towel, and Spark Plug, the wheeler dealer, said, "Let's buy a kite instead."

Spam Fighter laughed so loudly when he heard this that we all felt stupid. He lectured us on how building a kite will teach us the importance of following instructions and being diligent in finishing a task, however easy or boring it may seem.

He then took over the role of helping us build a kite. He brought out a new kite set, and appointed P Leader as our guide. P Leader read the instructions, clarified a few questions with Spam Fighter and in a matter of minutes he gave us our individual roles and soon had us all deeply engrossed in building the kite. Now that we were working to our strengths, it took us just a few minutes. We had assembled a colorful kite with a long tail that looked exactly like the one on the box cover. We attached the 50 meters of thread to the kite, and it was ready to be flown.

We were all excited at our handwork and ready to fly the kite. Off to the beach we went. It was a nice windy day, and without much hassle, the kite was airborne. It was an uplifting experience, and I was the epitome of happiness. To spice up things, I tried to steer the kite toward the seagulls flying curiously around it. We were thrilled as the kite flew higher and higher in the sky and we enjoyed its dance with the changing winds. Soon, our 50 meters of thread was all used. We settled down and enjoyed watching the kite dance merrily in the sky.

With the basics of kite building and flying in place, Spam Fighter showed us tricks on how to make the kite dance. Soon, with each of us shouting out what to do, the kite was one minute doing the tango, the next minute a Punjabi bhangra dance, and then, suddenly, it could dive like a seagull. Spam Fighter also showed us the technique to stabilize the kite as the direction of the wind suddenly changed. After a while, when we were in control of the kite, Spam Fighter went back to the Space Center and left us to enjoy flying the kite on our own.

Our enthusiasm, clumsiness, and uncoordinated hand and body movements soon took over and my legs got entangled in the thread. In a few seconds, the kite found a will of its own. We lost control of the kite, and it was soon on its way to freedom. We ran after the kite and when we got it back, fortunately, there was only minimal damage that we could quickly fix, and the kite was airborne again. After enjoying this wonderful experience for a few more hours, we landed the kite and returned to the Space Center.

The Spam Fighter tells us that he wants the kite packed as perfectly as possible so he can return it to the owner. This is an impossible task for someone like me who has been untidy and messy his whole life. With our newfound patience and a fair amount of dexterity under P Leader's guidance, we manage to dismantle the kite. As there are a lot of knots in the kite line, we have to remove them. After a generous use of expletives, we're finally done and quite happy with the team effort to pack the kite back into the box.

Before we move on to the next activity of the day, Spam Fighter asks me what I've learned from flying a kite.

I think for a while and reply, "I learned how a delicate kite in perfect weather conditions and in the hands of a skilled flyer is a graceful object. But, in a split second when weather conditions become tough, it becomes an uncontrollable monster. This reflection is true on so many levels of how my emotions can change rather suddenly."

Spam Fighter appreciates my answer.

I'm curious to move on with the next activity and softly murmur, "We now have the art of kite flying under our belt. What's next on the program?"

Spam Fighter says, "You're in for a treat. I'm also responsible for a program called Cyber Insecurity that focuses on preventing the Space Center from being bombarded by spam from outer space."

"How?" I ask.

"Every second of the day, we're bombarded with useless information or spam from cyberspace that percolates into our lives and leaves us mentally exhausted. We waste so much energy on fighting spam that it takes away the focus on our leading role of developing the Space Program, which is to find a new source of nuts in outer space."

I comment, "The Cyber Insecurity Program sounds so much like my challenges in dealing with the spam I have in my life and how it impacts my emotions."

Spam Fighter nods and continues, "I know that. Dr. Eye Can has briefed me on the problems you have dealing with the loads of spam that invades your life. He also told me about how, as a result, you have been forced to go on Social media and Communication diets to deal with it. I am happy to hear that these diets work and have helped and the effect is now you have simple spam filters to help you grimace less. I know a lot about spam and have specialized in how to deal with it. I look forward to showing you my own ingenious spam filter. I was forced to develop it to keep out as much spam from my life and now it helps others to. But before I gift it to you, the motto of the Cyber Insecurity program is 'Cut the Crap.'"

He hands me an elegant black leather folder with a gold belt to secure it. I carefully open the buckle and read aloud what's written in the most elegant handwriting on the brochure:

Welcome to your spam filter
Learn to tackle your Cyber Insecurity
Spam is ruthless. Destroy it.

After we browse through the brochure and find out that using the spam filter will help me go on an Information Ration, Nut Cracker chips in: "Oops! Going on an Information Ration is a 'mission impossible' for Kiran."

"Why?" asks Spam Fighter.

Nut Cracker looks at me and says, "For Kiran, nerding with information is on par with love for Cooking, Eating, and Smiling. Kiran has a huge information appetite and can, with ease, consume enormous amounts of information for his own knowledge and entertainment. I call him an 'Information Decorator,' since, like his designer cooking skills, he can take a simple piece of information and to irritate his loved one he can spice it up with the most absurd facts to create the most incredulous stories."

"My spam filter will help him go on an Information Ration," says Spam Fighter.

I look angrily at Nut Cracker for his hurtful comments. Casting a worried glance at Spam Fighter, I say, "I've learned a lot from Dr. Eye Can over the last few months, to smile more and grimace less, but going on an Information Ration, as Nut Cracker says, could be mission impossible for me."

Spam Fighter, eager to ease the growing tension in the air, says, "Have no fear, Spam Fighter is here. Let's go back to the ES room. Follow me."

We follow Spam Fighter into the ES room but, this time, into a new area that he tells us is a Space Center Training room. As we enter, we're met with a blur of whizzing noises, loud chatter, and blinking lights. We see several youngsters busy working on computers, wearing strange-looking glasses, testing flying drones, and engrossed in more high-tech stuff.

"This is a training center for my Biting Apprentices, whom I prefer to call space warrior apprentices and we're getting them ready for the next generation of skills that will be of great value in the Space Center. The apprentices are very intelligent, and quite a few have the ability to dream about the future in a way that many of us can never imagine. Night Suit, whom you met in the Library, has graduated from our training center."

He leads us back to the ES room and tells us to enjoy playing around with the gadgets and pointing to a bowl says, "Have your fill of The Space Center's cookies. They taste awful, as I don't mill any spices here that can make them taste better. We build Spam Filters here. If they are used like Pixie Dust when you're online, they will make your insecure life in cyberspace more secure."

While the others get immersed in playing Space Warriors, I apprehensively fiddle with the Spam Filter folder. The manual is about 50 pages. It looks similar to a "Lose something or the other in 21 days" self-help book. There's no way I'm going to read the manual and assemble the Spam Filter.

Spam Fighter comes up to me and says, "Kiran, relax. The Spam Filter will make your life easier. Also, remember, when you assemble your own Spam Filter, while you must pay attention to the instruction manual, unlike in the kite instruction manual, you don't have to follow the instructions to the letter. Instead of reading through pages and pages of the manual, Nutty Nana has made a 4-minute "How to build your spam filter" video. The link to the video can be found at the end of the manual. We've designed our Spam Filter with different spam filter levels. So, you can adjust them and choose what's best to protect you from the sources of the spam that is causing you to grimace or smile at any particular moment in time."

I'm relieved to hear these words after our dreadful kite-assembling episode. I locate the video link, and am happy to see that there are a few tips from satisfied Spam Filter users that are worth their weight in gold for us. I read them aloud:

'Information Ration
- Do not read any digital content for the first few hours after you get up.
- Ruthlessly reduce the amount of time spent on reading and watching news.
- Drastically cut down time spent trawling the internet, searching and reading trivial content.
- Keep away from social media.
- Keep your mobile phone and computer far away as often as you can.'

"Well," I comment, "Starting the Information Ration is going to be really tough. But I do see it has many benefits."

Looking my pixies, who have now gathered around me, in the eye, I say, "I'll need all your help to succeed in this Information Ration."

Spam Fighter says, "The building of the kite shows there's much to learn as a team. I'm sure you can go on an Information Ration and become a huge fan of it soon."

To bring an enjoyable day to an end, he continues, "On the SafarE, we'll spend many days at the Space Center and learn many Cool Moves to strengthen Ex-Factor. My plan is that when you spend time here, we can focus on training these emotional muscles."

He hands Ex-Factor a 4 by 4 Training Plan that has a diagram of space warriors demonstrating how they do Cool Moves to train their emotional muscles to be more Alert, Focused, Humble, and Thoughtful and be less Argumentative, Chaotic, Egoistic, and Restless. "I'll include you in the Space Training Program where we can nerd with a lot of cool cyber stuff and try out Information Ration to see if they can help strengthen your Ex-factor," he reassures me.

I smile as I say, "The days at the Space Center are going to be the best days of the SafarE."

I thank Spam Fighter for an awesome day. "I think the Spam Filter gift is great, but we need to get back to DontDoNation and try it out. I think I understood what it should be used for. I think that with the Spam Filter, going on an Information Ration shouldn't be so difficult now."

After a lovely day, exchanging our experiences, we walk back to the bungalow. On our fridge is a note from Mrs. Bolt, "Hope you enjoyed the Induction Program. Tomorrow at 9 am, we'll meet at the Bored Room and start planning the next program of the SafarE that's called Fragile UnDevelopment."

⌒

To find the smile punch line of The Space Center, I reflected on the number of months I had spent trying to figure out how to reduce the flow of information that was cluttering my life. A rigid Information Ration freed up so much of my time and got rid of a lot of leeches and chattering monkeys. I could spend this time saved on meaningful activities like absorbing knowledge from the Gold Minds that inspire me to bring Oh back into my life.

CHAPTER 11

ONE FRAGILE VAS

After a year on my odyssey, I was not only reenergized, but also the proud owner of a roadmap filled with stories, concepts, and toys, as well as Cool Moves to learn and Uncool Moves to unlearn. I was well on my way to Cape of Oh but seemed to have no clear directions on how to reach there.

Every day, it became more apparent that the path to Cape Oh wasn't linear or straightforward. I realized that during my journey, I would meet and have to tackle a plethora of challenges linked to my imperfect qualities. I worried about these challenges, as I knew that a few of them had the potential to disrupt my life in much the same way that the Hurricane that captured Oh a few years ago had done. To ensure that I remained committed to the chosen path, I realized it was very important for me to have a toy by my side throughout my odyssey. A toy that would help me remember how fragile I was in Cape of Oh No, how complex and chaotic my life could get, but one that at the same time would spur me on to smile more and grimace less so I never return to Cape of Oh No again.

CONCEPT 16

ONE AGILE VAS

At 9 am sharp, we knock on the door of Nut Quarters. Mrs. Bolt opens the door and offers us masala tea. We take the tea to the Bored Room where Team Inspiration is seated, and after exchanging pleasantries, we're ready to get our hands dirty and start planning the next program of the SafarE. Nut Cracker, unable to contain himself asks, "Why is it called the Fragile Undevelopment Program?"

With an unusual smile on her face, Mrs. Bolt says, "Let's wait to find the answer to that question."

She welcomes us all and suggests we spend some time reflecting on our experiences during the Induction Program. As she presents a summary, we all agree that we've had a taste of how we can strengthen Ex-Factor who has become the focus of the SafarE. In addition, all of us recognize the need to improve our skills for communication, coordination, and connecting as a team. We also realize that other abilities, such as improving our time management, creative thinking, and conflict resolution skills will also help us grow.

When Mrs. Bolt sees that we're getting restless and ready to hear more about the next program, she says, "Over the next week, we'll enjoy the Fragile Undevelopment Program. Who would like to share their thoughts on what can make the Fragile Undevelopment Program fun and memorable?"

I put my hand up and Mrs. Bolt says, "Over to you, Kiran."

I stand up and whisper in embarrassment, "When you're born with a surname like Vas, you'll probably be called exotic names that rhyme with it. Cracked Vas was a name I was called frequently by family, friends, and foes. My ego would be ruffled by such words, but I pepped my spirits up by reminding myself that a vase is also something special. When I first heard about the Fragile Undevelopment Program, I was drawn to the similarities between me and a Ming Vase. That's when I gave myself the exotic name - One Fragile Vas. Like a Ming vase, I too was fragile, yet beautiful. I could add many more charming attributes to compare myself with a vase. Yet, I realized that 'beauty lies in the eyes of the beholder.' Unfortunately, over the last few years, I had neglected myself and remained a bystander as I watched my life shatter into pieces."

There was silence in the room. Not many saw the relevance of the analogy I had presented, other than the familiar sounding word vase. Nutty Nanna laughed and said, "What does a Chinese vase have in common with an Indian living in Denmark? I can't wait to hear what you have to say next."

Unperturbed by the few snide remarks and giggles, I continued resolutely. I was confident that I had a great concept brewing. "Just imagine, that out of the blue I find a shattered mosaic of One Fragile Vas on the path to the Cape of Oh. I stop, and look around desperately, but there is nobody other than me who can help to pick the pieces of One Fragile Vas up and glue them together again."

There was still no reaction, so I went on, "I continue browsing through the shattered mosaic, and find quite a few pieces that appear attractive. As I keep them aside, I realize it is up to me and Team Smiling Billionaire to continue to sort through the pieces and find the attractive ones that convey good stories about Fragile Vas. I also realize that instead of trying to reconstruct them into One Fragile Vas, it would be better for me to build an entirely new mosaic – One Agile Vas, one that has an Ex-Factor we all dream of and whose charming smile is powered by Oh."

"What does agile mean?" asked Nut Cracker.

"Agile in this context is the opposite of fragile. I hope that all of us can develop new qualities and skills to learn and grow together as a team so we can handle all the challenges that we will face on our odyssey. In the process we will strengthen our Ex-Factor and all the four pillars of our Nut Worth."

Once again there is complete silence in the room. I pause, stretch myself, and continue, "I know I can build the mosaic of One Agile Vas. But I need your help. With careful planning, dexterity, patience, and a lot of experimentation with Cool Moves, we can, together, find the right combination of attractive pieces in my life to build that new mosaic. I now realize that these pieces are my perfect and imperfect qualities, and we need to tweak them a bit to succeed in building the new mosaic Agile Vas. More importantly, I know that the process will take a lot of trial and error. But there's a risk in trying to force together two pieces of the shattered One Fragile Vas that aren't compatible with each other. They will crumble further, and we may never be able to construct One Agile Vas in the way we all dream of. On the other hand, the good news could be that they have no place in One Agile Vas anyway."

There was a murmur of agreement in the room. "How do you intend to do this?" asked Colonel Cocktail in his now signature booming voice.

"The process of constructing Agile Vas will involve trial and error. So, to turn this tedious task into a bit of fun, I thought we could play a simulation game. It would be great fun if we all could work together and use our experiences to find the two pieces of the mosaic that fit together best. Once we have these two pieces, we will need a glue to hold them together. In this way, over a period of time, we will add more pieces and the mosaic of Agile Vas will begin to take shape. I know almost instinctively which individual pieces of the shattered Fragile Vas we'll find attractive. They're mostly my growing list of perfect qualities and toned-down imperfect qualities."

I stop to take a bite of an apple, but as I look around, I still see that most of the audience have an incredulous look on their faces. I continue, nevertheless.

"Once I imagined that we had the core of the mosaic pieces of One Agile Kiran in front of us, I started looking around for a glue to hold them together. But there was none! I realized that the appropriate glue that will hold One Agile Vas together can be none other than Oh. Together, we can create a billion smiles, every day!"

"I love this idea," said Nut Cracker. "Let's get going; Let's not waste time."

"Wait a second," I cautioned, "I have a problem over how to make this concept work. The problem is that as Oh is extremely fragile now, he's not powerful enough to help me glue One Agile Kiran together. This is where I need your help."

Mrs. Bolt stands up and says, "Thank you, Kiran, for these new analogies. Let's give Colonel Cocktail the floor to share his thoughts on this program and how we can help you construct One Agile Vas."

The Colonel clears his throat and sounds off, "The odyssey to bring Oh back into your life as we all realize by now, is a formidable task. I buy into Kiran's point that, as of now, you all are fragile in many ways. This is reflected in Oh also being so fragile."

He went on to suggest that we create a baseline of our fragilities and use the next few days to plan the overall SafarE, creating a detailed plan for the Fragile Undevelopment program.

"It will mainly aim to identify the areas you're fragile in, then undevelop them, and, finally, retrain them on the SafarE," the Colonel explained. "A poorly planned and improperly executed Fragile Undevelopment Program will mean that we have to manage with a poor baseline of the emotional muscles that we need to train. That will leave you underprepared for the odyssey. In that case, you run the risk of becoming Fragile Kiran again and Oh never wanting to come back into your life. So, let's get cracking and make a good plan for both the overall SafarE and the Fragile Undevelopment Program."

We all nodded our heads in agreement. Mrs. Bolt interjected, "Kiran, it's okay to be fragile. The sign of strength is to acknowledge that you're fragile, and like you did, seek the right help to make you agile again."

I loved Mrs. Bolt's words, as I had been sparring a bit with my pixies over this during the last few days. "Thank you, Mrs. Bolt. We all were relieved that we had Oh back into our lives, even though he was fragile. There was now an unspoken pixie pledge among us that we would all do what it takes to make Oh strong again so he could play a pivotal role in making me smile more than I grimace."

Seeing the determination in our faces, the Colonel took this as a sign that we all had accepted the importance of planning the SafarE. He continued, "Fortunately, we don't have to start our planning from scratch, as we have a lot of input from your stories that P Leader and I will use to draft a plan."

On hearing that he's going to spend a few days in the Colonel's company, P Leader's face lights up. "We'll be in touch," says the Colonel, and they leave the Bored Room. Once they're gone, Mrs. Bolt closes the meeting and leaves us to our own devices. The rest of us wander off to explore Nutty Woods. Over the next few days, as we relax and catch up with each other and share stories that keep us in high spirits, P Leader occasionally comes out of his meeting room and connects with us to clarify a few areas of our fragilities and any suggestions we have to undevelop them.

⌒

To find the smile punch line of One Agile Vas, I spent hours thinking about how to accept my fragilities for what they are and make use of my God-given talents to live a life in which I smile more and grimace less. I also accepted that a plan is a plan and when the conditions of a plan change, we have a new plan.

DIGITAL TWINS

As we're getting used to a relaxed life in Nutty Woods, one evening, two days later, while chilling around the bubbling Red Cooking Pot, P Leader arrives with a roll of paper. With a huge grimace that we attribute to an obvious lack of sleep, he rolls out his plans on a table and asks us to join him.

As we take our places around the table, he slowly walks us through the plans. We try to follow every word he says, and, after a while, we grasp the big picture of what we must do for the rest of the SafarE to improve our chances of bringing Oh back into our lives.

When his pitch is done, all our hands go up to ask him questions. He tells us to be patient and then hands out printouts of his Fragile Undevelopment list that had details of perfections, imperfections, strengths, fragilities, roles, responsibilities, templates, checklists, detailed steps, assumptions, risks, dependencies, constraints, and more. One by one, he walks us through each page in our plan and clarifies all our questions.

We spend a lot of time on the Fragile Undevelopment list he has created and all the Uncool Moves we have identified that need to be undeveloped. We consider what Cool Moves will be needed to develop them again. We're all in agreement of what is on this list. When, at last, he comes to the timeline, P Leader says, "The Colonel and I estimate that the SafarE will take us about nine months of hard work to train Ex-Factor for the rigorous time ahead on the odyssey."

The thought of staying nine months in Nutty Woods and training day in and day out didn't excite any of us. One by one, we aired our views and concerns and questioned the long timeline.

P Leader is not swayed by our concerns and sarcastic comments. He holds his ground, calmly clarifies all our concerns, revisiting the risks and rewards of having a well planned and executed SafarE. He also says the plans will need to be updated at frequent intervals to reflect reality. He's so convincing, motivating, and inspirational as he eases all our concerns, that, in the end, we all agree with the plan.

I could sense that we're still not sure how we'll know when we've finally freed Oh from the negative mesmerizing power of his former captors. and brought him back into our lives. No one seems to be ready to address this concern and sound stupid.

Fortunately, Nut Cracker comes to our rescue, and in a round-about way.

All the while P Leader had been rambling on about his plan, I had an eye on Nut Cracker who was fidgeting more than usual and sporting a pensive look. I came to know later that while we were all dreaming about One Agile Vas, he was silently processing the Ex-Factor he identified in some of my most Incredible Stories and was linking them to see how they could be used to find and free Oh from the negative mesmerizing power of his former captors.

When P Leader's pitch is over, Nut Cracker stands up and says he has an idea, "I still don't know what we need to do to free Oh from the negative mesmerizing power of his former captors. So, I have my own solution. While you rambled along, I loved the sound of Fragile Undevelopment. It reminded me of this buzzword in business called Agile Development. So, I played around with it and thought that if we could create a mockup of Oh based on the Missing Oh Report, we'll have a picture of what he looks like today. It will be pretty fragile."

While most of us were lost on Nut Cracker's train of thought and struggled with more buzzwords, P Leader saw the potential in Nut Cracker's idea. "I guess," he said, looking at Oh all huddled up in a corner, "Oh is fragile now, and will be recuperating for many more months till he's agile or in more simple words - able to stand on his own two feet. As long as he's fragile, he won't be able to participate actively in the SafarE and join us in training scenarios where we free him from his former captors. How do we solve this? Nut Cracker?"

"Piece of cake," says Nut Cracker. "Inspired by our visit to the Space Center, I thought - what if we could simulate scenarios where we help Oh escape from his former captors? It would be really cool if we could have a digital twin or a mockup of Oh, that could participate in simulation and real training scenarios. We could then simulate and test all our Cool Moves on the mock up, to verify the impact on him and predict how Oh will behave in similar scenarios. This will give us good insights in a simulation environment to see if Oh is becoming stronger everyday. What do you think?"

"I have no idea," says P Leader, "But I'm sure you have."

Nut Cracker smiles. "To start training the mock up of Oh, let's imagine he trained on the weakest possible Ex-Factor of Kiran. Then I can simulate Cool Moves that he trains on and we can analyze his smiles and grimaces and use this data to plan how to undevelop our fragilities that make him grimace and then train them afresh. The simulation process can continue till we transform him into a stronger version of Oh. At that point, he would have the agility to escape from his former captors."

"An interactive mockup of Oh?" queries P Leader. "All these nomenclatures or avatars of Oh are confusing but will help make our SafarE plan more realistic. Let me have a quick chat with Oh. Let's take a short break." A few minutes later when we're all back, P Leader says, "Tell us more. Oh and I really like the idea."

Nut Cracker paces around the table and says that he has all the components and a concept called Jugaad to build the mockup of 'Oh as he looks today.'

"Interesting," I say. "How will you do that?"

Nut Cracker takes a deep breath. "I will, with the help of Spark Plug and Mr. If On-Lee, use the concept of Jugaad or frugal engineering and build the mock up of Oh."

"What is Jugaad?" asks P Leader.

Nut Cracker takes a note from his pocket and says, "In the Library, the definition I got was a colloquial Indo-Aryan word, which refers to a non-conventional, frugal innovation, often termed a 'hack.' It could also refer to an innovative fix or a simple workaround, a solution that bends the rules, or a resource that can be used in such a way. It is also often used to signify creativity: to make existing things work, or to create new things with meager resources."

I nod in agreement. "I love Jugaad, as the concept has been the source of many ideas emerging from my innovative mind, right from my childhood in Bengaluru. Tell us more about your idea."

Nut Cracker puffs his chest, and elaborates, "Let's call this mockup of Oh 'Jugaad.'" We agree.

Nut Cracker continues, "Remember Oh is an algorithm, so think of Jugaad as a temporary algorithm that we will use instead of Oh in the Smile Making Machine during the SafarE. To start with, I'll load all the stories you've ever created and a copy of your weakest Ex-Factor into Jugaad. We can get this Ex-Factor data from Dr. Eye Can.

"Next, I'll write some code to reboot your Smile Making Machine. Once Jugaad is humming along nicely, using the old stories, we can train him to recognize, at each point when you say Oh, whether that triggers a smile or a grimace. The more we train him, the more accurate he becomes in predicting when you're about to say Oh and whether that makes you smile or grimace. Soon, he'll also become an expert in predicting the possible impact of a smile or grimace in an increasing number of situations. From there on, we can start optimizing how he can make your smiles last longer and grimaces shorter."

"Wow," mumbles P Leader. "Tell us more."

"In practice what Jugaad will do in a story that's about to unfold is: he will first try to predict the outcome of the story. Then he'll inform each of us what we have to do to respond to a call of action in the story to the best of our collective ability. After that, he'll also orchestrate the way we execute the action to achieve the outcome that's desired.

"Over time, as Jugaad gets to know all our individual and collective perfect and imperfect qualities better, he'll be the silent algorithm that possesses all the information that makes you smile more and grimace less. But the real game changer will be that Jugaad will also have information about which emotional muscles you need to train to strengthen Ex-Factor so Oh can be freed from his former captors."

"Wow! That is a monumental task you've set for Jugaad," I say. "I'm concerned about whether he can live up to these expectations in my chaotic life."

Nut Cracker shrugs and continues "Have no fear, Nut Cracker is here. When we're all happy about Jugaad's ability to orchestrate us and Kiran is smiling more and grimacing less, we'll know that Jugaad is performing the job he was designed for."

As he sees the incredulous look on my face, unperturbed, he says, "Don't worry, I haven't forgotten about Oh. We're not going to abandon him or replace him with Jugaad. When we're satisfied with the role Jugaad is playing in our life, throughout the SafarE, I will then find a way to transfer the data we've used to train Jugaad to Oh. Cool Move by Cool Move, he slowly takes over from Jugaad and will shoulder more and more responsibility, performing like the algorithm in the Smile Making Machine. After the bootcamp, as we progress on the odyssey and he becomes stronger with a bit of guidance from Ex-Factor, he can begin to gradually free himself or reduce his dependency from the mesmerizing power of his former captors."

As Nut Cracker sees that we're slowly getting hooked on his idea, he shows us a sketch of Jugaad, who is a humble ball with a flexible mouth hanging on a string.

"Nut Cracker, you nailed it," I say. "I finally understand how we can start to free Oh from the former captors and spare him from the trauma of being our guinea pig during the SafarE. In this way, he and Jugaad are like digital twins, and he can recuperate in peace and leave the hard work to his twin Jugaad till he's ready to take over responsibility for it again."

Nut Cracker sits down, thrilled with our positive response. We bombard him with more why, how, what, and when questions. He ignores us and, after a sip of chilled water, continues, "I can build Jugaad along with Spark Plug and Mr. If On-Lee, but all of us will need to work as a team to train him to live up to his responsibility."

With that, the three inventors depart to work on their creation.

～

To find the smile punch line of the mock up of Oh , I appreciated the power of out-of-the-box thinking and how the right use of concepts with a technology twist can make me smile more.

MEET JUGAAD

The next morning, as we're enjoying steaming cups of coffee, a red-eyed Nut Cracker appears and asks us if we're ready to meet Jugaad.

"You bet," we all say in unison.

He takes something out of his pocket and shows it to me. I look at Jugaad in dismay. I've been expecting something flashy, but what I hold in my hand is a ball that's all bandaged up. It looks cute though.

Nut Cracker ignores my grimace and gets geeky. He starts explaining how we can simulate Cool Moves to train Jugaad on the SafarE. As he drones on, we get the gist of what he's saying; he wants to use Jugaad to help us shortlist only those Cool Moves that we feel will have the most impact on making us smile more than grimace. We can then focus on those moves during the SafarE.

He seems to sense though, that his words sound like gibberish to us. To demonstrate what he means, he asks Spam Fighter to boot up Daisy, his computer. When Daisy is all lit up, Nut Cracker types a few commands. We see an animation on the screen. "Meet Jugaad," he says with a broad smile.

Meet
Jugaad

He then presses a few keys, and all of us pop up on the screen, and, in a few more clicks, he has all of us doing Cool Moves. We sit back and enjoy a visual of us perspiring a lot, but enjoying the smiles and grimaces we produce on Jugaad's face. Once Nut Cracker sees that we all have bought into the idea, he says, "In practice, when we're all satisfied about Jugaad's ability to orchestrate our calls to action, and Kiran is smiling more and grimacing less, we'll know that Jugaad is performing the job he was designed for here in Oh Landia.

"Then we teleport ourselves back to DontDoNation where we can confirm whether these Cool Moves have the same impact on your smiles and grimaces as they have in Oh Landia. If they do, we'll know they work, and I'll load them into Oh. Then, bit by bit, he can take over the orchestration role from Jugaad.

"If however, they don't work, we refine the Cool Moves in Oh Landia again, and repeat the trial and error process till we're confident that they work in DontDoNation. In this way, with careful planning, dexterity, patience, and a lot of experimentation with Cool Moves, Oh can slowly take over from Jugaad as the algorithm in the Smile Making Machine. Once we're back on the odyssey, it's just a matter of time before he can start to free himself from his former captors."

We were all still in awe of Nut Cracker's incredible idea and were smiling broadly now. Seeing that we had got over our disappointment over the plain-looking Jugaad, and that we were all happy with him and the role he will play in helping us free Oh, Nut Cracker hands Jugaad over to my loving guardianship. Protecting him with great care, I ask the Wizard of Oh to transform him into a pixie. The wizard looks into his book of *How to Design a Digital Twin*, chooses one, and with a swoosh of his sword, converts Jugaad into a pixie that looks like a red and green bandaged ball with flexible lips that can turn into a smile or grimace in the wink of an eye.

As I enjoy the sight of Jugaad, flying around the room acquainting himself with this strange new world, a minute later the wizard who has been digging in his bag, takes out a small box that is exquisitely wrapped and presents it to me.

"Kiran, over the last few days, I have been imagining what Oh would look like. This is my image of him."

I carefully unwrap the parcel and I find a beautiful figure carved in wood. It has a head that is shaped like an O supported on a body shaped like a H. It's face has a smile that melts my heart. "Thank you wizard, I say. "This is a toy that I will cherish and will be my muse on my odyssey.

"You are welcome Kiran. This is what I imagine Oh will look like when he is finally freed from the negative mesmerizing power of his captors and enjoys making you smile again for the rest of your life."

Meet
Oh

I call out to Jugaad to come and sit on my shoulder and holding Oh in my hands I know that with a combination of an ethereal creature that lives in my imagination and a physical toy that lives in my physical world, I have a two new sources of inspiration that that will go a long way in inspiring me to find Cool Moves to make me smile more than I grimace.

I stand up and say, "All that's left now before we start the next program of the SafarE, is to call Dr. Eye Can and ask him to place all of your pixies back inside me. What should we call our next program?"

"Jugaad" was the unanimous answer from my team.

I call Dr. Eye Can and brief him on Agile Oh and Jugaad and how we had all fallen in love with both of them. Dr. Eye Can has many critical questions that I try to answer. Finally, he says, "There's no doubt in my mind that as you gradually free Oh from the negative mesmerizing power of his former captors he'll help you flourish as an Extrapreneur. I can't wait to meet him and see you all again."

When I put the phone down, Mrs. Bolt says, "Well, we have a plan for our SafarE, and our Fragile Undevelopment Program seems to be a success. We have a Jugaad who will help us collate a portfolio of Cool Moves to master. So, in our next Jugaad Program, we can focus on training Ex-Factor and Oh to become strong enough to free Oh from his former captors. Remember, you are late bloomers in ADHD, Leadership, and Entrepreneurship. Just see what we've accomplished as a team in these few days. I think it's amazing that a simple contraption like Jugaad is all it takes to free Oh and help Kiran reach his three goals: Find ways to bring Oh back into his life; Pioneer the Art of Extrapreneurship and develop as an Extrapreneur; Become a Smiling Billionaire."

We're all delighted when Dr. Eye Can arrives in Oh Landia and displaying the quality of hyperactivity immediately sets up for a Close Kiran Surgery and asks the wizard to fire up the Red Cooking Pot. When he sees Oh again, his heart melts. He takes Oh aside and has a heart-to-heart conversation with him. After this, he asks Nut Cracker to brief him on Jugaad and the role he and Oh will play in my life. Then, he speaks to each of the pixies and does a Smileoscopy on each of them and finally on me. When he has all the information he needs, he asks the wizard to commence the Close Kiran Surgery.

When the surgery starts, he selects a number of random Cool and Uncool Moves for me to play. I start with the ones I love and admit I still don't enjoy quite a few of them, but I follow the process. As I play, the wizard slowly continues to place all the pixies inside me in their rightful home. Finally, he places Jugaad and Oh in my gut and attaches all the pixies to my ethereal umbilical cord and starts loading Jugaad with my stories.

All the while, Dr. Eye Can is recording all my nitty gritty thoughts, feelings, actions, and words I was uttering and sharing them with the wizard who then instructs him about what spices to hand over to be added to the Red Cooking Pot. As he adds the spices and stirs the curry being curated in the Red Cooking Pot, it coughs and gurgles and the wizard and doctor observe how the newly added Oh and Jugaad interact with each other and the other pixies. After a few hours of stirring and observing the scenes being played out in the Red Cooking Pot, all the pixies one by one settle down in the pot and when the curry, which the wizard calls "A dish fit for a pixie" is bubbling nicely and smelling divine, Dr. Eye Can closes the lid on the Red Cooking Pot and says, "Let's enjoy a great meal together."

When we are content, he sets me up for a Smileoscopy and says the only thing left before we start our next program, whatever Team Inspiration decides it to be, is to solve the Ex of your Ex-Factor and calculate your Nut Worth equation. But I'm a doctor, not a mathematician, so someone else has to help you solve your Nut Worth equation."

Spark Plug stood up and in a dead serious voice says, "The Nut Worth Equation is the sum of all Kiran's smiles minus grimaces. So please smile a lot, as the larger his smile the greater is the value of his Nut Worth Equation. QED."

The Wizard of Oh, very uncharacteristically for his usual quiet self, is quick with a retort. "It's not that simple. Gather around."

He slowly empties the contents of his bag on the table. Then he rolls out a map of Oh Landia. A map that has a lot of details, but I spot a picture of Oh on the far righthand corner. When the map is firmly held in place on the table, he gradually starts turning the small pieces lying on the table, so we can admire their details. To our amazement in a haphazard fashion, piece by piece we witness the delicate shapes of the Mines and Mills, Team Inspiration, Team Perspiration, the Biters and Chewers, Charlie, all my stories, concepts, toys, and others whose paths we have crossed on the odyssey so far. The wizard has also made thirty emojis for the emotions. Soon, there are more than a hundred pieces of what now looks like the Oh Landia puzzle in front of us.

When we're done admiring his handwork, he says, "The answer to the Nut Worth Equation or the path to Oh, is an iterative process, and there are no correct or wrong answers. But concrete proof that you all are making progress is the quality, not just the quantity, of every one of your smiles. Inspired by Kiran's concept of the shattered mosaic, I have coded each of these pieces with data that you can access in your own way to succeed in Ohism. The Oh Landia puzzle will help us as a team in a good old fashioned way, to choose our own pieces to build a solid foundation for Ohism. Only when we have this foundation, that I hope can be built during this SafarE, then, step by step, we can add more complex pieces that will take us closer to Oh."

We all loved the Wizard's puzzle ideas and Team Perspiration had already started their own game. After a while, when all of us are enjoying ourselves, Team Perspiration is bickering over what pieces the foundation should contain. The wizard hands Kiran a piece of paper and says, "I heard about how difficult it is for you to follow instructions and build something as simple as a kite. Here is the *Smarties Guide to Oh Landia* that provides an explanation to most of the complex pieces of the Oh Landia Puzzle. I think it is called a glossary in DontDoNation. When you have a solid foundation and are on a stable course on your odyssey, this is my image of you balancing all your perfect and imperfect qualities on your way to the Cape of Oh."

He hands me the cutest version of myself I have ever seen. "This is my version of the Real Kiran," he says and retires to the background.

Meet
Kiran

Dr. Eye Can starts the Smileoscope, and, after a while, the Smile Quotient Meter comes to life and displays readings of my Ex-Factor and Nut Worth. The doctor, wizard, and Ms. Bolt analyze the readings together and when they're all satisfied with the readings, Dr. Eye Can says, "Hats off to you, Kiran. Your Ex-Factor is strong enough for the next program of the SafarE, that I understand is called the Jugaad Program. I'm leaving you in the capable hands of Mrs. Bolt. The Close Kiran Surgery is done."

When he removes his gear and sets me free, Dr. Eye Can says he has loaded Jugaad with all our stories, reconnected my ethereal umbilical cord with the Ales, Guts, Jugaad and Oh and everyone is waiting inside me for the next program and the roles they have to play.

Before he signs off on the Close Kiran Surgery, he brings out his original odyssey travel checklist from our first session together and all the data he has gathered from our first consultation together. In conversation with Mrs. Bolt and the wizard, he updates the lists and his data and, with a lot of high fives among themselves, brings an end to the Close Kiran Surgery.

As he packs his bags, Dr. Eye Can says, "Kiran, as Spark Plug said QED. As I mentioned when I first tended you or Mr. Perfectly

Imperfect, when people like you get a piece of knowledge that can alter the course of their lives for the better, with a network of family and friends, they find ways to unpack the power of this knowledge and learn to survive and thrive in their daily lives. You're doing just that and more. Well done! It has been a pleasure to work alongside you to bring Oh back into your life. The next time you need me, I can be found under the name Dr. Yes You Can from the Clinic Tune Yourself With Professionals." And, with a puff, he's gone.

CHAPTER 12

My Coolest Heavyweight Cool Move

A common observation of people bearing an ADHD label is that we often have more open projects than we can close. For me, authoring *Perfectly Imperfect* was one hell of a heavyweight Cool Move that I used to pressure test this observation and work hard to improve my Attention Deficiency and Hyperactive Disorder qualities.

Wow, I authored and published *Perfectly Imperfect*. It took me 12 months to work on this book and 12 more months before I had the guts to decide to publish it and share Oh with the world. The truth that I understand now in this process is that the only thing Oh has ever wanted from me is to smile. Oh is the glue that holds me and my ADHD, Leadership and Entrepreneurship pixies together, and, as partners, we can create a billion smiles every day! The minute we forget about our partnership, my Ex-Factor weakens and I run the risk of losing Oh again.

All this while I worked day in and day out figuring out my Ex-Factor and doing Cool Moves. I can proudly say that writing *Perfectly Imperfect* got me away from my Cape of Oh No and well on the path to my Cape of Oh, wherever it may be. I have experienced both smiles and grimaces, but I can confidently say that every grimace was worth the energy it drained out of me to give me one more reason to smile. I still don't know if I will ever truly discover what the right combination of emotions in my Ex-Factor should be. In fact, I know it will constantly keep changing. One thing for sure is that authoring *Perfectly Imperfect* made me fall in love with the fine qualities that come with ADHD and respect the rough qualities that come with it.

In my search for Oh, a simple word that is said by a lot of people multiple times a day everyday and can be pronounced in a billion different ways by billions of people around the world, the simple Open Kiran Surgery freed my shackled mind, stimulated my stale senses, and opened up my heart. In this process, I found the reason why I love to smile and earned the right to bear the title, Kiran Vas, ADHD, Author. Oh inspired me to develop a tool kit that I'm proud to share with people like me and look forward to continuing to inspire you to find your own version of Oh and work hard to attain your own Heavyweight Cool Move.

In the words of Dr. Eye Can, "If I can, I believe you can. The question you must ask yourself now is, 'Do you believe you can?'"

APPENDIX

Disclaimer:

For the actual definition of terms used in the book please use an English language dictionary of your choice. This is how I use the terminology in *Perfectly Imperfect*.

What follows is a set of seven appendices. Each appendix is a collection of acronyms, mnemonics, metaphors and background information that are the corner stone of my stories, concepts, toys and visual games. I use a glossary structure for easy reference. This structure also ensured that they stuck like Velcro in my brain and helped me work with them as I wrote the book, and continues to help me reflect and use them proactively in my daily life.

Appendix A: Archetypes

The archetypes used:

1. The Hero: Kiran Vas/Mr. Perfectly Imperfect/Mr. Sunshine/ Mr. Smiling Billionaire

2. The Conflict: Before my diagnosis of ADHD, I was in a constant internal conflict on who, why, and what, was burning me out. With my diagnosis of ADHD, I knew ADHD was one of the root cause and I suddenly I had my first tool to start resolving my internal conflicts.

3. The Puzzle: To stop burning out, and to find ways to burn brighter, I need to understand my myriad of perfect and imperfect qualities and like a puzzle choose the pieces that fit together.

4. The Playground: My playground is my odyssey in Oh Landia, a virtual world. Oh Landia is the home of all my Ohs. It is my ethereal safe place where I can, along with my ethereal team, find ways to stop burning out and start burning brighter.

5. The Victim: Oh, the secret algorithm behind my smile that has been taken captive by someone who has an interest in keeping me chronically grumpy and who does not like me to smile.

6. The Adventurer: Kiran Vas, who goes on several adventures to find Oh.

7. The Villains: A few of my Oh No Emotions who have a vested interest in capturing Oh and thrive when I am chronically grumpy.

8. My Helpers: The Guts or my hobbies of Cooking, Eating, Smiling. These are a natural source of smiles when I engage

with them. They play an important role in helping me to find, free, bring, and keep Oh in my life.

9. My Weapons: The Ales, or my passions for ADHD, Leadership, and Entrepreneurship. These are a natural source of smiles when engaging with them. They play an important role in helping me to find, free, bring, and keep Oh in my life.

10. My Real-life mentors: aka The Miners and Millers, area group of my closest family and friends who have stood by me in all situations in life. It is from them I learn the rudimentary principle of leadership and entrepreneurship.

11. The Philosopher: Dr. Eye Can, a virtual me with whom I enjoy monologues and who inspires me to go beyond what I think I can do with my talents.

12. The Wiseman: Wizard of Oh, an expert in Ohism

13. The Detective: Ex-Factor, is my secret combination of my perfect and imperfect qualities whose power Oh uses to smile or grimace.

14. The Doer: Cool Moves, plays a key role in helping make my Ex-Factor strong and attractive to draw Oh back into it.

Appendix B: Timeline

This is a summary of the timeline I use in the book.

1. 1967 - 2018: I am living the dream life in Cape of Oh Yes. During this period, I enjoyed a privileged life and achieved most of my dreams. Oh, drawing on my strong Ex-Factor, is the source of an infinite number of smiles. But my source of smiles started drying up slowly from 2012.

2. 2018 - 2020: I am living the worst of my nightmares in the Cape of Oh No. This period by far is the hardest period of my life to date. Oh, drawing on my weak Ex-Factor, is the most fragile version of himself and struggles to make me smile.
3. 2021: I start my odyssey to Find, Free, Bring and Keep Oh in my life.
4. 2022: I start living out my Mission, Purpose, and Goals
5. 2023 - Published author and committed to reaching the Cape of Oh

Appendix C: Stories

I have a built-in database of millions of my own stories archived within me that I call my Story Archives. In these stories, I've played all the 14 archetypes in different stages of my life. As I analyzed my stories, I became convinced how powerful they were and knew deep down that within them lies the secret I need to discover so as to strengthen my Ex-Factor.

To strengthen my Ex-Factor, I need to train my Emotional Muscles that will help me to work with my emotions and as my Ex-Factor becomes stronger, I will gradually create more Oh Yes Stories and less Oh No Stories and smile more and grimace less.

*My dream to smile more is to create **more Oh Yes Stories** with the tagline*

Alert, Confident, Courageous, Competitive, Diligent, Enthusiastic, Energetic, Focused, Friendly, Funny, Grateful, Humble, Heroic, Playful, Thoughtful.

*To do this I need to **train my emotional muscles***

Admiration, Adoration, Amusement, Appreciation, Awe, Calmness, Excitement, Interest, Joy, Nostalgia, Relief, Romance, Satisfaction, Surprise, and Sympathy.

*In the same way to create less **Oh No Stories** with the tagline*

Aggressive, Argumentative, Chaotic, Egoistic, Envious, Greedy, Materialistic, Helpless, Impatient, Irritated, Forgetful, Frustrated, Guilty, Lethargic, Restless,

*I need to **train the emotional muscles** that will **help me reduce my grimaces** when I experience the emotions of*

Anger, Anxiousness, Awkwardness, Boredom, Contempt, Confusion, Craving, Embarrassment, Disgust, Disappointment, Distress, Fear, Horror, Pain and Sadness.

Appendix D: Concepts

This is a list of a few key concepts:

1. Ales is an acronym for my ADHD, Leadership and Entrepreneurship. They are called Nut Cracker, Leadership, and Entrepreneurship and encapsulate all my perfect and imperfect qualities linked to my ADHD, Leadership, and Entrepreneurship.

2. Biters and Chewers are metaphors for pixies in Oh Landia who work for the Nut Miners and Nut Millers. The concept of Biters helps me remember that whenever I encounter an exciting idea or proposition, I should first take a quick bite

of it. I should only hyper focus on it after deciding whether I like the taste or not. Similarly, the concept of Chewers reminds me that even if I like the taste, I must remember to chew slowly on it to understand the flavors or benefits it adds to my life.

3. Cape of Oh is a metaphor of an exciting horizon that is the destination of my odyssey.

4. Cape of Oh No is a metaphor for the place I lived in during the hardest period of my life filled with grimaces.

5. Cape of Oh Yes is a metaphor of a beautiful place that I lived in for five decades during which I enjoyed a life filled with smiles.

6. Cool Moves (New and Old) are everyday actions that create energy. New Cool Moves are new actions that I learned to do after I was diagnosed with ADHD. Old Cool Moves are old actions that have traditionally always been a source of smiles and I must continue doing them regularly.

7. DontDoNation is my reference to planet Earth.

8. Emotions, I use thirty Oh Yes and Oh No Emotions that are linked to thirty Oh Yes and Oh No Stories. These thirty emotions are my baseline to train my emotional muscles.

9. Emotional Muscles, these are the muscles that I need to train to smile more and grimace less.

10. Energy Grid is a concept that helps me remember that I'm like an energy grid and can generate, distribute, and store energy that I can use to smile more and grimace less. Each mine and the mill on the energy grid has a clear purpose to help me reach my goals.

11. Fine Qualities/Perfect Qualities are qualities that help me create Oh Yes Stories.

12. Guts, this is the mnemonic for Cooking, Eating and Smiling, my passions, that I have visualized as my pixies. Cooking, Eating and Smiles are a natural source of smiles for me, which are almost effortless.

13. Innernet, is my own internal version of the internet in which millions of my stories are stored.

14. Miners and Millers, a group of my closest family and friends who have stood by me in all situations in life. I called them Miners as they give me entrepreneurial advice, and Millers as they give me leadership advice. Together using the metaphor of mining for raw materials and milling the raw material for its value, they inspire me to extract the most value from my ADHD, Entrepreneurship, and Leadership qualities.

15. Missing Oh report, a concept that I created to help me describe what Oh looks like or to put a face to a name.

16. Nutty Woods is a place in the heart of Oh Landia where the scene of the basecamp and bootcamp unfolds.

17. Nut Worth is an aggregation of four mutually-exclusive, collectively-exhaustible yet integrated sources of the four pillars, – Physical, Mental, Financial, and Social – of my wealth. When they're in balance, they ensure I smile more than I grimace.

18. Nut Worth Equation is the sum of my Smiles minus my Grimaces. There will never be a right or wrong answer to this equation.

19. Oh Landia is my ethereal world and the home of all my Ohs.

20. Odyssey is a series of adventures that I go on to Find, Free, Bring, and Keep Oh in my life.

21. Oh is my secret algorithm that makes me smile.

22. Oh No, Ooh No, Oooh No Stories and Emotions are metaphors for three types of my grimaces.

23. Oh Yes, Ooh Yes, Ooh Yes Stories and Emotions, are metaphors for the three types of smiles.

24. Red Cooking Pot is a symbol of my mind and body. It serves as a portal for me to access what was going on in my innernet.

25. Portal to Oh Landia, is an imaginary portal that I use to enter and exit as I travel between Oh Landia and DontDoNation.

26. Rough Qualities/Imperfect Qualities are qualities that make me create Oh No Stories.

27. SafarE, the name of my bootcamp. Its name is inspired from a safari I went to in Tanzania in 2014.

28. Smiling Pauper, my state when I have run out of smiles.

29. Smiling Billionaire, my state when I am creating a billion smiles every day!

30. Smile Making Machine helps me to remember if I want to reach Cape of Oh, I need to run my life like a business and not a hobby, as only then can it pay me back great returns in terms of smiles. .

31. Sweet and Sour Spot is a spin on the term 'sweet spot'. I use the term to find the optimum combination of the individual perfect and imperfect qualities the Ales. When the Ales execute a Call to Action from the Sweet Spot, they are in harmony and make me smile and when they execute a Call to Action from the Sour Spot, they are in conflict and make me grimace.

32. Uncool Moves (New and Old) are everyday actions that consume my energy. Uncool Moves are a source of grimaces.

33. Vulnerability Log is a list of areas in my life in which I'm still vulnerable.

34. WWoW is my acronym for wandering aimlessly, worrying unnecessarily, and wondering about the nerdiest things in life.

35. 4 by 4 Training Plan is a plan made with Team Inspiration to help me focus on training 4 Oh Yes and 4 Oh No Emotional Muscles at their Mine or Mill.

36. 80/20 Principle, or the Pareto principle that states 80% of all outcomes are derived from 20% of causes.

Appendix E: Toys

This is a list of a few key toys.

1. A Lot of Smiles help me focus my resources on Cool Moves that will give me the best returns when I invest them to achieve my three goals. It has three interconnected parts - A Lot Filter, Smile Formula, and Dumb Bells.

    a. A Lot Filter, a custom designed filter that helps me focus on selecting Cool Moves to train to strengthen my Ex-Factor. To get the most benefit from a Cool Move I must be ready - To Learn a Lot, To Plan a Lot, To Practice a Lot, To Integrate a Lot

    b. My Smile Toy is a filter that helps me ensure that Cool Moves I choose to train must often be Simple, Meaningful, Intelligent, Lucrative and Educational and must also be Scalable, Marketable, Inspirational to develop my Leadership and Entrepreneurial qualities to create a billion smiles every day!

c. The Three Dumb Bells is a key to choosing the right mix of Cool Moves to achieve my goal. The three categories are: a Flyweight – Oh Yes or Oh No Cool Moves that will take less than three months to integrate or get rid of from my daily life; Middleweight – Ooh Yes or Ooh No Cool Moves that will take between three to six months to integrate into my daily life: and Heavyweight – Oooh Yes and Oooh No Cool Moves that will take more than a year to integrate into my daily life.

2. Pre-Mortem is a process where I imagine I've died and then make an "If only I had list" that contains all the things I wish I had done or not done.

3. Smile and Grimace P&L, my north star as I navigate my way to become a Smiling Billionaire. My Smile and Grimace P&L helps me measure and monitor all my investments in Cool Moves to ensure they're taking me closer to becoming a Smiling Billionaire.

4. Smile Making Machine, a fantasy machine within me and its algorithm Oh that magically uses my Ex-Factor to churn out smiles and grimaces.

5. Smileoscope and Smileoscopy: The Smileoscope is a toy and the Smileoscopy is a procedure that Dr. Eye Can uses to ascertain the quantity and quality of my smiles.

6. Smile Quotient Meter and Smile Quotient: The Smile Quotient Meter is a toy that measures the smiles and grimaces produced during a Smileoscopy. The Smile Quotient is a number obtained when I divide the number of smiles by the number of grimaces.

7. The Surgeries performed by Dr. Eye Can and the Wizard of Oh are noninvasive surgeries to find Oh.

a. Open Kiran Surgery is a surgery inspired by an Open-Heart Surgery and a toy that gives me a structure for when I go deeper on my inner journey to discover more about the Ales than I have ever dared to.

b. Close Kiran Surgery is a surgery inspired by an Open-Heart Surgery and a metaphor that gives me a structure to bring to a natural close the times I go on an inner journey to discover more about the Ales than I have ever dared to.

Appendix F: Pixies

Note: Ethereal, I use the word to describe a story, concept, toy and more that lives in my imagination and belongs to Oh Landia my ethereal world. Oh Landia is where my pixies live. They are delicate, mysterious, profound, and as I integrate my stories, concepts, toys through visual games, I encapsulate wisdom in each of them that will help me smile more and grimace less.

1. Dr. Eye Can, this is virtual me. I use Dr. Eye Can as my sounding board when I'm having monologues with myself, trying to solve a problem or dreaming up a new idea. It's a metaphor for the fallacy that I can do everything by myself.

2. Cool Moves helps me visualize the concept of Cool Moves.

3. Ex-Factor helps me visualize what my Ex-Factor is. It reminds me to be a detective and always be on the lookout for what missing qualities need to be added to my Ex-Factor.

4. Nut Cracker is a visual of my ADHD and helps me encapsulate my growing knowledge of ADHD.

5. Jugaad is a visual for me to remember to always be creative and resourceful and have fun while I find unconventional solutions to reach my goal.

6. P Leader is a visual of my leadership qualities and helps me encapsulate my growing leadership qualities.

7. Spark Plug is a visual of my entrepreneurial qualities and helps me encapsulate my growing entrepreneurial qualities.

8. The Wizard of Oh is a visual of a wise man and reminds me that I will also need help from an expert in Ohism.

Team Inspiration – The Millers

a. Mrs. Bolt in her Mill, the Library where she mills, and her Pixie Dust called Book Worm, reminds me that it is the art of learning to seek knowledge and applying this knowledge to many aspects of my life that will help me to discover new amazing ways to smile more.

b. Colonel Cocktail in his Mill, the Vault where he mills, and his Pixie Dust called Wealth, reminds me it is the art of strategy, tactics, discipline, and operational excellence that will help me strive to achieve my goals in life.

c. Miss Chef, in her Mill, The Dining Room, where she prepares mouth watering buffets using her Pixie Dust called Mischief. Miss Chef reminds me it is the art of cooking for which I have a natural talent, that can help me process some of my most complex thoughts and find solutions.

d. Nutty Nanna in her Mill called Pickle Street mills her Pixie Dust called Raja. Nutty Nanna mentors me to find simple ways to appreciate the beauty of life.

Team Inspiration - The Miners

a. Acrobat in her Mine, The Obstacle Course mines her Pixie Dust called Enjoy. The Acrobat mentors me to train my mind and body to overcome obstacles in my daily life and learn ways to smile more.

b. Dragon Slayer in his Mine, The Forest mines his Pixie Dust called Pacifier. The Dragon Slayer mentors me to overcome some of the inner and outer dragons that impact my peace of mind.

c. Mr. If On-Lee in his Mine The Experiment mines his Pixie Dust called No Expectations. Mr. If On-Lee mentors me through the art of entrepreneurship to process some of my most complex business ideas to see if they're worth investing resources in.

d. Spam Fighter in his Mine, The Space Center builds Spam Filters, that is his equivalent to a Pixie Dust. Spam Fighter mentors me through the lens of cyberspace on how to reduce the amount of spam in my life.

Team Perspiration

a. Ear Wax is my sense of hearing. I use Ear Wax to filter out the constant stream of noise pollution that surrounds me and distracts me from focusing on what I need to do to achieve my three goals.

b. Hard Nose is my sense of smell. I use Hard Nose to help me keep far away from the situations in life that for many historical reasons make me grimace.

c. Taste Buds is my sense of taste. Taste Buds helps me remember to experience the magic of the five tastes: sweet, sour, salty, bitter, and savory that help me enjoy life.

d. Tough Skin is my sense of touch. Tough Skin helps me remember that life will always throw hard knocks at me. I use Tough Skin to help me protect myself from the worst damage these knocks can impart on me.

e. Worried Eyes is my sense of sight. I use Worried Eyes to help me spot the most beautiful opportunities in life and keep an eye out for trouble of the sort that I am always interested in being part of.

Appendix G: General Terms

This is a list of a few terms that add tremendous value in my life as I learn to use them proactively .

1. Agile is a term that helps remind that I must always be flexible and adapt with the best New Cool Moves to respond to the changing conditions in my life.

2. Call to Action is an internal instruction to the Ales to perform a task that needs their individual or collective qualities. Their magic happens and you execute the action perfectly and burn brighter.

3. Charlie and Charlie Time, my 15-year-old Cocker Spaniel who is my best friend and knows my secrets that I shared during the approximately 15,000 km we have walked together. Charlie Time is when I walk with Charlie and I let him lead the way and I follow.

4. Crappy Alarm is a virtual alarm that I visualize that goes off automatically when my life becomes overloaded with crappy information that makes me grimace.

5. Digital Twins is a term that I use to remind me that any physical obstacle I need to overcome in my life can be visualized and simulated in my imagination to find ways to overcome these obstacles before trying them out in real life.

6. Finger-Licking Good Curry is a curry that I cook from scratch to process my emotions as I solve a problem. It challenges me to get my Ales and Guts to work in coordination , and also requires me to get all the five senses working as a team. When the curry is ready, I relish eating it with my fingers.

7. ICE Pack are interactive visual games designed to harness the power of imagination, enabling me to seamlessly integrate my stories, concepts, and toys. Each game is designed to provide me with a specific value that helps me to learn to survive and thrive with ADHD. The value compounds as I become more proficient at interconnecting the value of each individual game into a larger whole.

8. Leeches and Chattering monkeys are a group of toxic people who drain me of energy when I interact with them.

9. Mr. FONGES is my acronym for fear of not falling asleep.

10. Mr. Spectacles is a term and a visual I use to help me accept that I need medication to survive and thrive with ADHD. Mr. Spectacles helped me visualize that medication like a pair of spectacles for my fuzzy eyes helps me see things more clearly.

11. My brand of ADHD, Leadership and Entrepreneurship refers to my personal ADHD, Leadership and Entrepreneurial perfections and imperfections.

12. Ohism is a term that encompasses find, free, bring and keep Oh in my life.

13. Pixie Dust, there are eight Pixie Dust Spices in Nutty Woods. Each of them is the signature spice of Team Inspiration who've spent years perfecting it and reflects their philosophy of life in a few words. Each pixie dust can be used in countless situations in life when I need inspiration to solve problems that potentially make me grimace more than I smile.

14. SAD is my acronym for Stress, Anxiety and Depression

Manufactured by Amazon.ca
Acheson, AB